The Villages of Aberdeen
The Spital

The story begins where *Round About Mounthooly* left off, tracing the history of the once marshy Howe o Spital from dreaded leper colony to reluctant fire station and recording much around the area that has vanished; the Mardyke, the Poorhouse, the granite yards, the barracks, the trams and Advocates Park.

The Spital itself, Aberdeen's mystery village, is then tackled. The author disentangles fact from romance and finds a place of panoramic views, haunted houses, remarkable architecture, a fabulous chapel and much more. 'Corseted between Big Brother (Old Aberdeen), and even Bigger Brother (Aberdeen), she writes, 'the Spital has retained its individuality and a touch of the enigmatic down the years.'

This, the first history of the Spital, is rich in research and high in readability and profusely illustrated. A companion volume, *The Spital Lands* is in preparation.

By the same author

'Villages of Aberdeen' series

Footdee
and her Shipyards

Round About Mounthooly

Front Cover
The Spital looking towards Old Aberdeen
From the original watercolour by J.A.Sutherland

The Villages of Aberdeen

The Spital

Diane Morgan

Denburn Books
ABERDEEN

First Published 1996
Reprinted 1997

British Library Cataloguing in Publication Data
A catalogue record of this book is available from the British Library

ISBN 1 898645 03 5

Design and Layout by
Jimmy and Pat Sutherland

Produced on the Xerox Docutech digital publisher by
Printagraph, The Print Factory, Aberdeen.

Acknowledgements

First and foremost I must thank George Gordon and Ronald and Helen Leith for sharing with me their great knowledge of the area. Without them this volume would have been much the poorer.

I would like to acknowledge the help of those who advised on a whole range of subjects that had a bearing on the Spital area: on architecture, Sandy Reith and John Souter who as always has given me the benefit of his great knowledge; on the parish of St Peter's, Dr Leslie J Macfarlane; on the Convent of St Margaret's, Mother Verity Margaret; on the lepers, Anne Johnston; on the advocates, Dorothea Bruce; on King's Crescent journalists, K J Peters; on the granite industry, John (Ian) McLaren; on the Gordon Highlanders and Captain Beaton, Doug Mitchell and Norman Adams; on John Duncan, cattle auctioneer and A S Donald ice cream manufacturer, their respective grandsons Hugh Duncan and Mervyn Donald; on Grampian Transport, Lynne Anderson; on St Peter's Nursery, Catherine Cameron; on the YWCA, Hazel Smith; on fire stations past and present Dennis Scott and Donny Harper; on the 'link' road, Councillor Jack Dempsey; on his memories of Councillor A Fraser Mackintosh, ex-Lord Provost Alex Collie; on East End FC, Brian Stephen; on the Red Lion, Sandy Pirie; on boxing, Felix Graham and John Gillan; on Advocates Park and whippet racing, George Tait.

My thanks to everyone who has most kindly responded to written or verbal queries and I would particularly thank the following who have told me of aspects of life in and around the Spital, or have provided information about properties there: Mr and Mrs John Argo, Sandy Argo, Mr and Mrs E Bandeen, Jacinta Birchley, Harold S Bishop, Gordon Cardno, Mrs Dennis Christie, Dr. Iain Davidson, Iris Donald, Mr and Mrs Tommy Donaldson, Ean Emslie, Dorothy Gerrard, John Gordon, George Keith, Chrissie Leith, Ivy Leith, Muriel McCulloch, Susan McGowan, Consuela McKenzie, Mr and Mrs Alex Slessor, Norman Smith, Elizabeth Weston, Alison Whimster, and Jimmy Yule. I would like to acknowledge the help of the staff at the Local Collection, Aberdeen City Libraries, of Miss Judith Cripps, city archivist and her staff, and of everyone at the Special Collections, King's College, University of Aberdeen. A special thank you to Stuart W Allan, curator, Gordon Highlanders' Museum, and Charles Hunt, Keeper of Art, Aberdeen University, and everyone concerned at Aberdeen City Libraries who provided such splendid prints.

Returning to *Round About Mounthooly* for a moment, I was delighted at the number of people who wrote to tell me of their reminiscences, and I must apologise for omitting to mention the Mounthooly underground toilets. John Gray of California provided interesting memories of the Spring Garden-Gallowgate area, as did Dr May Williamson on Powis Place. A very special thank you to Garth Jessamine, an irrepressible fount of knowledge on the legendary Bendelow-Jessamine family.

Once again I must express my debt to my book designers, Pat and Jimmy Sutherland, who have worked with much devotion to prepare this volume for publication; to Frank Donnelly who once more has provided excellent photographic backup; and to my husband, David I Morgan, who has patiently chauffeured me up and down the Spital on countless occasions. There are less frustrating things to do on a Sunday afternoon than to try to find out where Nos 1-15 the Spital have gone.

I am grateful to everyone who has provided illustrations outwith the author's collection and have acknowledged them individually. The front cover and the line drawings are by Jimmy (J A) Sutherland.

Diane Morgan, 1996

Contents

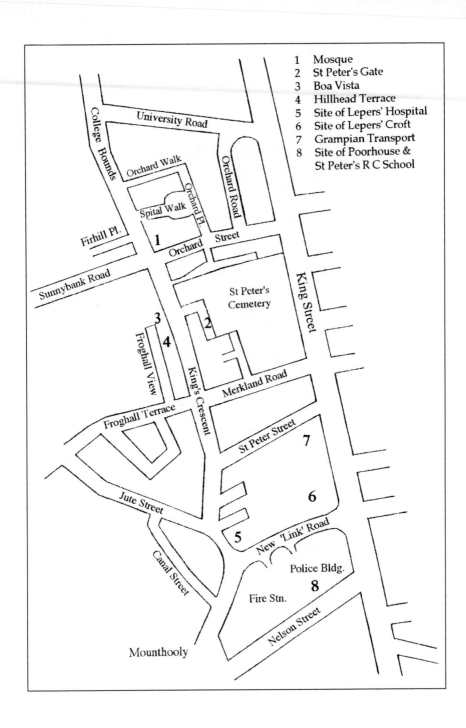

1   Mosque
2   St Peter's Gate
3   Boa Vista
4   Hillhead Terrace
5   Site of Lepers' Hospital
6   Site of Lepers' Croft
7   Grampian Transport
8   Site of Poorhouse &
    St Peter's R C School

Introduction

The Spital takes its name from St Peter's Hospital, a twelfth century eventide home or hospice for aged priests which sat near the brow of the hill between Aberdeen and Old Aberdeen. The abbreviated form of the word presently attached itself to everything in the neighbourhood. A charter of 1310 mentions the croft of Spyttalhillis. The fifteenth century Chapel of St Peter's, sited near the hospice, became the Spital Kirk while the village that grew up beside it was the Kirkton of Spital, later just the Spital. But the road running through the village was the King's Highway or the Oldtown Road. The Spital as a road name was a nineteenth century development. Even as late as 1821, Wood's Map plots the word 'Spit-tal' astride the thoroughfare in the manner of a place-name, not running along it like a road name.

This thoroughfare, for all the attentions of civil engineers and public works contractors, stubbornly remains a narrow road climbing Aberdeen's most formidable urban hill. Anyone who stands at the offset junction of Froghall Terrace and Merkland Road will appreciate that its eastern and western slopes are as formidable as those of north-south axis.

The Spital vies with Fittie and Mounthooly in the number of ways it was spelt, and most of them are scattered throughout these pages. By the nineteenth century spelling had stabilised at 'Spittal'. 'Spital' appears tentatively in the 1860s, but it was not until the village was annexed by Aberdeen in 1883 that the contemporary spelling came into official use.

Deep-ingrained Spital myths persist. The best-known is that the house, now No 45 the Spital, was a leper hospital, from whose lower reaches a tunnel led across to St Peter's Cemetery and/or the Gallowshill along which the corpses of the lepers were trundled. The fact that No 45 post-dates the last leper by roughly two centuries, and no one who has lived there has ever found the tunnel makes not a whit of difference. I have now heard this tale so often that I think I am beginning to believe it !

1

A leper hospital did exist, nearer Aberdeen, in the old Howe o Spital where, at time of writing, the King's Crescent Fire Station is making a reluctant debut. There is some evidence that there was a leper presence on both sides of the Howe, perhaps prompting tales of a tunnel. There is aye watter far the stirkie droons. It has been suggested that the leper hospital gave its name to the Spital, but its candidacy is a weak one. St Peter's Hospital was established and archaic forms of 'Spital' were in use long before the leper colony came into being.

The other enduring legend tells of a German spy disguised as 'a nun', who signalled nightly from the heights of St Margaret's Convent to a U-boat, lurking in Aberdeen Bay. I have not dared ask Mother Verity Margaret, there throughout the dark days of the war, to comment.

Spital street numbering provided an unexpected challenge. In the old days numbers were consecutive but zigzagged bewilderingly from one side of the road to the other. They had an irritating habit of changing, some, after *anschluss* with Aberdeen in 1883 and virtually all of them in 1903 when there was a general reorganisation in the city. An attempt has been made to master this numbers game, essential for the accurate interpretation of the earlier valuation rolls and census returns.

The Spital, in keeping with an established trend in this series, has turned itself into two books. The present volume starts where *Round About Mounthooly* finished, heading north through the Howe o Spital to the Spital itself and the threshold of Old Aberdeen. But the Spital once stood at the centre of the vast Spital Lands, encompassing Sunnyside, Froghall and Sunnybank, to the west, and the old King Street Road, Pittodrie and the Links to the east. Their fascinating story was intended to form a part of this book. Needless to say, they are in the throes of becoming a book in their own right, a companion volume, *The Spital Lands*.

Part One

Howe o Spital

Cottages, King's Crescent

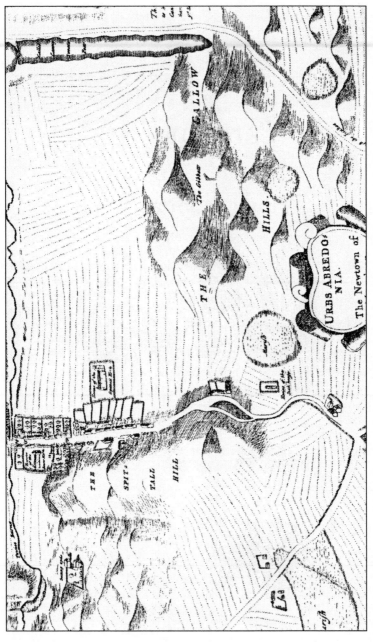

The Spital with the Spital Lands on either side, from Parson Gordon's Plan of 1661. The fork at the Gallowgate-head is bottom centre left. Above it, right, is an anonymous fermtoon, and above that, The 'Ruins of the Sick houſe' within their enclosure, with the circular mire (Mariſh) to the right. Beyond 'The Gallow Hills' extend towards the Links. 'The Gibbet' is perched on what is now the top of Erroll Street.

Chapter 1

The Leper Folk

Such as goe out at the Gallowgate port towards Old Aberdeen, haff way almost, may see the place where of old stood the Lepers' Hospitall, called the Seik-hous, hard by the way syde.

Description of Bothe Touns of Aberdeen. James Gordon, 1661

At the start of our journey we find ourselves back with our old friend the Mounthooly Roundabout, the Gallowgate-head of old, where the ancient highways forked. The left-hand fork went to Inverurie via Causewayend, which has already been explored, Kittybrewster and many other hamlets; the right-hand, to Old Aberdeen and beyond via Mounthooly and the Spital. This is the road we take now, the *via regia* of ancient charters, the royal way, the kingis hy yett, the king's common highway, the Old Aberdeen Road, the Old Town Road, the Spital Road. One of the busiest thoroughfares in Scotland, it was, in spite of its numerous names, little more than a narrow track that went up hill and down dale over notoriously difficult terrain.

Immediately beyond Mounthooly, this track ran through the Howe o Spital, the area we now know as King's Crescent. The local historian George Gordon gives an evocative description of how it once would have been:

Low lying, bounded by hilly ground on the west and the bleak expanse of the Lepers' Colony on the east, the Howe o Spital was a dark, boggy morass in wet weather; a place most travellers hastily passed through in daylight and avoided during the hours of darkness for fear of lurking footpads.

This was leper land. Just mention the Spital and people will say, 'Ah, yes, the lepers.' Long gone and mostly anonymous they are, nevertheless, the Spital's best remembered residents! Their colony lay south of the

5

present St Peter Street, or Love Lane as it used to be called, just inside the Inner Marches, in croft land, which, together with 'the biggit land' at the burgh's heart, the Green, the Castlegate, the Broadgate and the Gallowgate, formed 'the royalty' of the town. The leper colony thus lay within the burgh's control, important given the contagious nature of the disease, yet remote enough to offer a place of perpetual quarantine, the isolation essential to prevent the spread of this dread, incurable disease. As the fifteenth century Scots poet Robert Henryson wrote in *The Testament of Cresseid*: 'There is na salve may save thee of thy sair'.

Leprosy had come to Scotland by the early twelfth century and may have reached Aberdeen by the late thirteenth, but there is no mention of the leper colony until a charter of 1363 which concerns not the lepers themselves, but the sale of three crofts. Few roads then had names, and crofts are identified by their proximity to other crofts or familiar landmarks; but the charter does mention a *vicus furcarum*, the street of the forks, which must be the Gallowgate. The *furca* was the name given to the fork-like yoke fixed around the neck of criminals on their way to the gallows. (*Furca et fosse* was the ancient right to impose death by gallows or pit, the latter presumably filled with water). An intriguing but irrelevant thought; the common meaning of *furca* is a two-pronged fork and the Gallowgate led to the Gallowgate-head with its prominent forks to Cassie-end and Mounthooly.

The charter also makes mention of the *via regia*, the Old Aberdeen Road, going from the town of Aberdeen towards the houses of the lepers, on the east. The interesting thing about this document, written in Latin as was customary at the time, is that the word *domus*, a house, used to describe the lepers' dwellings, appears only in the plural *(domos* and *domibus)*. There seems no reason to use the plural if the singular would have done, so we can perhaps envisage a little cluster of thackit biggins, in the Howe, that dip of King's Crescent, where the playing fields used to be, and where the Fire Station has been located.

The next development of which we have a note took place in 1519. Or did it? In his *Description of Bothe Touns* of 1661, James Gordon, Parson of Rothiemay, reported that a chapel, dedicated to St Anne, patroness of lepers, stood next to their sick house or hospital. 'The citizens licencit one Mr Alexander Galloway, then person (parson) of Kinkell, for to build the chappell, anno 1519'. Gordon may have been told about the entry in the Aberdeen Council Register for the January of that year which stated the same thing in rather more detail, to wit that the provost, baillies and Town Council granted to certain poor ladies (a sisterhood of nuns) 'in honour of God and the glorious matron Sanct Ane', that piece of green land lying on the north side of their sick house. That was done at the instance of the 'rycht

Saint Anne, South Porch, Chartres Cathedral. According to tradition, the mother of the Virgin Mary.

venerable and worschipfull' Master Alexander Galloway who promised to build a chapel and oratory on 'ane pece of ground perteining to the said seikhouse', again in honour of God and Saint Anne. The city fathers and their successors 'perpertualy in all tyme cuming' would be the patrons of the chapel.

The architect Dr William Kelly, a very thorough researcher, understood two separate pieces of ground to be involved here. Master Galloway, a skilled canon or church lawyer, acting on behalf of the nuns, had persuaded the Council to gift that 'piece of green land' - the first piece of ground - north of the sick house (why we don't know - perhaps the sisters would live there and minister to the lepers). He would, in return, build a chapel and oratory dedicated to Saint Anne on ground - the second piece of ground - which was already within the leper colony.

Was this chapel ever built? And who was the persuasive Master Alexander Galloway, parson of Kinkell? Galloway was one of the North East's most gifted and versatile sons, a true child of the Renaissance and in his day, right-hand man to the great bishops, William Elphinstone and Gavin Dunbar. Inspired perhaps, by watching the building of King's College Chapel during his student days - he was one of the first graduates of King's - he developed a rare talent for architecture, long before that term came into use. Around the time that he would have been working on St Anne's Chapel, we know Galloway was designing and overseeing work on the Bridge of Dee which he eventually handed over to the people of Aberdeen in 1529. In the early 1520s he was also busy on the handsome and unique Greyfriars Chapel, and, as a canon of St Machar's Cathedral, on his own manse in the Chanonry in what is now the garden of No 12 Tillydrone House. He designed Bishop Dunbar's ornate tomb which still can be seen in St Machar's graveyard, protected these days by a monstrous cloche, and for his own parish kirk of Kinkell, Inverurie, among others, he built a unique sacrament house. And perhaps unusually for a man of the cloth, he advised the Council on the city defences in 1529.

Galloway's most memorable work, however was the famous ceiling of St Machar's Cathedral, created during the years 1519-22. It depicts the

7

heraldic emblems of pope, kings, dukes, nobles, bishops and burghs, forty-eight crests all told, drawn up in three hierarchical columns, containing, at least to the politically aware of the day, the occasional coded compliment and insult. Devising and implementing this unique scheme must have taken a considerable amount of time. No handy reference books on heraldry in those days! Galloway would have been familiar with many Scottish heraldic devices, but he presumably had to research the more recondite details of European heraldry, perhaps consulting and making sketches from the two or three continental armorial manuscripts then extant, during his visits abroad on church business.

We well may wonder if he ever found time to build the Chapel of St Anne. It was never again mentioned, either in the records, or in title deeds. Yet had it existed it must have been an outstanding landmark, bearing some stamp of Galloway's genius. Parson Gordon never actually saw it. Of the leper hospital and chapel he said in 1661: 'now both thes buildings are gone, and scarcelie is the name knowne to many'. It seems improbable that the chapel could have vanished so completely by Gordon's time for much of Galloway's heritage has endured. Many of the works mentioned above survive to this day, as Greyfriars Chapel would have done, had it not been demolished in 1903, in the face of much local opposition, to allow for the building of the west front of Marischal College. Admittedly the site of 'St Anne's Chapel' is marked on the 1868 ordnance survey map immediately

The site of the leper colony in 1996. The King's Crescent Fire Station is in course of erection.

8

west of the Lepers' Hospital and opposite Nos 9 - 11 King's Crescent, but on what proof I know not. For someone as busy as Galloway, the construction of a chapel at the colony, given the dreich site, the spongy terrain and the contagious congregation, would not have been the most attractive of projects, and he may have given it a low priority.

And what was the fate of that 'piece of green land' that had been granted to the nuns and which lay on the north side of the sick house? Hay's Mortification, a charitable bequest of 1609 and the origin of the Bridge of Don Fund, may provide a clue. By this mortification, Sir Alexander Hay, in repayment of a family debt, granted the burgh of Aberdeen feu duties and annual rents from various crofts for the upkeep of the Bridge of Don as the Brig o Balgownie was then called. The mortification, in listing the crofts from which the necessary revenue was to be derived, mentions one, unnamed, lying near 'the lepers' house', between the umquhile (late) Mariota Umphray's Croft now belonging to King's College on the south,

with the *via regia*, the Old Aberdeen Road, on the east. Canal Street, as noted in *Round About Mounthooly*, was laid out on Umphray's Croft. The unnamed croft and its neighbour, the lepers' house, were therefore north of the future Canal Street, with the Old Aberdeen road to the east. If the topography of Hay's Mortification is accurate, this particular lepers' house must have lain on the west side of the Old Aberdeen road, perhaps on that very 'piece of green land'. A marsh and the lepers' croft which was under cultivation (but not by the lepers) inhibited development to the east, so that 'piece of green land' possibly formed an extension to the colony. Though it lay on the other side of the Spital Road there is evidence that it was well to the north. In the eighteenth century a 'piece of ground' across on the west side of the road, complete by then with a house of two storeys and barn, has a habit of popping up in transactions dealing with the Mardyke or the Mardykes Croft as the old leper land had been more attractively renamed. It sounds like the same piece of ground and is described as 'joining in with St Peter's keys'. This was one of several ancient stones, incised with keys, marking the boundaries of the old Spital parish of St Peter's with the

Saint Peter with the keys of heaven. South Porch, Chartres Cathedral.

9

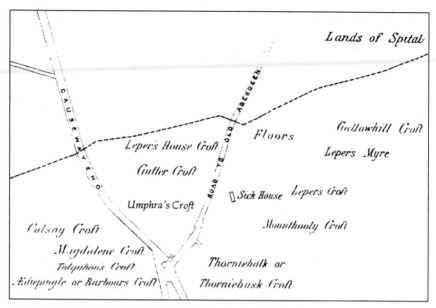

A conjectural plan of Aberdeen's crofts, by P J Anderson. He shows the Lepers' House Croft to the west of the Road to Old Aberdeen, and the Sick House, Lepers' Croft and Lepers'Myre on the east side. He places the Gallowhill Croft north east of the Myre.. From 'Charters Relating to the Burgh of Aberdeen', 1890. (Umphra's Croft has been imposed).

burgh of Aberdeen. It was as far north as you could get within territory owned by the town. Its successor, March Stone No 61, sits further south, in a King's Crescent garden.

The leper colony would have changed in appearance over the years. The simple huts, deteriorating with age, may have been replaced by a larger, single dwelling on the east side, perhaps the 'seikhouse' or 'hospitall' which is mentioned from the sixteenth century onwards. In May 1604 the Kirk Session ordained that Helen Smyth:

ane puir woman infectit with Leprosie to be put in the Hospitall appoyntit for keiping and haulding of Lipper folkis betwixt the townis and the keyis of the said hospital be deliverit to hir.

The existence of keys suggests a building of some substance. Even in 1808, the doors of the sturdy stone-built new fisher cottages in Footdee still had snecks rather than locks. Incidentally, a charter of James VI of 1591 mentions the 'hospitall and house' of the 'leprous persons'. Hospital and sickhouse were surely one and the same, but does this phrase indicate a house as well as a hospital, or merely a hospital-cum-house? We will never know.

By the sixteenth century a 'croft and yard adjacent to the seik folkis house' and 'croft and myre pertening to the lipperfolk', already briefly alluded to, were being mentioned in various documents. The croft was 'laboured' by a tenant of the Town Council's who owned the land, with any revenue derived from it contributing to the weal of the lepers. Although the lepers' buildings would have huddled near the roadside, the tract of land which bore their name was sizeable. It stretched, in today's terms, from the future Nelson Street area almost as far north as St Peter Street, and from east to west 'betwixt the Gallowhills and the Spital Road', as Kennedy tells us in his *Annals of Aberdeen* of 1818. This is quite far east but the distance, as the crow flies, is not so great. The Gallowhills were just east of what is now King Street, around the Erroll Street-Trinity Cemetery area. The gibbet itself occupied a prominent position near where the Cemetery lodge now stands and would have been visible to the lepers down in the Spital Howe. Kennedy tells of a sixteenth century leper hospital near Edinburgh, whose inmates were forbidden by the magistrates from leaving the hospital, or having its door open after sunset, under pain of death:

That this might not be deemed an empty threatening, a gallows was erected at the gable of the hospital for the immediate execution of the offenders.

The lands of the Lepers' Croft today. The view is from the Gallowhills, the eastern extremity, looking across Errol Street and King Street to King's Crescent and the Spital. The flat stone on the grass to the right is a march stone marked with a cross.

11

There is no evidence that such a fate awaited Aberdeen's lepers. Nevertheless, the gibbet must have cast a long shadow across the Gallowhills to the colony in the Howe.

What of the lepers themselves? Anne Johnston, who with colleagues in the city's Archaeological Section carried out an excavation of the King's Crescent site in 1990, notes that it was not until 1589 that a specific leper is mentioned in the city records. In that year, the register of deaths for the Parish of St Nicholas records the death of an unnamed 'lepar boy in ye lepar houss of Aberdene'. Council Registers note the admission of three lepers between 1591 and 1612, while two others are mentioned in the records of the Kirk Session. Of these, the most prominent is Robert Abel:

(who) now at the guid pleisure off God is visiet with the seikness of leprosie and thairby onhabill to wyn his living or frequent honest menis societie...

Anne Johnston points out that the length of the entry in the Council Register and the fact that he signs it legibly indicate that he was a man of some status in the burgh. Abel had sought admission to the leper hospital in 1591, at a time when conditions in the Howe seem to have been particularly miserable. It may be, therefore, that he was determined to make improvements before winter began, with some assistance from the king himself. In August that year, James VI, in residence at Falkland Palace issued a charter in favour of the Aberdeen leperfolk:

we being informit of the smalnes of the rent appointit for the leprous personis in the hospitall and hous betwixt New and Auld Aberdeen unable to sustene thame in meet and fyre, quhairthgrow they leif verie miserablie, specialie in the Wynter season.

Because of 'the vehementis of the cauld', the lepers 'for halding in of their lyves' would make for the comparative comfort of the two adjacent towns, Aberdeen and Old Aberdeen, where they 'perrell the estate and helth of mony clene folkis'. We can imagine the terror of the folk of Mounthooly and the Spital when the noise of the clapper, and shouts of 'Unclean, unclean', were heard and a gaggle of lepers, some in tattered cloaks, some perhaps in mantles and beaver hats as in Henryson's poem, emerged from the Howe o Spital, begging cups in hand.

The king ordained that one peat from each load being brought to market in both towns be delivered 'to Robert Abell' and remanent of the said pure (poor) leprous persons'. Abel it seems, had not taken long to establish himself as the colony's leader. We cannot tell how the king's boon was implemented; perhaps peats coming into Aberdeen from Perwinnes Moss at Scotstown Moor were thrown to the lepers from carts as they passed through the Howe o Spital, hence the advantage of a leper presence on both sides of the road. No need then for them to go into either burgh to fetch peats. Incursions into the world of the quick by the living dead were not encouraged.

But the colony did have means of support. When admitted, a leper brought with him all his posses-sions which became the property of the hospital. In addition, the family may have organised the sending in of food and alms on a regular basis. Then there was the matter of income. King James had noted the 'smalnes of the rent appointit for the leprous personis in the hospitall', a reference to rent due from the tacksman or tenant of the adjoining Sickhouse Croft. It was one of the crofts of the burgh, in the northern (later described as eastern) territories, owned by the Town Council. The tenant would either cultivate or graze the croft

In 1589 the register of deaths for St Nicholas Parish recorded the death of a 'lepar boy in ye lepar houss of Aberdene'.

land and the rent paid was used for the good of the lepers. The following episode throws some light on the system.

In August 1574, the provost and baillies of Aberdeen appeared before 'my Lord Regentis grace' (the Regent Morton), and the Lordis of Secreit Counsall (the Privy Council) and were read a lecture on furthering the principles of the Reformation. They were instructed to ban festive days (like Christmas), always an unpopular edict, to punish blasphemers, to remove organs from kirks, as well as priests' stalls and 'bakkis of altaris' (choir screens) which, in a thrifty mix of iconoclasm and carpentry, were to be made into pews, or failing that, sold for ready cash. The magistrates were told to see to it that parish churches were maintained and that the poor were not defrauded of alms. Then in a curious descent from the fairly general to the very particular they were instructed to 'uptak' from James Leslie, 'the present possessor of the croft and myre pertaining to the lipperfolk betwix New and Auld Aberdene' five years arrears of rent. With that and any other funds that were available they were to have the house 'theikkit (thatched) and reparit' for receiving lepers in time coming. It seems that none were in residence at that moment. Leslie's tack (lease) had one further year to run, and then the tack of the croft and myre were to be rouped to the highest bidder every three years and all the revenue, the 'haill proffite', was to be spent on maintaining the house and sustaining the resident 'lipperfolkis'.

Scotland is a small country, but even so, one can hardly expect the Earl of Morton and his colleagues to have such a detailed knowledge of overdue rent. The magistrates probably alerted the Privy Councillors to the situation and thus got the backing of a government decree before chasing Leslie for rent. Seeking a new tenant, however, was always a chancy method of fund-raising. Attempts to roup a tack were many a time frustrated by the non-appearance of a bidder.

King James had spoken of Robert Abel and 'the remanent', the remainder, of the lepers. We don't know how many there were over the centuries, but details survive in the Council Register and Session Records of a few whose cases had attracted specific notice. Robert Abel, as noted, was a man of some standing. He had, among other things, stressed that he was 'a native townis man'. As Anne Johnston has pointed out, admission was normally restricted to local people. Isabel Fynnie, 'quha is becum leprous', and who was admitted in 1594 stressed her North East connections. She was the spouse of Johne Symsone of Elrick.

But the Council did admit lepers who had not the advantage of being born and bred in Aberdeen. One such, in 1612, was the tragic Agnes Jameson. Her husband and bairns had left her, and were expelled from town, presumably a quarantine measure. Agnes had 'no kynd of lodging, meat nor drinck', and was dependant on the charity of 'guid Christanes'. Allowing her temporary accommodation in the hospital, rather than have her contaminate 'clean folks' was a humane decision, tempered by caution. She was not, however, permitted any share of the rent that fell due to the leper house.

Agnes was the last leper on record. We have already met Helene Smyth who had the keys of the hospital delivered to her in 1604 and that does suggest that in its latter years, the hospital worked on an *ad hoc* basis. Parson Gordon's Plan, published fifty years after Agnes Jameson's admission shows the 'Ruins of the Sick house', on the east side of the Spital Road, just beyond Mounthooly, a long building running north to south, enclosed by its yard, and surrounded by croft lands while the 'Marish' or mire lies to the east. This is the only sketch we have, and it may be largely conjecture. Of the shadowy chapel dedicated to the 'glorious matron Sanct Ane' and the lepers' house on the west side of the road there is no sign.

The 'Lepersmyre or Sickhouse Croft' continued to be set in tack or leased out by the Town Council, or to be accurate, by the Master of Guild Brethren's Hospital, which was under the Town's patronage. This was not a hospital in the modern sense, more an old folks' home which by the mid-seventeenth century accommodated half-a-dozen decayed burgesses. The Master's accounts show that his income included revenue from the croft which was mortified in favour of 'the Sickfolk and Lepers'. One tenant of the Sickhouse Croft in the later seventeenth century was a mason, John Ronald, who paid the modest annual 'duty' of £30 Scots.

Leprosy died out as that century progressed so the croft's revenue was subsequently mortified to 'the poor of the said burgh'. Eventually, in 1715, the Town Council and the Master of the Guild Brethren's Hospital sold the croft for £870 Scots. Some three years later, since 'ther are now no lepers in Scotland' it was decided to add this money to funds bequeathed some years earlier by 'severall pious disposed gentlemen' for the purpose of maintaining 'persons deprived of the use of their reason'. The Sickhouse Croft entries now vanish from the accounts of the Master of the Guild Brethren's Hospital. The mental hospital envisaged by the 'pious disposed gentlemen' never did materialise, but in 1741, these funds were donated to the newly completed infirmary at Woolmanhill whose direct descendant is Aberdeen Royal Infirmary, Foresterhill.

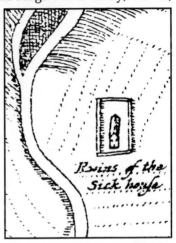

'Ruins of the Sick houfe'. Detail from Parson Gordon's Plan of 1661.

Plans to redevelop the area traditionally associated with the leper colony on the east side of King's Crescent made the 'dig' of 1990 imperative, especially as a major link road between King Street and King's Crescent, was due to be constructed across the only remaining open land on the ancient site. The results were disappointing, though not unexpectedly so, given some vagueness about the precise position of the colony. Some twenty-six post and stake holes, possibly medieval, were found in one trench, but the excavation was inhibited by 'substantial overburden' - an overlying stratum - not surprising in an area where there had been a number of granite yards. But before the coming of the granite merchants and others, there were a number of interesting developments at the former leper colony. To these we will turn next.

15

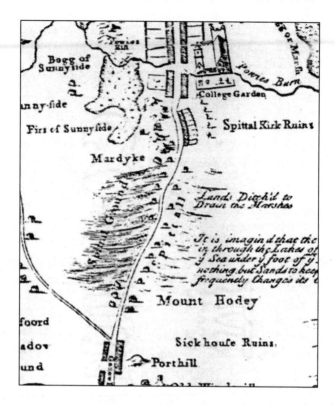

G & W Patersons' Survey of New and Old Aberdeen, of 1746 places the 'Sickhouse Ruins', between the Porthill and 'Mount Hodey'. The Sickhouse Croft was rechristened Mardykes thirty years earlier but the new name had not yet caught on. The Patersons noted the Mardyke only in relation to 'that piece of ground' on the west side of the Old Aberdeen highway. They place it quite far north.

Chapter 2

The Land of the Mardyke

The President of the Society of Advocates in Aberdeen having formed a road between King Street and Spital are prepared to feu off the ground on very moderate terms.

Aberdeen Journal, 13 October, 1852

In the summer of 1715, just a few months before the Jacobite Standard was raised on the Braes of Mar, the old leper lands in the Howe o Spital acquired a new owner. Aberdeen Town Council, represented by the august personages of the Provost, Baillies, Thesaurer and Master of the Guild Brethren's Hospital, conveyed these croftlands to William Lindsay who had been a goldsmith burgess of Aberdeen since 1695. He paid £870 Scots for the property which now had a more upmarket name; the 'croft of land formerly called the Sickhouse Croft or Lepers Myre' was 'now called Mardykes Croft' - and sometimes simply 'the Mardyke'. A little earlier, in the February of 1715, the marches between the Sickhouse Croft and the neighbouring Gallowhills Croft owned by a shipmaster, John Lumsden, had been redded up. 'The several marches betwixt the two crofts were discerned' by the arbiters, a farmer and a former provost, 'having always God and a good conscience before our eyes'. John Walker, goldsmith, a former apprentice of Lindsay's, and William Harper, 'serviteur to Jerom Smith, periwigg maker, Aberdeen' were witnesses, and Lindsay paid Lumsden £48 Scots for a slice of ground that he wanted to incorporate within his own territory. The dividing line between the lands was indicated by stones each marked with a cross. Lindsay was given leave to build a dyke

17

A flat boulder, 'marked with ane cross' remains on the Gallowhill.

on top of the march stones, 'provided always the cross marked on the said stones be not covered'. Hence the name, March Dykes or Mardykes.

It's not easy to say how much of the Mardyke was actually enclosed. Building dykes would have been a Herculean labour, given the extent of the lands. Their eastward stretch was noted in the last chapter; in the deeds of the time they are described as beginning at a march stone on the east side of the highway going to Old Aberdeen, holding eastwards past numerous march stones, all of them marked with a cross, some of them 'new infixed march stones' until 'it come to a march stone at the end of the hanging brae' (just north of Erroll Street). The boundary line then proceeded 'eastwards or thereby from march stone to march stone

March stones incised with an identifying 'logo' such as a cross or St Peter's keys were not uncommon in early times. This march stone, indicating the boundary of lands owned by the Knights Hospitallers, displayed in Vaucouleurs Museum, northern France, has the distinctive cross of the order cut into it.

18

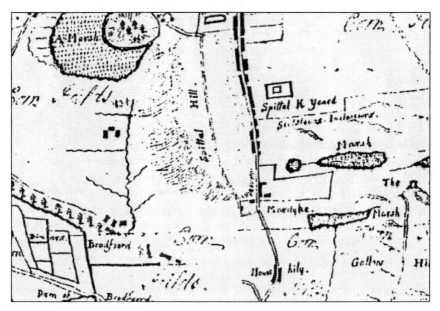

The Survey of New and Old Aberdeen, circa 1750 by Baillie Andrew Logie, the Council's 'in-house' draughtsman shows the Mardyke with 'that piece of ground' in its enclosure on the west side of the road. The two little black squares are presumably the house and barn. Behind the enclosure a little track runs parallel to the Old Aberdeen Road.

all marked with a cross' until a march stone at the road leading to the Gallowhills is reached (Urquhart Lane). The course now holds south for a little, then turns west and back, march stone by march stone to the Howe o Spital. Many stones were still visible, lying in open fields the latter part of the nineteenth century. They are shown on the 1868 ordnance survey map, though some would have been removed when King Street was laid out. Today, one of these stones, clearly 'marked with ane cross' lies on the Gallowhills, and there are several other stones in the area.

Included in the sale of 1715 was 'that piece of ground lying to the west of the said road going to Old Aberdeen'. Again it was described as 'joining with St Peter's keys', and was surrounded by a dyke on all sides, except the north. At each neuk there stood a marchstone, each one marked with a cross, thus 'coding' this enclosure as a part of the Mardyke. Provided that he left 'a sufficient highway' for the Old Aberdeen Road, and 'a sufficient road' for the two other little thoroughfares that flanked the enclosure - one of them, behind the property, ran parallel to the Old Aberdeen Road towards the Spital Brae - the Council permitted Lindsay to level the ground, not any easy task given the terrain...'and to build houses there and otherwise to make use thereof as he should think fit'. In fact he built 'a house

19

of two storeys and a barn', though whether or not it was occupied by Lindsay himself, trying his hand at a little gentlemanly farming, or by his tenant at the Mardyke, Robert Cassie, is not clear. This enclosure, which once may have been an extension of the leper colony, became known as Lindsay's Folly.

In 1715 Lindsay was a busy man. If not quite in the same league as Alexander Galloway, he was at least something of a latter-day Davie do A'thing, the Town's versatile master of works of a century earlier. In 1706, and not a moment too soon, the Council had decided that the city's water supply must be improved, and entered into a contract with an Edinburgh plumber 'anent bringing in water to the burgh'. The chosen source was a spring in Carden's Haugh, a wooded area on the outskirts of the town at that time, but now at the west end of the Grammar School policies, and long vanished underground. The water was to be pumped through various pipes to wells ('fountains') in the town and Lindsay, the man on the spot, was engaged as overseer, advising on the casting and laying of the lead pipes and the installation of the water engines that would pump the water to the wells. This may seem a slightly rugged project for a goldsmith (they usually crafted in silver rather than gold, though they worked in lead as well), but Lindsay proved a highly successful water engineer. In May 1708 he petitioned the Council for a long term contract. He had, he said, 'keeped the springs in ther course to the toune, and the fountaines running within the towne, ane full year'. The magistrates agreed that he 'hade done good service to the towne, and been most useful in bringing in the water to this burghe' and appointed him at £200 a year - Scots money presumably, since at this time sterling was so designated - 'to oversee the said worke during his lyftym…and remaining and residing the burgh'.

The Council were in funds that year. A number of Dutch East Indiamen had been wrecked north of the harbour and the magistrates, as local admirals-depute, had received a considerable sum in salvage. They decided to splash out, crowning their successful water project in some style. In September 1708 Lindsay was appointed to design and cast a brass statue three and a half feet high, with 'four antick (antique) faces' on the corners, from all of which water should play when desired, and 'to sett up the same on the fountain in the Castlegate', the most prominent well in the burgh. He was to be paid £60 sterling, 'on(e) half within eight days, and the other when the work is finished'.

Although Lindsay received his advance of £30, it was not until 1710 that he produced the Mannie Mark 1, as we can call it, though it was just a timber statue 'coloured and gilded'. The brass statue ' was not yet ready' but the magistrates decided that it 'might serve', told him to erect it, 'also the jetdo's' and paid the second instalment of his fee. The 'fountain' gave good service and 'the jetdo's' (jets d'eau) seem to have functioned admirably. In his *Brief Survey of Aberdeen* of 1853 Archibald Courage noted that 'from the head of the statue, and from the mouths of the grotesque heads on the corners, jets of water are made to play on occasions of public rejoicing'.

But to return to Lindsay's busy career. In 1713, shortly before buying the Mardykes Croft he had become deacon of the Hammermen Incorporation, deacon-convener of the Seven Incorporated Trades and in the following year a member of the Town Council itself, one of the two elected Trades councillors. In

An 'antick' face from the Mannie's' plinth in the Castlegate. The central face is flanked by two faces in profile. The 'jetdo's' spouted from here on festive occasions.

1714, in addition to his post as overseer of wells, he was appointed overseer of public works, responsible for the maintenance of the city churches, bridges, calsays, the Tollbooth and more. He was also appointed overseer of the defences and armaments of the burgh. Not that these were tested for, with a Jacobite rising in the offing, all the gunpowder in town was requisitioned by the Hanoverian government.

The Rising of 1715 began in earnest for Aberdeen on 20 September when the Earl Marischal rode in to town and at the market cross proclaimed the Old Pretender, King James VIII. The following day Lindsay would have been present when the Earl and his retinue were entertained by the strongly Jacobite Seven Incorporated Trades. A Town Council of similar persuasion now took over, and remained in power until the Rising fizzled out a few months later. Lindsay was appointed one of the town's four 'taxers', responsible for ingathering money from the citizens when the Jacobites demanded a 'loan' of £2000 sterling, of which £500 to be handed over immediately. There is no record of how successful he was in this unpopular task. Equally demanding, though altogether different was the duty entrusted to him in January 1716 to 'take care of the Bridge of Dee when the storm breaks and provide materials for breaking the ice'. Storms had been prolonged, snowfall heavy, the River Dee was frozen and there were fears for the structure of the Bridge of Dee.

A few months later, in June 1716, he was sacked 'for weighty considerations'. This implies that he did not carry out his task to the Council's satisfaction. Or it may be that the Hanoverian magistrates, who replaced the short-lived Jacobite administration that April, had decided on a purge of Jacobite sympathisers. Whatever the reason, council officials were instructed not to pay him any further moneys, and by 1721 he was in Edinburgh where the magistrates, taking a leaf out of Aberdeen's book, had employed him to improve the capital's water supply. It seems, however, that he was able to hold Aberdeen Town Council to his 'lyftym' contract as overseer of wells and to exact payment of his salary. For his part, he returned on three subsequent occasions to deal with problems. By 1733, however, he was occupied with other pressing matters and advised the Aberdeen magistrates that he was 'content to give up his contract as overseer of the wells' for the payment of £40 sterling. But he would undertake to give free advice in writing 'anent the wells and their courses' and also 'repair in person to Aberdeen in caices of necessity'. The agreement sounds amicable enough.

During his Edinburgh years his finances, for reasons unknown, had spiralled downwards. In 1729 he raised 3000 merks Scots, just over £150 sterling, using his properties as securities 'in friendly borrowing' with a heritable bond in favour of John Rickart of Auchnacant, a wealthy Aberdeen merchant and a future benefactor of the new hospital at Woolmanhill. To no avail. By 1733 he had gone bust. 'My affairs having fallen into disorder on account of my funds and effects not answering to pay my credite. I am not able therefore to give immediate satisfaction to all my creditors'. With this sad statement he again made over his properties, this time to the solicitor, Alexander Thomson Jnr, a leading member of the Society of Advocates in Aberdeen and trustee for his creditors, as a security for his debts.

Lindsay's financial embarrassment is hard to understand. He was a man of property. As well as owning the Mardyke, he had a nice little set-up 'at the Trinities' with 'tenements of foreland and inland, with closes and gardens', between 'the old shoar, now converted into the Fish Mercat', and the Trinity Church, nowadays the area around the junction of Market Street and Guild Street. And as we have seen, he was no slouch when it came to making deals with the magistrates. He even revived the fortunes of the hammermen whose funds were at low ebb when he became their deacon in 1714. From the extant kitty of £3000 Scots, he set up a successful capital accumulating fund, which Ebenezer Bain, historian of the Seven Incorporated Trades described as 'one of the chief instruments in their (the hammermen's) financial prosperity'. The hammermen did not forget. Lindsay died in 1753 and was commemorated half a century later when a

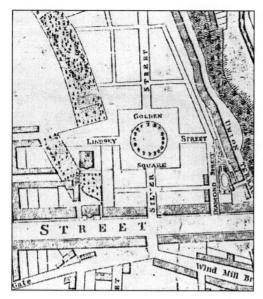

The Golden Square area, including 'Lindsey Street', from John Smith's Plan of Aberdeen of 1810.

number of streets were laid out on land owned by the hammermen west of the Denburn Valley. Names such as Golden Square, Silver Streets North and South, Diamond Street, Ruby Place, Crown Street were appropriate to the craft. But the street running east and west from Golden Square was named Lindsay Street. The western section was absorbed when Crimon Place was created, though the eastern section still links Golden Square and Diamond Street.

One other small memory of this remarkable citizen remains. His wooden Mannie Mark I was stood down from its perch on the Castlegate Well in 1791 and replaced by the present lead statue (subsequently shunted to the Green, then restored to the Castlegate in 1972). So if the Mannie we know today is not by Lindsay, the 'grotesque heads' on the four corners are his, though one at least has been replaced in modern times. Moray Stone Cutters carried out the operation and it is impossible to tell it from the others.

This Mannie is not by Lindsay, but the grotesque heads probably are.

Alexander Thomson Jnr retained Lindsay's properties until 1745, when he rouped them. A colleague of Thomson's, Thomas Mosman, treasurer of the Society of Advocates in Aberdeen, the only person to turn up at the roup, offered £2020 Scots on behalf of the Society, which was accepted. The Mardykes Croft at that time was tenanted by a Gallowgate-head farmer and horse hirer. It was Mosman's successor as treasurer, John Clerk, who took sasine or possession of the properties on the behalf of the Society in 1747. Clerk was responsible for administering them until after 1774 when the Society's first Crown Charter authorised the acquisition of lands under its own name. Clerk pronounced himself 'very willing' to hand them over. The Advocates in Aberdeen, the town's solicitors, were said to have obliged King James V1 with an unsecured loan in return for which the monarch granted them the right to call themselves advocates. Given that local lawyers were referred to as advocates nearly twenty years before the birth of King James, certain doubts have been cast on this apocryphal tale. Like the Seven Incorporated Trades and other guilds, the Society looked after its own in those pre-welfare state days and a fund for 'decayed, indigent members and their relatives' had been set up as early as 1685. Income derived from land ownership was to play an important part in keeping this pension fund buoyant.

For a century and more, the Society was happy to lease the Mardykes Croft for agricultural purposes. The term 'Sickhouse' remained in common use for long years after its demise as is evident from contemporary maps, and from a lease of 1753 when the Society rouped the Mardyke to an Aberdeen farmer, George Duncan, for nineteen years for an annual payment of £106 Scots. In the margin in a most unlawyer-like scribble was a note by which Duncan undertook to make 'sufficient ditches in the laigh grounds of the sickhouse myre' for purposes of drainage, and to leave 'the whole grounds in good heart' at the end of his tenancy. There was no room to write out the usual spiel about 'the croft of land formerly called the Sickhouse Croft or Lepers Myre now called Mardykes Croft' - but 'Sickhouse' had been preferred to 'Mardykes'. Another point of interest is that Duncan, perhaps inspired by having such learned landlords, had learned to write, or at least to sign his name. An earlier transaction relating to the lease is signed by a number of fluent legal hands and includes the swirling signature of Thomas Mosman. Duncan can only offer a shaky GD. But in the deed of 1753 he signs his name in full, firmly if roughly, twice, both at the end of the deed and, as required by law, in the marginal note.

Squeezing provisos about ditching and draining into a margin as an afterthought does not indicate that the lawyers were preoccupied with the repetitive niceties of legal style to the neglect of agricultural necessities.

Their attitude to land management was by no means *laissez-faire*. In those heady days of the agricultural revolution being an 'improver' was all the rage. The Advocates in Aberdeen liked estates. Most of them had one. Of the lawyers we have met, Alexander Thomson Jnr had two, one at Banchory Devenick, one at Newmachar. (His father owned Portlethen; another member of the Society, the father of Baillie Andrew Logie owned Loanhead). Thomas Mosman would succeed his brother William, an artist of distinction, as laird of Middlefield near Woodside, while Clerk owned the estate of Kincardine. James Watson his former apprentice, son-in-law, and successor as treasurer owned Binghill, near Peterculter. A later treasurer, Hugh Hutcheon of Hutcheon Street fame, one of the progenitors of George Street, owned Broadford. But like William Lindsay, a number of Advocates in Aberdeen overreached themselves and plunged spectacularly into bankruptcy.

And if the Mardyke was the first land acquired by the Society, it was by no means the last. It owned Foresterhill for a time from 1790, and Wester Hatton from 1827 which was improved out of recognition from a runrig guddle of infields, outfields and faughs to a handsome property of trig fields of profitable crops. Society records show that the advocates were conscientious lairds who were known to require assurances that their tenants were 'steady and respectable' as well as being able to offer an acceptable rent. And over the years, they were much concerned with ditching and draining in the Mardyke and elsewhere.

In a neat consolidation of 1767 the Society acquired the croft of Gallowhill

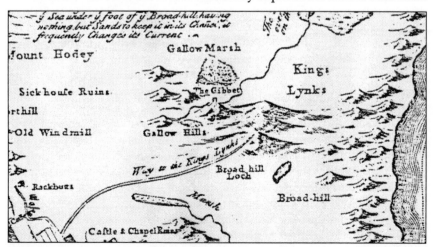

The gallows, from which the Gallowhills took their name, from the Patersons' Survey of 1746. The last victim, Alexander Morison, a wright, was executed and hung in chains in 1776 for the murder of his wife.

25

formerly owned by the shipmaster John Lumsden. It lay to the north east of the Mardyke which was now becoming known rather more grandly as 'lands' rather than 'croft'. At £555 11s 1d sterling the Gallowhill was an expensive purchase compared with the Mardyke which had cost £166.13s 4d sterling some twenty years earlier. Land prices were increasing rapidly. Rationalisation went hand-in-hand with consolidation as the following advertisement shows. It appeared in the *Aberdeen Journal* on June 18, 1770, when George Duncan's tack was coming up for renewal:

That the Lands of Marrdyke presently possessed by Geo Duncan, and the Lands called Gallowhill presently possessed by David Luke and Murdoch M'Pherson, all Farmers in Aberdeen, belonging to the Society of Procurators (Advocates) of Aberdeen are to be set in Tack for nineteen years after Whitsunday 1771. Any person who inclines to a private Bargain may Apply to James Watson, Advocate in Aberdeen, present Collector (treasurer) for the Society. As also there will be sold or feued out as Purchasers shall offer that part of the Marrdyke lying on the West side of the road to Old Aberdeen with the Barn and ruinous House thereto, also belonging to the said Society.

The last sentence is revealing. 'That piece of ground', Lindsay's Folly, on the west side of the road, part of the these lands since the sixteenth century and tracing its origins back to leper times, was to be sold off. It was superfluous to requirements, and William Lindsay's two storey house had become ruinous. The articles of roup reveal a little more; that Lindsay's Folly was bounded on the north and west by ground belonging to George Moir of Scotstown, proprietor of the Spital Lands; that the property was to be set up at £40 sterling; and as well as being advertised in the *Aberdeen Journal*, the sale was to be proclaimed 'three severall times thro' this Town of Aberdeen by Tuck of Drum'. In spite of such publicity there were no takers. Eventually in 1772 Lindsay's Folly was purchased by Thomas Simpson, a Spital wright who paid only £30 for it.

It was around this time that much needed road improvements were carried out in the Spital Howe with the Town Council 'enlarging and straightening the Old Aberdeen highway' in 1776. In this good cause a piece of ground was sliced from the Mardyke and the Society was compensated by the reduction of a few shillings from their teind tack duty.

The Mardyke had a new tenant by the end of the eighteenth century. William Naughten, an Aberdeen maltster, took up a sixteen year lease, with the aim, doubtless, of growing his own bere or barley. He paid Hugh Hutcheon, treasurer of the Society at that time, an annual rent of £54 sterling. Rents, like land prices, were escalating in those years. George Duncan's annual rent in the early 1750s had been less that £9 sterling.

But it was a development across at Lindsay's Folly that would trigger off changes in the Howe. The Moirs of Scotstown and Spital had the superiority of Lindsay's Folly, and in 1838, Dame Isabella, the seventh Moir laird of Scotstown, and her husband, Sir Michael Bruce of Stenhouse, feued half an acre of it to a Caithness man, John Sutherland who had a licensed grocery business at No 29 North Street. He lived 'over the shop' at No 27 with his wife Mary and daughter Mary Anne, but in 1836 sold out to Simpson Shepherd, bearer of a name that would become well known in the licensed trade. The family moved to Glenburnie which stood a little west of the present Grammar School lodge. A grassy patch now marks the site. Two years later the family flitted again, to the Howe o Spital. John Sutherland is now described as 'late merchant'; though only forty-eight, he had retired. But he was by no means idle. By the end of 1838, he had levelled part of his feu at Lindsay's Folly and built an imposing house of fine granite, with a flight of stairs leading to the front door. George Gordon describes it:

Everything connected with the house was on a large scale; the public rooms of the ground floor were of extremely generous proportions, as were the six bedrooms and the kitchen area; in addition there were liberal servants quarters and an ample cellarage. Facing south-east and set back about sixty feet from the Spital Road, it was a pleasing situation and from the upper windows an uninterrupted view of the sea and the surrounding countryside could be obtained.

A reconstruction of Viewton Place as it would have looked during John Sutherland's time.

27

Through having a shop in busy North Street, John Sutherland would have appreciated the rural ambience of the Spital Howe, no great distance away, with the neat fields of the Mardyke and open country opposite. Moreover, while living at Glenburnie, he would have walked daily along Skene Street and been aware of the handsome houses that Robert Mackie had built in Mackie Place, and the new townhouses of Skene Place, now Nos 1-4 Skene Street. Perhaps thus inspired, Sutherland dropped the name Lindsay's Folly in favour of Viewton Place. The view, we know was admirable, and 'Place', sometimes used to describe a grand house sitting in its own grounds, had an upmarket ring about it. Sutherland had indeed laid out grounds and built substantial walls round his property. From the feu charter we learn that the ground to the south, belonged to King's College, to the west partly to Lady Bruce (Dame Isabella) and partly to Widow MacDonald. To the north, the remaining portion of Lindsay's Folly was possessed by Alexander Smith.

The members of the Society of Advocates must have observed the metamorphosis of Lindsay's Folly with interest and noted the other changes taking place all around the Lands of Mardyke. In April 1848, a number of them had been in the procession that wound from the town hall at the Castlegate down to Nelson Street when Baillie James Forbes laid the foundation stone of the new East Poorhouse on croftlands that had be-

The palatial building in the foreground is the East Poorhouse. The group of houses to the left is Canal Street, with the Spital Road snaking north. The house standing on its own between Canal Street and Old Aberdeen (at the top of the illustration) is Viewton Place. Behind the Poorhouse the fields of the Sickhouse and Gallowhill Crofts stretch eastwards towards the Links. From George Washington Wilson's Bird's Eye View of 1850.

longed to the Wrights and Coopers Trade. These lands marched with the Mardyke's southern boundary, and not so long ago had been tended by the nurseryman, James Gordon. Around them, the remaining croft territories of the burgh were being covered over by housing and manufactories, with the Lochlands, George Street and the Causewayend Road and their linking roads playing their role in accommodating a population which had soared to over 63,000 by 1841 and would double again by the end of the century. It was time for the Society to reassess the Mardyke and Gallowhill lands with a view to greater profitability.

Housing seemed to be the way forward. Viewton Place provided an elegant example of what could be done. Why not lay out a few streets on the *rus in urbe* principle, the country estate in town, that Archibald Simpson had carried out so successfully in Ferryhill? The Society seemed not at all discouraged by the fact that nearby King Street, which had sliced through their lands and created a number of problems in so doing, was very slow to attract houses and businesses, even slower than Union Street. But the Howe o Spital had the advantage of being nearer George Street and St Nicholas Street, the city's prime business and shopping area. There was another bonus point. Many of the members of the Society were alumni of either Marischal or King's Colleges and aware that plans to unite the two universities, which had failed so often in the past, were likely to come to fruition soon. A new phase of activity was bound to be inaugurated in the Howe as students and masters walked the ancient highway between the two colleges. How convenient to have a house, or lodgings in the Mardyke.

By the early 1850s the Society was well ahead with ambitious plans. More land in the immediate neighbourhood was acquired in 1851 by the acquisition of a croft due north belonging to the Tailor Trade and in August 1852 the *Aberdeen Journal* carried the following advertisement:

The Society of Advocates in Aberdeen, having formed a road between King Street and Spital are prepared to feu off the ground on the north side of the road on very moderate terms. The ground to be feued is upwards of 100 feet in depth and slopes to the south.

Thus appeared the thoroughfare, soon to be named by the Society of Advocates in its own honour. The slope to the south was a problem and there was talk of getting rid of the Howe altogether, or at least of levelling it up by infilling the dips with rubbish, and 'superfluous stuff from the railway'. (The Great North of Scotland Railway's line from Kittybrewster to Waterloo Quay, running through Mounthooly, would replace the Aberdeenshire Canal in 1854). But there was no rush to take up feus in Advocates

Road, and the rest of the Gallowhill and Mardyke lands remained under crop for the time being.

A report of 1854 by the Society's surveyor, James Forbes Beattie, reveals that the lands were now divided into five lots. Lot 1 had been levelled for building stances and probably included Advocates Road. Lot 2 sounded as if it were ready to become a building site. It had been left uncropped and covered with danders. The three remaining lots were still under cultivation and in good condition. But by 1864 Beattie had drawn up ambitious plans for a residential scheme, and the Mardyke and Gallowhill crofts had vanished altogether. Opposite the present Jute Street, a new street was shown with a row of terraced cottages between it and Advocates Road to the north. The cottages were set fifteen feet back from the new street, giving ample room for front gardens. On the south side of the new street, a row of larger houses, also with spacious feus, was planned. The whole, when complete, may have resembled the Victoria Street we know today. The Spital Road ran to the west and another new street was proposed to the east, a buffer against King Street. Alas, this promising 'Advocates Square' never materialised, and by 1897, what remained of the lands of Gallowhill and Mardyke was sold to the Town Council for £3000.

Across the way, John Sutherland's wife did not have very long to enjoy Viewton Place. She died in 1842, and his daughter Mary Anne married the Reverend James Black of Kirkcaldy the following year. John Sutherland would have approved of the match for like Black he was an Auld Licht Anti Burger, a member of one of the early secession kirks that had split away from the established church of Scotland before the Disruption of 1843.

For the remainder of his long life, John Sutherland enjoyed the not inconsiderable distinction of being described as 'a man of independent means'. It seems that his 'Free Kirk' principles in no way inhibited him from making money. 'He was an astute investor who early realised the value of following the cult of equity', writes George Gordon. Market prices were advertised in the *Aberdeen Journal* for the first time on 26 December 1838, and Gordon argues that Sutherland must have been among the first to transact business with Aberdeen's fledgling Stock Exchange, dealing with the city's early stockbrokers, Henry Oswald at 45 Marischal Street, and Johnstone and Gordon at No 25. He invested widely, in banks, railways, insurance and most significantly in Scottish Canadian and Scottish Australian investment companies, the ancestors of some of our well known Investment Trusts.

In spite of his wealth, John Sutherland lived quietly, without ostentation, at Viewton Place. He had no carriage which members of the Society

30

of Advocates must have thought rather *infra dig*. When he died in 1882 at the age of ninety-two, however, he left the equivalent of £3 million according to today's values. The Society of Advocates in Aberdeen must have been rather impressed.

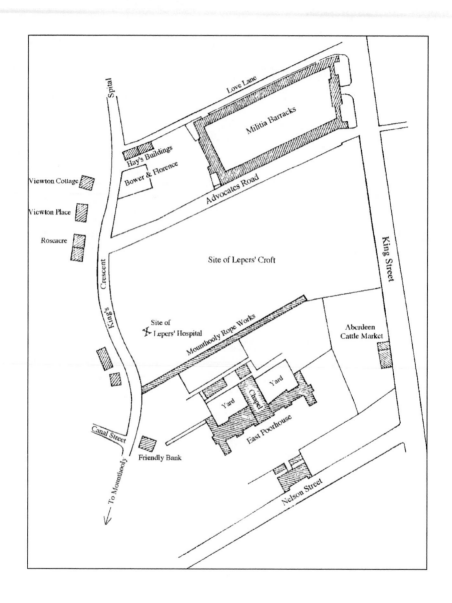

Chapter 3

From Miry Hollow to King's Crescent

I most distinctly and emphatically object to the shutting up of (Advocates) Road...
Colonel Thomas Innes of Learney

In 1861, the Commissioners of Supply for the County of Aberdeen, local lairds with a responsibility for roads, bridges and the like, announced plans which impinged on the Lands of Mardyke. They, or at least some of their number, were minded to erect a Depôt for the County Militia Regiment, the Royal Aberdeenshire Highlanders. Mr Leslie of Powis thought the price too high but Colonel Henry Knight Erskine of Pittodrie, a relative through marriage of the Moirs of Scotstown and Spital, insisted that the present Depôt was quite insufficient 'and urged that the matter did not admit of being delayed'. That opinion was straight from the horse's mouth. He commanded the regiment. Part of the site contemplated was within the Spital Lands, near the junction of Love Lane, still a little country road, and King Street, not much developed beyond Queen Street, thus offering 'advantages of open space and free communication'. It was, moreover, 'at a convenient distance from the exercise ground and musketry range on the Links' which lay just north of the Gallowhill. The remainder of the land was partly owned by Aberdeen Town Council and partly by the Society of Advocates who, it seems, was not averse to feuing out the necessary ground to the Commissioners.

That November the *Aberdeen Free Press* reported :

The frontage of the former Militia Depôt retains its original entrance.

These barracks will form a building of very considerable extent...enclosing a drill court 370 feet long and 140 feet wide. The design is quite plain, after the regular barrack fashion, only that at the angles there will be a couple of towers giving the buildings a somewhat baronial look. The estimated cost of carrying out the design is £9265, (the inevitable under-estimate) and while this may seem a large outlay for a mere regimental depot, it had to be borne in mind that storage and other accommodation has to be provided for the whole regiment.

The Royal Aberdeenshires were a volunteer regiment with a core of permanent staff. The accommodation was initially intended for the latter, while the storage space would be used for the equipment of the volunteers who were to drill there. Formed in 1859, these enthusiastic part-time soldiers, would now have a suitable home for their equipment and stores. Gunpowder, in the past, had been kept in the loft of St Paul's Episcopal Church in the Gallowgate.

The Depôt was mostly two-storey with the front entrance, to King Street, attrac-

Colonel Henry Knight Erskine, Commandant of the Royal Aberdeenshire Highlanders.

34

tively landscaped as it is to this day. Here officers' quarters and administration were located, while at the rear were storerooms, stabling, the surgery, NCO quarters, a washhouse, and the ablutions room, nicely situated between coal house and cook house. The mason work was undertaken by Messrs J Fraser and Son - 'the energetic Mr Fraser' had laid the foundation stone - and carpentry work was carried out by Messrs Daniel Macandrew & Son, whose busy and versatile Loch Street firm was encountered in *Round About Mounthooly*. The Depôt looked like a fortress and it was one. The walls were loop-holed to allow those inside to 'command the exterior of the walls at every point'. (They could, even now, if the loopholes were unblocked). Sheds and ranges of open shelters occupied the long sides of the rectangular drilling-court, flanked by Advocates Road to the south and Love Lane to the north. Before long the open shelters had to be converted into barrack rooms. Parliament had recently decreed that new recruits had to be drilled as soon as possible, hence the importance of the drill-court. Quartering them seems to have been an afterthought.

Though the plans had been drawn by William Ramage, architect, formerly assistant to Archibald Simpson, the whole scheme was the brain child of a member of the local gentry, Captain Thomas Innes. 'He induced the county to spend £12,000 in building training barracks', his obituarist noted. As a young man Innes had been called to the Scottish bar, where he practised for ten years. His real interests, however, lay elsewhere. He abandoned his legal practice and in 1855, during the time of the Crimea scare, he obtained a commission in the Royal Aberdeenshire Highlanders. He was then forty-one.

Colonel Innes of Learney, courtesy, City of Aberdeen Libraries.

The Militia Depôt - it did not become the Militia Barracks for some years - was completed by 1862, just in time for the Depôt battalion to lead the march past in front of 30,000 onlookers, the grandstand filled with the great and the good, during the first Wapinshaw of modern times held at the Links. Major Innes, as he now was, had been the driving force behind this display of weaponry and rifle practice which would become an annual event, and was responsible for the re-introduction of the ancient name, which some folk thought an affectation. The Depôt regulars paraded

The Military and Volunteer Review was the star attraction of the Wapinshaw held at the Queen's Links in 1862. The Highlanders in the foreground are the Depôt battalion which led the march past. The prominent building, centre, rear is the Bannermill. From the painting by Henry Pont.

alongside all the local volunteers in whose creation Innes had played a leading role. As was recalled in his obituary - not due to be written for another fifty years; 'He worked hard in inaugurating the Volunteers and in promoting arrangements for the defence of the county against foreign invasion.' In his hands Aberdeenshire was safe from the enemy.

The quadrangle bounded by Love Lane, Nelson Street, the Spital Road and King Street was beginning to take on a definite style. To the south the Militia Depôt was counter-balanced by an equally institutional building, the East or St Nicholas Poorhouse, which opened in 1849 under the auspices of the St Nicholas Parochial Board which was charged in those days with the care of paupers. (St Nicholas Parish was, in effect, the city of Aberdeen). The Poorhouse, standing in nearly six acres of ground, fronted on to Nelson Street and stretched back towards the open fields of the Leper's Croft, as the 1868 ordnance survey still stubbornly called the Mardykes. The governor's house at the west side of the front entrance boasted a parlour, bedrooms and a bathroom, but the kitchen was somewhat inconveniently placed on the east side of the entrance, in the lodge. The inconvenient layout of the governor's house may have persuaded Aberdeen Parish Council, the Parochial Board's sucessor, to acquire the nearby house of Friendly Bank to serve as the governor's residence at a later date.

Immediately to the rear of the governor's house and lodge were two small wards for probationary paupers, females to the east, males to the west. Three long courtyards separated this frontage from the main block of the Poorhouse, running east to west, with its extensive dormitories, work-rooms and day rooms for the inmates. There were also children's bedrooms and a school. Again there was strict male and female segregation. At right angles to this block, the long chapel and dining hall, ran from north to south, acting as a barrier between the male and female airing yards, both of which provided seats for the weary. Beyond the airing yards, and parallel to the main block was another east-west block this time containing work rooms, bakehouse, a large oven, the bread room, kitchen, wash house, laundry, drying room, carpenters' shop, storerooms, as well as male and female refractory cells for the badly behaved and a *post mortem* examination room for the dead. At the rear, two small wings running northwards, balanced the governor's house and lodge at the front. They contained, the coal store, scullery, pantry, larder, milk house, another workroom, and the ashpit. All told, there was accommodation for two hundred men and two hundred women, be they aged, infirm, dissolute or able-bodied. And there were places for children too.

The paupers, unlike the lepers, their near neighbours of earlier times, did not have to be born locally to qualify for entry. Even so, the Poorhouse,

An artist's impression of the East Poorhouse, based on contemporary maps and a lithograph of 1889 by Andrew Gibb & Co which indicates a tower similar to those at the City and Woodend Hospitals.

in its early days, did not always run to capacity. The 1851 census returns show just over 200 inmates, among them washerwomen, farm servants, a stocking knitter, a deserted wife and others as noted in *Round About Mounthooly*. Figures for 1874 show ninety-eight men, 148 women, twenty-five boys and twenty girls. Occasionally it was home to the talented. In 1888, William Bromfield, who composed 'St Kilda' died there. By the early years of the twentieth century, however, the number of inmates risen to around 400.

In 1875 the Society of Advocates, who initially feued part of the Mardyke to the St Nicholas Parochial Board for the building of the Poorhouse, now provided outdoor work opportunities by feuing to the Board, an additional three acres behind the Poorhouse grounds. 'It will be cultivated by the fatuous and other paupers kept by that Institution', the *Aberdeen Journal* reported. Cultivation went into full swing, providing not only enough vegetables for home consumption, but to sell as well, making a profit, in 1906, for example, of over £90. Pigs were reared as well as vegetables. The growing of Brussels sprouts seems not to have been successful and on one occasion we find the governor authorised to purchase 3,000, of them. That order list also included 1000 yards of picture cord and hooks; enough surely to cover every wall of the Poorhouse with paintings of a suitably uplifting and instructive nature.

A sizeable community such as the East Poorhouse, with its various needs generated good business for tradesmen and retailers throughout town and in the immediate neighbourhood. William McKinnon's Spring Garden Iron Works carried out a number of unspecified repairs most years, while Stephen Goodbrand supplied hosiery. Considerable quantities and ranges of materials, purchased from local warehousemen kept the workshops busy. But it was not all work. Apart from the annual strawberry treat, concerts were provided by the choirs of the local churches, and flowers and magazines were handed in. *The People's Friend* was supplied by the publisher on a regular basis. The East Poorhouse children - fifty-five boys and fifty-seven girls at that time were allotted a special place in Union Terrace to see the Royal procession when King Edward VII, accompanied by Queen Alexandra, were *en route* to open the new Marischal College façade in September 1906.

Nor was admission to the Poorhouse necessarily for life. Many inmates did die there, ninety-one in 1907, but others left voluntarily, or were taken away by relatives; still others were boarded out or sent into service; some were returned to their home parish; others absconded, some were dismissed. Ordinary and special leaves of absence were granted, the latter for example, for funerals of kinsfolk. The names, of those 'returned drunk' from such excursions were invariably noted. Not all residents were paupers. Boarders, itinerant musicians for example, who would later use the East North Street 'modler', were put up for a small fee.

The atmosphere at the city's first Cattle Market, built soon after the Poorhouse, in 1850, and on adjoining ground to the east, was likely to have been rather cheerier. The concept of a market was an innovatory one, for at that time fat cattle were sold to butchers and fleshers, by private bargain, either at the twice yearly country fairs, or straight from the farm. The choice of site on the King Street-Nelson Street corner seems curious at first glance. It was not particularly handy for the harbour, and was far removed from the transient terminus of the new south railway at Ferryhill, while the proposed permanent terminus at Guild Street would offer only marginal improvement. But King Street, which became the King Street Road north of Love Lane, was the popular route into town for farmers from the north of the county; and the Market was handily placed for calves, sheep, and pigs transported from Inverurie and the Garioch, into Aberdeen by barge. Tallis's Plan of the early 1850s reveals just how close the Aberdeenshire Canal's landing area at Nelson Street and the Cattle Market were. The letter-head on page 43, though dating from a time long after the Canal had gone, shows that there was a Nelson Street entrance.

Beasts continued to be sold on the traditional one-to-one basis at the new Market, but the business was now simplified and centralised. One

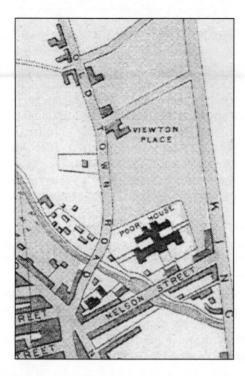

Tallis's Plan of the early 1850s. Note the proximity of the Aberdeenshire Canal, flowing under Nelson Street, to the Cattle Market, on the Nelson/King Street corner. The scattering of houses across the Old Town Road from the Poorhouse is Canal Street, while the anonymous house sitting in solitary splendour to the north is Viewton Place. (Hay's Buildings, almost opposite have been wrongly identified as Viewton Place).

young cattle salesman would streamline the trade even further. The enterprising John Duncan, born in 1840 in the Spital, was dealing privately in stock by the time he was in his early twenties, and began to build up a substantial trade with Orkney and Shetland farmers. By 1867 he had decided to acquire a stance at the Market, and on 27 November of that year, the following advertisement appeared in the *Aberdeen Journal*:

Aberdeen Cattle Market

John Duncan, Spital, begs to intimate to Farmers and others engaged in the Cattle Trade, that he has commenced Business as Cattle Salesman in the above Market, having had considerable experience for a number of years back in buying and selling Cattle on his own account; and to those favouring him with Consignments he hopes, by strict attention to Business, and by securing full value for Stock forwarded for sale, to merit a continued share of patronage.

There followed a formidable list of sponsors, a cattle dealer, numerous fleshers and J & W Martin, Butchers, Aberdeen. In a postscript Duncan advised that he had acquired the stance of the late Mr Isaac, cattle salesman 'which he has fitted up to show Cattle to advantage'. In fact he would chain cows up so that the buyer could poke and prod and assess each animal's degree of finish.

It was not long before Duncan abandoned the private sale, and at much the same time as Alex Middleton of the Belmont Mart, Kittybrewster, began to pioneer the auctioning of cattle in Aberdeen. In a few months time, it was as 'Live Stock Agent and Auctioneer' that he was advertising a 'Sale of Fat Stock, every Saturday at 12.30pm, in the Cattle Market, Aberdeen'. At one such sale, for example, that of 23 September, 1868, the *Aberdeen Journal* reported upwards of one hundred head of cattle, and a large attendance of buyers, but sales were slow, except for the better class of cattle, one superior bull fetching £86. 'Supplies of sheep not so large as previous weeks, but fully equal to demand'.

David Kerr Cameron in *The Cornkister Days* describes how Duncan's mart would have evolved:

First he erected 'flakes', portable fencing, to mark stock divisions, then came the rostrum and, finally, more permanent structures took shape. John knew a good beast when he saw one and like many old auctioneers expected the same skill in others. He was, it was said, the fastest seller in the north.

In 1878 he sold 102 head of American cattle at prices ranging from £21 to £29 10s in half an hour, such was the demand; but it was some time before the openness of the public mart was fully accepted by the North East's conservative farmers; as the *Aberdeen Daily Journal* recorded at the time of his death: 'by his straightforwardness and probity, Mr Duncan in the early days overcame the prejudice that lurked for a time in the minds of many'.

By the early 1870s he had left his home at No 37 Spital for No 6 Roslin Terrace a stone's throw from the Cattle Market on the other side of King Street. Here the first two of his seven children, six sons and a daughter, all of whom would do well, were born. By 1875, with his family increasing, he had moved again, to a more spacious dwelling. Across on the high, airy west side of the Spital Road, John Sutherland's handsome Viewton Place had stood in splendid isolation for nearly twenty years. By 1854, however, Robert McKilliam, a prosperous manufacturing confectioner with premises in Union Street and the Upperkirkgate, had bought a piece of ground immediately to the north which, like Viewton Place, had once been part of Lindsay's Folly. Here McKilliam built a substantial ten-roomed house which he called Viewton Cottage, and here he stayed for the best part of twenty years. It was to Viewton Cottage that John Duncan came in 1875. By

Duncan's Zetland House. It later became an X-Ray centre and is now Grampian Health Board Staff Social & Recreational Club. Courtesy Hugh Duncan.

that time - it had been back in 1866 to be exact - the section of the Spital Road between the Mounthooly Railway Bridge and Love Lane had been christened King's Crescent. It was some distance from King's College, and the name probably derives from the fact that the College and its successor, Aberdeen University, were superiors of much land in the area.

After four years in Viewton Cottage, Duncan was on the march again. He had acquired ground on the corner of the King Street Road and the newly laid out Merkland Road, within spitting distance of the Cattle Market. Here he built an imposing townhouse, with stabling to the rear. He called his new residence Zetland House - then the official name of the county of Shetland - acknowledging that his prosperity had derived, at least in part, from the sale of cattle from the Northern Isles. A brief stroll past the Poorhouse vegetable garden, the Militia Barracks and James Hutcheon's gloomily named King Street Cemetery Granite Works, and he was home from work. At the time of building Zetland House, he had also become tenant of Whitestripes Farm on the Grandhome estate beyond the Bridge of Don, and both properties would remain in his possession for the rest of his life.

In the early 1880s he became official cattle salesman to Queen Victoria, who, the *Aberdeen Journal* reported, 'would send to the City Mart some of her choice wealthily-fleshed black skins from Abergeldie, and there was always exceptionally keen competition for their possession'. His stationery

42

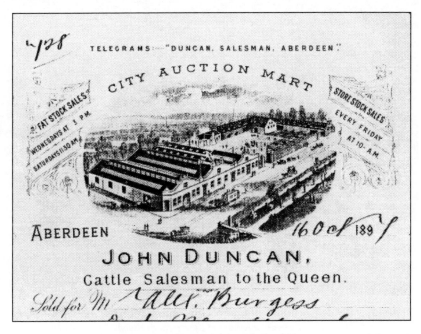

TELEGRAMS:— "DUNCAN, SALESMAN, ABERDEEN".

CITY AUCTION MART

FAT STOCK SALES WEDNESDAYS AT 1 P.M. SATURDAYS 11.30 A.M.

STORE STOCK SALES EVERY FRIDAY AT 10. A.M.

ABERDEEN

JOHN DUNCAN,
Cattle Salesman to the Queen.

John Duncan's letterhead incorporates a fine illustration of the Mart. Note, left, cattle entering by the Nelson Street gate. On the extreme left, the trees of the East Poorhouse can be glimpsed and on the extreme right, across King Street, the entrance of the Boys' and Girls' Hospital, now the RGIT Ltd Offshore Survival Centre. Courtesy, Sandy Burgess.

thereafter bore the proud legend: 'Cattle Salesman to the Queen'. By 1884 he had resolved to buy the Cattle Market and his lawyers approached the owners, Aberdeen Town Council, with an offer of £1850 which was accepted. The Market had undergone a few improvements since its early days. Refreshment rooms and cattle sheds had been erected in 1869, and Duncan, 'full of progressive ideas and business capacity', made further improvements. The Market became the City Auction Mart.

At the time John Duncan was living in King's Crescent, a curving row of houses had been built south of Viewton Place. The first house was erected in 1863 by Joseph Tennant, a King Street draper. The feudal superior, Aberdeen University - King's and Marischal Colleges had at last joined forces - was anxious to set the same high standards that King's College had imposed on feuars when Canal Street was laid out fifty years earlier. Joseph Tennant was instructed, by the terms of his feu charter, to build:

43

Roseacre, right and its neighbours, viewed from Advocates Road. The tall handsome trees are a feature of the neighbourhood.

a substantial dwelling house, similar to those in Roslin Terrace, Aberdeen, fronting the said Spital Road and retired backwards therefrom fifty feet or thereby, the said house being built with stone and lime and covered with slates and of the value of at least £300 sterling.

Tennant obliged with a compact seven-roomed house and carved a name for it, Roseacre, on a stone near the top of the house. His feu charter contains more gems. The University had it in mind to open up a new road through its land, the future Jute Street, running westward between the Spital Road and Froghall Cottage, and was giving out feus for a number of houses in the empty ground between Joseph Tennant's house and the new road. All of them had to be of the same standard and uniformity was to be preserved. None were to be higher than Roseacre, and 'none…shall project forward beyond each other'. Moreover, the long front gardens shall not be used by feuars in any part for bleach greens or drying poles (that was for the rear) but as flower gardens only. A true appreciation of what townscape is all about! Feuing plans were drawn up by the distinguished architect, J R Mackenzie, and in 1868, the cottages south of Roseacre appeared, curving down to the Jute Street-King's Crescent corner.

The mirror image houses Nos 23-25 on this corner were built by two sisters, Jessie and Mary Anne Johnston who had inherited money from their father, a Culter landowner. One sister was married to Robert Cran, an

44

accountant, the other, to a merchant, Ewen McDonald who had journeyed, barefoot, from Uig in Skye to make his fortune in the North East. There was still a rural feel about the place, and the cottages had an uninterrupted outlook across to the Links and the sea. The tenements, built across the road for the workforce of Bower & Florence, granite merchants, were not then in existence.

The Jute Works at Froghall were being built in 1873. In that same year the University also feued ground encompassing what became the part of King's Crescent south of Jute Street, and much of the future Jute Street, which it had intended to open up itself, to Loch Street builder, Daniel Macandrew. The *Aberdeen Journal* of 22 April 1874 confirmed the name of the new street, 'in accordance with the wishes of Mr Macandrew', who now lost no time in designing and building stylish new villas, with piended slate roofs, bracketed eaves, swan-neck consoles and corniced ridge stacks. Ready by 1875, these were pioneer concrete buildings, among the first such in Scotland as was the Tivoli, built in 1872 as Her Majesty's Theatre. Macandrew rented out three of these new houses, Nos 17, 19 and 21 King's Crescent, and kept the fourth, No 1 Jute Street, Crescent Villa, on the corner, for himself. They are all now Category 'B'-listed. Daniel Macandrew was a man of considerable ability. He had served apprenticeships both as architect and joiner, and among his many building contracts were those for the library at King's, now the Visitor Centre, and the anatomical buildings at Marischal. A Free Kirker, he had, as a young man at the time of the Disruption of 1843, drawn up and gifted plans for Old John Knox Free in Gerrard Street to the con-gregation.

Daniel Macandrew, courtesy, City of Aberdeen Libraries.

Between Mount Pleasant on the Canal Street corner and the first of the concrete houses, a row of traditional cottages had appeared during the 1860s while the last house to be built in King's Crescent was at the far end. In 1879, the Rev John Comper of St Margaret's Episcopal Church in the Gallowgate built a fine family home, St Margaret's Brae, immediately north of Viewton Cottage. In spite of its address, 39 King's Crescent, it is beyond the old boundary and its story more logically belongs to the Spital.

Macandrew's pioneering concrete houses form the white group, centre, with the 'Roseacre' group beyond. Left, traditional cottages at the Mounthooly end of King's Crescent. Extreme right, offices for Fire Brigade safety staff are under way in 1996.

While attractive new houses were going up in King's Crescent, a quagmire remained underfoot. Early in the nineteenth century 'the Howe o Spital was a pandemonium of mire and darkness', according to the *Aberdeen Journal* and things got worse after the Fusion of the Colleges in 1860 when the numbers of students tramping the Spital Road increased dramatically. On 3 January 1872 the *Journal* reported:

It is lamentable to see year in year out in wet weather several hundred students wading along the ancient highway between Marischal and King's Colleges. It is suggested to cut a portion of the high Spital Hill and fill in the 'miry hollow' known as King's Crescent between that part opposite St Nicholas Poorhouse and Love Lane. This measure would give an easy gradient, and causeying the whole like King Street would give a dry-shod way to many a hard-grinding student. A small subscription from 1000 students would enable the footpath all the way from Mounthooly to College Bounds to be raised a few inches and laid with Caithness flagstones or concrete. The distance of about 800 yards at 5/- a yard would cost £200.

Nothing came of this. But pedestrian traffic had increased further with the formation of Jute Street and the opening of the Jute Works, and at last

46

in 1876, the Council agreed to lay the granite footpath with proper channels on both sides of the street from Mounthooly Bridge to Love Lane. As George Gordon has noted: 'Up to that time one of the more essential of the outside fixtures of the dwellings in King's Crescent had been the mud scrappers; a few still remain as a reminder of a muddier age'.

Back on the east side of King's Crescent, the Society of Advocates, had given up hope, perhaps precipitously, of a desirable housing development, an Advocates Square, and seem to have been reconciled to an industrial use for the Lands of Mardyke and Gallowhill. John Clark, their factor, declared sadly of Advocates Road; No feus 'have yet been disposed of, and there appears to be little or no demand for any as sites of houses'. As early as 1866, the Society feued land to John Florence, an experienced stonecutter then in his thirties, specifically for use as a granite yard. Earlier in the century, granite had been laboriously cut and polished by hand and in those days, as John Fyfe, the grand old man of granite put it, 'the granite trade of Aberdeen consisted of three journeymen masons, two or three apprentices and a dog'. However, after Alexander Macdonald made his first tentative experiments in polishing granite mechanically in the 1820s, the trade had grown by fits and starts, swelling to a crescendo at the end of the century. John Florence's small yard, one of a dozen, scattered across Aberdeen in the 1860s, was tucked behind Hay's Buildings near the Love Lane corner. It fronted King's Crescent, directly opposite Viewton Cottage. To the east, bleach greens separated the yard from the rear of the Militia Depôt.

John Florence made an inauspicious start. His partner, John Westland, vanished from the scene soon after start up, and, re-emerged in partnership with another granite cutter, as Westland & Anderson, in Constitution Street. Worse still, on the morning of Christmas Eve, 1866 at about 7.15 the boiler of the yard's steam engine burst, with, as the *Aberdeen Journal* reported:

a fearful explosion. Some idea of the violence of the explosion may be formed from the fact that some of the bricks, pieces of stone and metal were thrown from a distance of several hundred yards, breaking a large number of windows in the houses in Love Lane and King's Crescent. In one instance a brick went through the shutters and windows of a house in King's Crescent about 50 yards distant and penetrated through the partition of the room into another apartment. A large piece of metal which required five men to lift was thrown to a considerable height over adjoining houses. Fortunately no one was hurt.

John Florence was not one to be easily deterred. He now put his business on a sound footing by entering into partnership with the entrepre-

The workforce of Bower & Florence's Spital Granite Works, King's Crescent circa 1912. Wallace the watchdog is in the foreground, one of the firm's seven overhead cranes in the background, and over the rear wall, the barracks built by Colonel Innes.

Left, James Bower. Right, James Florence, courtesy, City of Aberdeen Libraries.

neurial James H Bower. Bower, had made his money from the lucrative Scotch coal business, the railway companies, and the Caledonian Lime Company, to name but a few of the irons he had in the fire. He recognised the potential of the expanding granite industry and Florence's energy and ability. The firm was relaunched as Bower & Florence, Spittal Granite Works, in 1867, though in fact Bower at this time had bought out Florence's financial interest for £900. True to the principal of living over the shop, John Florence acquired Roseacre, its third owner, in 1873. Bower was less handily placed. He owned the estate of Pitmurchie near Torphins. (The house is now a private nursing home). To be fair, he also had a townhouse in Golden Square. What John Sutherland in Viewton Place must have felt about the din of a granite yard across the road is not recorded.

Expansion, not explosion, was now the watchword of the firm. In 1873 Bower & Florence built a handsome, bow-fronted granite office, at the corner of Advocates Road and King's Crescent, and the following year extended their yard which involved the Advocates, their feudal superiors, in a contretemps with the Militia of which more anon. In 1875 the firm louped Advocates Road when the Society feued them almost two acres due south of the yard. Here they built a curving crescent of substantial tenements for the workforce, though again it was J H Bower who put up the money. To this day, the great depths of their basements indicate something of the original hollow of the Spital Howe. Each tenement housed seven or eight families and the crescent was in two blocks, Nos 40-44 and Nos 46-52 King's Crescent, the division caused by a nameless road laid out to give access into the Mardyke lands, to the Advocates' Square that never was. Guarding its entrance and well-placed for the Bower & Florence workforce and their families were the twin corner shops, whose doors were sur-

49

Twin corner shops with matching corbels stand guard on either side of the cul-de-sac, laid out to give access to the Square that never was.

mounted by matching corbels, giant thumb marks in the granite. At No 44 was James Gray, baker, who lived across at Mount Pleasant in Canal Street while William Milne, the grocer, was at No 46. The shop was 'dry', not popular in a growing neighbourhood, and Milne's licence eventually came about by curious means. On 7 April 1882 Mrs Tod of 19 King's Crescent, wife of the assistant curate at St Margaret's in the Gallowgate:

was seen to rush from her house, her whole person alight, enveloped in flame. Her cries roused the neighbours and they rushed to her assistance by throwing cold water over her. Dr Jackson who was passing at the time gave what help he could ...It is believed that a live coal set her dress alight.

Mrs Tod died the following day. A few days later William Milne applied again for a grocer's shop licence. A previous application had been refused, in spite of a large number of signatures in support, and in spite of his having held an unblemished licence in another part of town for twenty years. Now Aberdeen Licensing Court heard from Milne's lawyer that during Mrs Tod's tragic accident the whole district had been searched for a bottle of wine without success. There was nothing available between Craig's shop in the Gallowgate and the Red Lion on the Spital Hill. 'If the

50

shop had had a licence some good may have been done for the poor woman'. William Milne was eventually given his licence which was subsequently held by his widow, and by his successor, James M. Duncan. Gray the baker across at No 44 was succeeded early in the twentieth century by a bakery branch of the North of Scotland Co-operative Company as the 'Co-opie' then was.

Bower & Florence went from strength to strength. In the late 1880s, *Scotland of Today* enthused:

The Spittal Granite Yard (is) admirably laid out and fully equipped with the most modern appliances. There is a large polishing mill, together with a complete plant of improved sawing and cutting machinery, all worked by steam power. Their productions in polished granite monuments (red, blue and grey), and in all kinds of tombs, columns, pilasters, house fronts, chimney pieces etc. exhibit merit in artistic design... The quality of the material used is of the highest class, the granite being brought direct to the works from the firm's valuable quarry at Peterhead. The trade is mainly of an export character, goods being extensively and frequently consigned to China, Australia, New Zealand and North and South America. Messrs Bower & Florence have also developed a valuable home connection.

These were boom days for the industry. In 1892, the value of finished granite exported from Aberdeen to America was £67, 000, while the total of all other goods exported from the city was only £42,500. That was the year that John Florence died, following a severe attack of flu. He was only fifty-five, and perhaps overwork had taken its toll. James H Bower continued as sole proprietor until his death in 1901, the year that the city exported over 70,000 tons of granite. James's eldest son, Haddon A Bower, now took over. He and his two brothers would carve distinguished careers for themselves in Aberdeen. Herbert, was a partner in Bower & Smith, Chartered Accountants, while George Haddon Bower was a partner in the legal firm of G H Bower & Gibb, Advocates in Aberdeen. George had married Amy, sister of the opera singer, Mary Garden, and it was one day while staying with Amy at Pitmurchie that Mary Garden consigned letters written to her by the composer Debussy to a garden bonfire. A few were saved in the nick of time.

The involvement of the Bowers, businessmen who could supply financial backing, was the exception rather than the rule in the granite trade. The industry in its Golden Age offered opportunities for the skilled, go-ahead artisan. John McLaren was one such. His story is typical of many granite merchants, though he was more successful than most. He had walked in from his home near Dunecht to serve his time as an apprentice mason with

51

Haddon Bower, left and John McLaren. Courtesy, Ian McLaren

Bower & Florence before the First World War. He later went to seek his fortune in the United States and in South Africa before returning to his old firm as one of their key men. Later he left to set up round the corner in St Peter Street, in partnership with Alec Norrie. In those days, as his son, John Mclaren Jnr (Ian), recalled, 'a good craftsman with little financial backing could acquire a patch of ground and quickly establish a business'. Ian McLaren continued:

Norrie, McLaren & Co were destined to be short-lived. Mr Bower, frustrated by the incompetent running and supervision of his works, exploded one day, 'for God's sake send for McLaren'. As McLaren had by this time realised that he was doing the bulk of the work in the St Peter Street yard with little help from his partner, he was prepared to return - but only in partnership with Mr Bower.

Bower & Florence, with John McLaren at the helm and with close on a hundred men (and a dog) on the staff, and with a large variety of contracts, continued successfully into the twentieth century.

More granite men arrived in the old Mardyke. John G Duncan, Sculptor and Monumental Mason, whose trade was increasing, moved to 'more commodious premises' in Advocates Road in 1890. In his 'well-arranged office' *Scotland of Today* tell us:

intending customers have always the privilege of inspecting a splendid assortment of all kinds of designs. The various machines and mechanical appliances, cranes etc. are large and of the most powerful character, while the whole of the operations are performed with the greatest ease, celerity and precision.

Small but successful, Duncan's employed about a dozen skilled man and regularly turned out 'a large amount of splendid work', for export, including fountains, pedestals and vases. Interestingly, as well as the local stone, in red, pink, white, blue and grey, Duncan imported red and green granite from Sweden and grey granite from Germany. By 1893, he was off again, across town to a bigger and better yard. The St Nicholas Granite Works had also been set up in Advocates Road by Archibald A Brown in 1890 and after Duncan's departure Brown had a new neighbour Thomas J Blann, who, before the end of the century was on his travels again, to the great granite yards of Merkland and Pittodrie. These were heady times in the industry when firms, now long forgotten, were here today and gone tomorrow, continually, it seems, in search of bigger and better premises, and more promising partnerships. A blacksmith was also in residence in Advocates Road, working on his own account, but also likely to be undertaking jobs for the yards.

The last granite merchant to arrive in the old Mardyke was James Rae who set up his Crown Granite Works behind the back greens of the Bower & Florence tenements in 1897. The lay-out of the yard crossed the vestigial road and probably created the cul-de-sac we know today. It remained anonymous and James Rae had to be content with 44b King's Crescent as the address of the Crown Granite Works. He was another over-the-shop boss, living at No 13 and later at No 23 King's Crescent on the Jute Street corner.

Not all industries within the enclave were connected with granite. Around 1880, a rope and twine manufactory, the Mounthooly Ropeworks, was founded by Stephen Goodbrand and Peter Skene with a workforce averaging around six men and thirty boys. The ropewalk was tucked neatly behind the Poorhouse, close to the putative site of the leper's hospital and the ephemeral Chapel of St Anne, and running east towards King Street, between the inmates' vegetable garden to the north and John Duncan's City Auction Mart to the south. Later a store, a heckling shed, a stable and a coach house were added. Goodbrand had bought Viewton Place, only a stone's throw away, in 1893, the year after John Sutherland's death. The steep access at Viewton would have made it difficult to bring a coach in about, so housing it at the Ropeworks was a sensible solution.

Stephen Goodbrand's name was for many years a household one in Aberdeen and his story is a classic example of the Victorian principle of self-

53

help. He started his working life as a heckler, combing out flax fibres at Hadden's Mills in the Green. There he remained until the firm went bankrupt in 1848. His talents had not gone unnoticed, and at the request of John Stewart, joint founder with Joseph Rowell of the Aberdeen Combworks, he became cashier of that firm, 'where he would be left with the entire charge and responsibility of the works' in the absence of the partners. Later he became cashier and manager of Andrew Sutherland's Woollen Mill at the top of Canal Road and held the same position under Mr Watkins, a former manager of Broadford, who bought the factory from the Sutherland family. It

Stephen Goodbrand, courtesy, City of Aberdeen Libraries.

was whilst he was employed by Watkins & Co that he found time to set up the Mounthooly Ropeworks. Peter Skene, his partner had been a traveller with the well known brush firm of Messrs Gray Watt & Co. whose manufactory was at the Mounthooly end of West North Street. On Skene's death, Stephen Goodbrand not only carried on the business single-handed, but started up a successful hosiery business at 176 George Street. Goodbrand, described as kindly, generous and lacking in ostentation, had remarkable energy and business capacity. He was a cousin of the Woodside flesher William Murray, another self-made man, whose business in the dead meat trade expanded from George Street and Hutcheon Street, throughout Scotland, into England and across the Atlantic to the Chicago stock yards. Goodbrand travelled widely in Europe and the United states as his representative.

Immediately north of the Mounthooly Ropeworks, on the conjectural site of the lepers' hospital, the Northern Bowling Club established a green in the 1890s. In 1914 the bowlers went off to Orchard Road where they remain.

We end where we began, at the Militia Depôt, which, over the years, would have a chequered career. In 1863, soon after its completion, there was an outbreak of typhus in the Gallowgate and Causewayend areas, and it was deemed safer to entrain the regiment for Fort George, and carry out summer exercises there, a routine that was continued for some years before the depôt was brought fully into use. Lieutenant Colonel Thomas Innes, who had received promotion in his civilian as well as his military capacity, coming into his own as laird of the family estates of Learney and Cullerlie. Four years later he declared war on the Society of Advocates. When Advocates Road had been formed over twenty years earlier, it was as a private road, for the sole purpose of giving access to feus on the Mardyke lands. Indeed, the architect - and future Lord Provost - James Matthews, who had laid out the road, advised the Society in 1854:

It would be advisable to shut off the new Street, in the meantime from public traffic. And I would recommend a timber fence of upright slabs to be erected along the south side, say three and a half feet wide with a Beech hedge planted on the inside.

Love Lane, only a few yards to the north, provided the necessary public access between the Spital Road and King Street. In August 1874, Bower & Florence who were anxious to extend to the east, toward the Barracks, sought to have the adjoining part of Advocates Road included in their feu. The Society agreed. As a courtesy John Clark, advised the military that Advocates Road would now be closed, reminding them that it ,'was never open for public traffic which has always been excluded' and 'in so far as I can learn, it is not required and has not been used for the purpose of the Barrack'. Innes's reply was a redoubtable piece of dog-in-the-mangerism. While indicating that the Regiment did not often require the use of Advocates Road for wheeled traffic, and that its closure was not a matter 'of sufficient importance' he immediately went on thunder that :

the access of that road is of very great importance and the maintenance of open space round the Barrack is most essential. I most distinctly and emphatically object to the shutting up of the road or curtailment in any way of the space which has hitherto been open to the passage and use of the Regiment on the South side of the Barracks'

As chairman of the Kincardine O'Neil District Road Board, Innes controlled the roads in that area (in all for fifty years), and took badly to any road within his sphere of influence being controlled by others. Soon, however, he was involved in a more serious crisis when, in the mid-1870s, the Government toyed with the idea of dispensing with the Barracks altogether; then the pendulum swung the other way in 1880 when additional space was urgently required after the Regiment was augmented by two companies. The War Office 's response was notoriously slow in such

The barrack square soon after 1870 looking east. The inner side of the range which fronts King Street is to the rear. The plaque, just visible, right, was dedicated by the officers and men of the Royal Aberdeenshire Highlanders to the memory of their CO, Colonel Henry Knight Erskine of Pittodrie. The south range, right has been converted into married quarters. Courtesy, Gordon Highlanders' Museum.

The barrack square before 1880, looking west. Top right is the Spital Hill where the Chapel of St Margaret's Convent would later be built. Like the north range, right, the south range, left, has been converted into married quarters. Courtesy, Gordon Highlanders' Museum.

matters, so Innes, now a full Colonel, took matters in hand, personally instructing the building of new barracks of three storeys with attics, and co-incidentally putting paid to the concept of maintaining 'open space round the Barrack'. The new building was sited at the rear of the main block and could house a further 300 men. It cost Colonel Innes £3000, but he ensured that the rates payable by the Government to the local authority would be made over to him until he was fully reimbursed. Bower & Florence had meanwhile expanded eastwards as intended, and so the granite yard and the barracks confronted each other, not face-to-face, but rear-to-rear on land that had of late been bleach greens. By this time, the barrack rooms along the north and south ranges, had been converted into married quarters for the NCOs and men of the permanent garrison. Numbers fluctuated, but officers apart, a typical permanent garrison in the late nineteenth century would consist of; one pipe major, one colour sergeant, one staff sergeant, one quartermaster sergeant, one sergeant drummer, two sergeants, three drummers, three corporals, one lance-corporal and four privates. The main body of men, still volunteers, lived locally, and reported to the barracks when required to drill.

In 1882, the Royal Aberdeenshires were amalgamated with two other regiments to become the Third Battalion, the Gordon Highlanders (Militia); two years later, new colours were presented to them by the Prince and Princess of Wales, the future Edward VII and Queen Alexandra. Colonel Innes had retired at the time of the amalgamation, having twice prolonged his period of service beyond the official age limit. 'The practice of renewed periods of command was a bad one,' wrote Lachlan Mackinnon succinctly about no one in particular. Innes was sixty-eight, and as it transpired, had another thirty years public service left in him. At the time of his death it was recorded that he 'made his influence felt in every public department with which his name was associated'. These were many; his chairmanships and directorships included those of the Commissioners of Supply, of various Road Boards, his local Parochial Board, Agricultural Societies and the Great North of Scotland Railway. He founded and laid out Torphins, completed Learney House, saved Richards & Co of Broadford from collapse and the River Dee from pollution; he abolished the tolls, reorganised the finances of the Milne Bequest which enhanced local teachers' remuneration, played a leading role in establishing the marts at Kittybrewster, as well as the Conservative Club and the Gordon Highlanders Institute in Belmont Street, where he personally bought the building, No 37, and set it up as a club. By an interesting co-incidence it had been built in 1778 by George Moir of Scotstown and Spital as his townhouse.

Innes was a leading member of St Paul's Episcopal Church, which no doubt explains why gunpowder was once permitted to be stored in the loft.

No 37 Belmont Street.

Never one to take 'no' for an answer he secured Highland dress for his Aberdeenshire Militia after it had been initially refused and subsequently wrote a history of the Regiment. He was senior Royal Archer during Edward VII's last visit to Scotland, and set in motion plans for a statue of the King to be erected in Aberdeen after the latter's death; but he did not live to see its unveiling at the Union Terrace corner in 1914. Colonel Thomas Innes of Learney, who as a young advocate had seen Sir Walter Scott walking with his stick in the High Street of Edinburgh, died in 1912 at the age of ninety-eight. Local big shots didn't come much bigger.

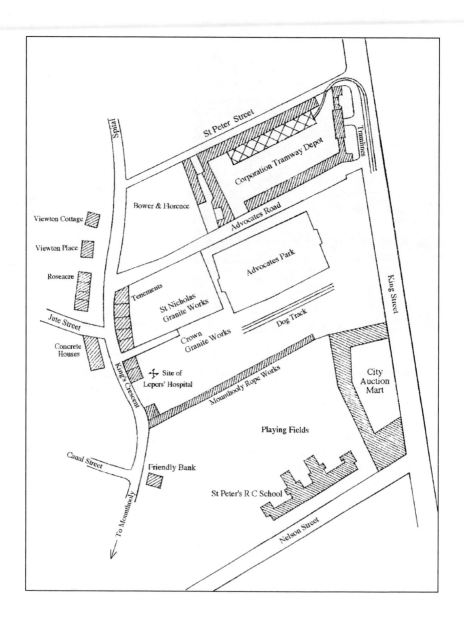

Viewton Cottage

Viewton Place

Roseacre

Jute Street

Concrete
Houses

King's Crescent

Canal Street

To Mounthooly

Spital

St Peter Street

Corporation Tramway Depot

Tramlines

Bower & Florence

Advocates Road

Tenements

St Nicholas
Granite Works

Advocates Park

Crown
Granite Works

Dog Track

Site of
Lepers' Hospital

Mounthooly Rope Works

King Street

City
Auction
Mart

Playing Fields

Friendly Bank

St Peter's R C School

Nelson Street

Chapter 4

The Great Quadrangle

Advocates Park: A football ground of fond and revered memory.

George Tait.

At the north end of the great quadrangle, life in the Third Battalion, the Gordon Highlanders went on at the Militia Barracks after Colonel Innes had taken late retirement. In the 1960s, Mr William Waterman, by then oldest living Gordon, could recall being billeted in the 'Advocates Barracks' after joining the Gordon Highlanders in 1892. At that time the Barracks 'under Pipe Major Grant' still appeared in the valuation roll as part of the Spital Lands. The Militia were now known as volunteer units - the term 'territorial' was yet to be coined, and indeed 'volunteer' has come back into fashion - and they remained a home defence force. During the Boer War, however, there came an innovation; for the first time volunteer units were allowed to go overseas. Three Volunteer Service Companies were recruited from the Third Battalion in 1900 and 1901 and marched away from King Street to entrain for Southampton and sail for Capetown. They were attached to regular Gordon battalions for a twelve months tour of duty, acquitted themselves well and won high praise from Lord Roberts, Commander-in-Chief of the British forces in South Africa.

After the Boer War ended in 1902, the Barracks reverted to its peace time role. It was in 1905 that twenty-one year-old George Stewart MacLennan, who had enlisted in the Gordons in 1899, was promoted pipe major, the youngest in the British Army. He had won the Oban Gold Medal the previous year in 1904 and on three subsequent occasions he would win the

61

The barrack square in 1899, looking west, with the Third Gordon Highlanders on parade. The building commissioned by Colonel Innes now looms behind the west range - which has gained a clock. The west, like the south range, left, was demolished when Aberdeen Corporation Tramways took over. Innes's building, which served as a hospital, remains, as does the north range, right. The Convent Chapel, top right, completed in 1892, in turn looms above Innes's building. Courtesy, Gordon Highlanders' Museum.

G S MacLennan, courtesy,
Gordon Highlanders' Museum.

Inverness Gold Clasp, the unofficial world championship. One of the most brilliant composers for the bagpipes, 'GS' had learned pibroch at his father's knee, and was a veteran by the age of ten, playing for Queen Victoria by Royal Command.

He was based at Castlehill, but one of his duties was to organise a pipe band at the Militia Barracks. Apparently in those days many army pipers had been tinkers in civilian life, piping being a tradition of the race, but it seems that 'GS' was not impressed by their playing. Hopefully he was able to raise standards. The family lived in King Street and in Powis Place. According to George MacLennan Jnr, his father successfully avoided married quarters throughout his army career. He could not countenance the thought of an officer coming into his quarters and giving orders to his family. On leaving the army 'GS' opened a bagpipe shop in the city, but died early, at the age of forty-five. The gun carriage which bore his coffin was drawn by six horses and was followed by a group of senior officers, 20,000 mourners, and by three pipe bands which played 'Lochaber No More'. This indeed was a cortège on a par with those of Priest Gordon and Dr Kidd of Gilcomston. Little wonder the city came to a standstill.

Two distinguished holders of the Victoria Cross were stationed at the Militia Barracks during their army careers. A Boer War hero, Sergeant Major William Robertson, was posted to the Third Battalion as Captain

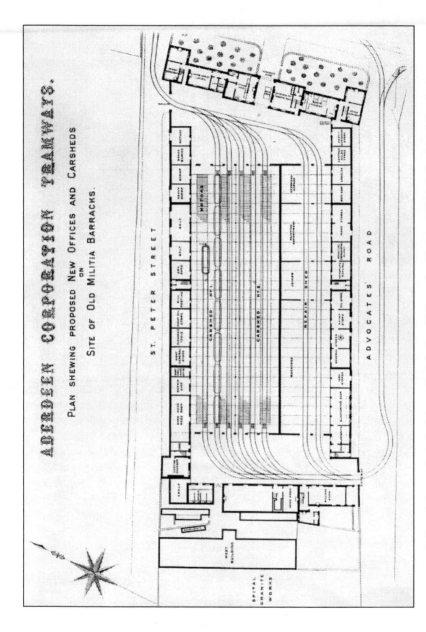

A plan of the car shed. It slots neatly into the old Barracks. Courtesy City of Aberdeen Libraries.

(QM) in 1904. He retired in the 1920s with the rank of colonel. The other holder was Lieutenant Alan Ebenezer Ker, who showed 'conspicuous bravery and devotion to duty' in France in 1918.

But we are running ahead of ourselves. Prior to the outbreak of the First World War, the War Office had relinquished the Barracks. By 1912 they were empty and in the ownership of Aberdeen County Council, successors to the Commissioners of Supply. But others were hatching plans. By late 1913, Aberdeen's burgh surveyor, William Dyack and the tramway manager, R Stuart Pilcher, were putting up a good case for the acquisition by Aberdeen Town Council, 'of the subjects in King Street known as the Militia Barracks for tramway purposes'. The two-and-a-half acre site, of which less than an acre was occupied by buildings, had great potential, allowing for the construction of 'new offices and car sheds' (a tramcar depôt) within the original rectangle of the Barracks.

The first phase could include, they argued, not only 'accommodation for twenty-two (tram)cars' but 'six motor omnibuses' as well. In fact, the first motor bus was not purchased until 1920 and for the following seven years the sides of early buses were emblazoned with *Corporation Tramways*. The car shed was to be of steel frame construction and would run parallel to the north range of the Barracks, along St Peter Street. There would be three single lines of tramway and pits would extend 'over nearly the whole area of the shed'. At the north range, a section of the married quarters would be converted to house dry sand, salt and oil stores, repair shop, shedmen's messroom, and the heating chamber. Scrap, brake blocks, bill-posting, the night general store, coke, coal, and the foreman's office could all be housed in the same range without conversion. 'The existing lavatories on the west side of the ground' too 'would be utilised without renewal'. Pilcher was aware that shoehorning his Tramway Headquarters as economically as possible into the old Barracks would impress the Council. And it was not a case of all work and no play. The west block, hitherto used by the War Office as mobilisation and accoutrements stores would provide 'excellent recreation rooms for the men'. The ground floor would be formed into a traffic mess-room and newsroom, with a billiard room and gymnasium on the first floor. The existing clubrooms in Castle Street were not convenient for they were 'cut off from our car routes during the winter months'.

In the second phase, the car shed would be extended to provide accommodation for a further twenty-four trams and as soon as it was complete, 'the old Baths as well as the car sheds at Constitution Street' would be vacated. This did not imply that Pilcher had a line in submersible trams. The Aberdeen Swimming Baths, redundant since the building of the nearby Beach Bathing Station, had been pressed into service by the Corporation Tramways. One wonders if the pond, drained of water, served as an inspection pit. The third phase, the provision of workshops, would involve converting the south, Advocates Road, range of married quarters, for stores, blacksmithing, armature repairs and saddlery. Separate entrances and exits at St Peter Street and Advocates Road, would allow the trams to circulate smoothly through the shed and avoid shunting. These planned workshops would replace the Dee Village shed which was becoming too small to cope with repairs. Pilcher's scheme also involved adopting the east range, fronting King Street as offices for the Tramways Department, replacing the offices in the Town House where six clerks had to work in a confined area, under artificial lighting all day. The front range would also include a parcel and time keepers' office, and a ticket stockroom as well as houses for two caretakers, in the north and south turrets.

With the total cost of the redevelopment estimated at just under £26000 - this included the site itself at around £2000 - the acquisition of the Militia Barracks was clearly no stopgap move. In 1898 Aberdeen Town Council had bought over the assets of the Aberdeen and District Tramways Company and their aims for public transport in the city were ambitious. Electrification was introduced the following year, and Pilcher, transport manager since 1906, foresaw the need to acquire all-purpose headquarters where the city's growing transport system could be centralised, and which offered space for expansion. The Town Council was agreeable to the purchase, and by May 1914 tenders for the car shed were approved. Within a few months, however, Pilcher's plans had gone on 'hold'. War had been declared and the army was back in the Barracks. That October the Council accepted that 'portions at present occupied by the Military, would be so for an indefinite period' and charged the War Office £50 a month and 'any such taxes that the Corporation were liable for during the period of military occupation'.

During the First World War, the old Militia Depôt played an important role in preparing young men for action. Numerous drafts of soldiers trained there and marched away, never to return. Memories remain. Mrs Chrissie Leith who was born in 1912 can still remember looking down from the side window of her home at No 48 King's Crescent watching the soldiers drilling in the Barracks' square. Mr John Gordon recalls a memory of his mother's who was brought up in St Peter Street; as a young girl she ran errands for troops confined to barracks. They showed considerable initiative, lowering a basket with cash in for cigarettes from the upper storeys. Cigarettes safely on board, the basket would then be drawn up.

Soon after the war ended, the car shed was up and running following the lines of Pilcher's Phase One. It would, however, be many years before

Pilcher's first car shed with the original north (St Peter Street) range of the Barracks at right angles.

the old Barracks became solely dedicated to the needs of Aberdeen Corporation Tramways. In June 1919 the Council found itself wrestling with a massive housing shortage. Between the early 1880s and the beginning of the First World War, the city had embarked on an extensive slum clearance programme, condemning around 2500 houses, and demolishing about 1800 of these. This far outstripped its provision of 'workmen's dwellings' under the Housing (Scotland) Act of 1890. Only fourteen tenements, providing 131 'houses', had been built in Urquhart Road and Park Road by 1914. House-building had been frozen during the war and one of several urgent measures taken to help the homeless after 1918 was the conversion of the King Street frontage of the Barracks and the south, Advocates' Road, range into eighteen single-roomed, twenty-six two-roomed and two three-roomed flats. One former resident, whose accommodation included one of the turrets, recalled that the family's single room was huge, and though the turret was small she squeezed her cooker in and it served as a kitchen. Residents found themselves sharing their new home with a few tramcars, rather more fleas - though at least the car shed was over at the north range as originally planned - and something else. It was during this post- war period that the ghost of Captain Beaton began to haunt the Barracks. He had received head injuries while in the trenches in 1915, and was invalided

*The south turret where
Captain Beaton hanged himself.*

home. After treatment and a period of recuperation in the music rooms of the High School for Girls, converted into a convalescent hospital, he was transferred to the Barracks to await further orders. One day, in March 1918, his new posting, back to France, came through. Perhaps his head wound had something to do with it, but he could not cope with the new situation. The following morning his body was found hanging in the south turret, used then as the officers' mess.

In his collection of ghost stories, *Haunted Neuk*, Norman Adams records the reminiscences of two ladies who remembered the Barracks from childhood. Mrs May Cooper, whose family lived in the former officers' quarters for eleven years, recalled that the tale of the soldier who hanged himself was common knowledge among the residents, while Mrs Helen Leiper actually saw the ghost. While visiting relatives in the Barracks when a child in the 1920s, she got bored with grown-up gossip and wandered upstairs. She stopped outside an open doorway and looked into a small sunlight room where there was an iron cot and a white bedcover. Sitting on the bed was a soldier in a khaki uniform. 'He had a bandage round his head and appeared to be winding another bandage around his hands. I never saw his feet…He rose without a word and vanished into thin air'. It wasn't until the late 1970s that she heard that others had seen the ghost.

The original north range of the Barracks from inside the car shed.

The Barracks' community remained in these 'temporary dwellings' far longer than was originally intended for it was not until 1924 that the larger council schemes began to take shape. But by 1930 the forty-six original apartments at the Barracks had increased to sixty, and heads of families included fishermen, shipyard workers, a stonepolisher, a letter cutter, labourers, a shipwright, a rivetter, seamen, and a tramway conductor, handily placed for his work, especially if he was on the Bridges route. Annual rents by that time ranged between £5.10s and £14.5s.

By 1925 bus services were expanding rapidly to keep pace with the demands of the new housing schemes. More buses required more parking and garage space, and with the Barracks currently out of the reckoning, the Corporation purchased premises at Canal Road, with room for seventy buses. By 1932, however, with residents rehoused, a big extension was carried out at the depôt, enabling the overhauling of both trams and buses to be centralised at King Street. But the Beach Garage - 'the old Baths' in Constitution Street - was retained for the time being.

To the west, the Barracks' old neighbour, the Spital Granite Yard of Bower
& Florence was doing well at this time.
John McLaren became sole owner after
Haddon Bower's death in 1927, and his
son, Ian McLaren remembers his first
holiday job as a thirteen-year-old, tracing regimental crests for Imperial War
Graves. His memoir, *Sixty Years in an
Aberdeen Granite Yard*, recalls the inner
world of the yard and provides an elegy
for the masons and polishers, those aris-
tocrats of the granite industry, and for
the great army of cranemen, scabblers,
sawmen, apprentices, sawboys and nip-
pers. Turners, he argues, were among
the most highly skilled of all, producing
from their lathes, everything from vases

Ian McLaren, courtesy, John Souter

to huge three ton granite rollers, with circular columns, fountains, balusters
and urns coming somewhere in between. The yard also had its own smithy,
where a toolsmith made tools from steel bars. 'Woe betide him if tools were
not properly tempered as he then incurred the wrath of frustrated masons
and suffered much verbal abuse'. Keeping the various strong and sometimes difficult personalities of the granite yard working together harmoni-
ously was no easy matter:

The front yard craneman, Alec Cranna, operated the hooter for starting and
stopping times. He was continually under attack by the men who accused him of
sounding the start too early or stopping too late. A A Brown, granite merchants, and
near neighbours across Advocates Road had a very loud hooter in which our chaps
seemed to have more faith. Against this opposition and competition Alec gave up
and as far as possible co-ordinated our whistle with Brown's blast.

One mason, Jimmy Gavin, was with the firm for so many years that the
shed he worked in was known as 'Jimmy Gavin's shed' long after he passed
away. His sons, Bill and George Gavin, both first class masons, were the
firm's eye doctors:

both very adept at removing sharp grit or broken fragments of shot from men's
eyes. Their instruments were pointed matchstick or, in difficult cases, a needle, with
the patient propped against a door post.

70

Difficult cases went to the Eye Institute in King Street. In those days before the National Health Service the firm had an 'Infirmary Box' which was passed round on pay-day. 'To pass the box was unforgivable', writes McLaren. He continues, 'Noise was all around':

the crunch crunch of the steel blades on shot, the clank of driving rods and the thump of worn bearings all of which were features of the old shot saws. Yards with a number of old time saws could create a high noise level around their immediate neighbourhood but in these days I suppose nobody thought of complaining. After all noise meant work and wages and that was very important.

Keeping a weather eye out for nickums was another task. The yard had a fixed roof with glazed roof lights and John Gordon recalls that as a boy, he and his chums would climb on to the roof and be chased by the foreman, worried in case they fell through the glass.

We now catch up on events at the south end of the great quadrangle. By the time of the First World War, the mighty East Poorhouse had been reduced to a heap of rubble. Mr Alex Slessor, brought up in the Merkland Road area, can remember as a child seeing piles of stones left lying on the site. What had happened?

Early in the century, Aberdeen Parish Council had decided to replace the East and West Poorhouses with a single building. To this end, they purchased the Oldmill estate west of the city, which, for half a century, had housed the local Boy's Reformatory. The boys were packed off into the country, to Oakbank on the High North Stocket, where the School continues, though in a rather different form. The Reformatory was then demolished and its stones used by the architects, Brown & Watt to build an imposing poorhouse, which survives to this day as the central block of Woodend Hospital.

There was much excitement about the move to Oldmill, which was set in spacious grounds, and would have its own farm. Brown & Watt supervised everything down to the most minute detail, deciding what should be transported from the East Poorhouse - including, 'eleven Baths with Fittings and Pipings, one Saw Bench and one Washing Machine' - and what should be sold as surplus to requirements. At last the great day came. On 14 May 1907 the inmates of the East Poorhouse were conveyed to Oldmill by the Great North of Scotland Railway Company to whom the Aberdeen Parish Council had awarded the transport tender. Railway enthusiasts need not be alarmed. No long lost line ran between Nelson Street and the Skene Road. The inmates were conveyed in the GNSR's fleet of motor buses at 5d per head, with children under three free of charge.

What were the reasons for this move? New houses being built in Ferryhill were beginning to encroach on the West Poorhouse whose thriving pig farm may not have been appreciated by the residents of this developing, upmarket end of town. Flitting to pastures new was understandable. The East Poorhouse, on the other hand, was still surrounded by spacious acres stretching from Nelson Street across the old Leper's Croft to Advocates Road, reflected in the substantial feu duties paid by the Parish Council not only to the Society of Advocates, but to the Wrights and Coopers and the Shipmasters Societies as well. On the face of it, it looked capable of expansion. One can speculate, however, that the East Poorhouse was suffering from structural problems, though this is not officially noted in the Parish Council minutes. Its front range was a stone's throw from the 'service' area of the Aberdeenshire Canal, where the waterway bulged out to allow barges to pull in to the side for repair, as shown on John Tallis's Plan on page 40. The two were side by side for some three years, ample time for Canal water to seep into Poorhouse territory, causing shrinkage when the ground later dried out. Add to that the fact that the type of foundations that were acceptable in 1851 were a good deal more casual than what is demanded by law today, and one is assembling all the ingredients for a nasty case of subsidence. A move was perhaps imperative.

Suspicions are further fuelled by the difficulties the Parish Council experienced in trying to dispose of the empty buildings. Not that there was any shortage of inquiries about the surrounding lands. In 1907, Hawthorn Football Club - Hawthorn Terrace, between Roslin Terrace and Urquhart Road, may have inspired the name - had offered a 30/-a year rent for the use of the old paupers' vegetable garden, which, it will be recalled, lay between the back of the Poorhouse and Advocates Road. The footballers were turned down, and the ground was leased to Aberdeen Town Council's Cleansing Department for cropping purposes. Aberdeen City Police Club, however, was permitted to use Poorhouse ground in Nelson Street 'for recreational purposes' while the house and garden of Friendly Bank was leased to the Church of Scotland at £25 per annum, as a Boys' Home. It became No 2 King's Crescent.

The local Territorial Forces Association expressed an initial interest, but their masters at the War Department demurred at the upset price of £7,500. Instead, they snapped up the West Poorhouse, more of a bargain at £5,250, and converted it into Fonthill Barracks, later the Prince of Wales Barracks and now 'army surplus'. The 'Parish' then approached Aberdeen Town Council who seemed about to take the plunge, then cooled off. Perhaps they had noticed something. The East Poorhouse began to take on the dimensions of an albatross, hanging round neck of the Parish Council. Early in 1909 they divided the site into three more marketable lots, an

72

inducement which fell on barren ground. Eventually, in November 1909, Aberdeen Town Council reappeared on the scene, announcing that it 'might consider seeing its way' if the Parish Council would dispose of the Poorhouse to them for the amount of burdens resting on it. In other words the Town would acquire the property for the cost of paying off any existing debts such as a bond. Far from expressing scorn at such a miserable offer, the Parish Council agreed and their minutes meekly note the sale, at £2500, £5000 below the upset price. This happened at a time when buildings in this busy industrial area were used and re-used. Several examples were discovered in *Round About Mounthooly*, and we have just noted the transformation of the King Street Barracks into a tramcar depôt. One might have expected to find an enterprising manufacturer setting up in a corner of the place, or at least, using it for storage. Instead and unusually, the buildings were taken down. The first one learns of this is from the Parish Records. A Mr Brand of Dundee, contracted to demolish the East Poorhouse, had demolished all the trees as well, which was not part of the deal. He had sold them as timber, and was required to stump up his £16 profit. His business, happily, still continues.

Thus was the Poorhouse reduced to the heaps of rubble which lay in Nelson Street for years. At last, in July 1914, the Council decided that the stones should be used for road-making. A month or two earlier an interesting plan had been put forward by a councillor, to 'erect dwellings for tramway servants' on the site - very convenient with the car shed at the Barracks only a short stroll away. This plan, however, was abandoned. Perhaps someone had a word in the councillor's ear. The War then intervened and for its duration the site became an army camp. Work started on the erection of temporary huts for the troops as early as November 1914, and the 17th Royal Field Artillery was granted use of ground on the north side of Nelson Street, for instructional purposes. In June 1919, a start was made on demolishing the accumulation of buildings now on the site, and clearing and levelling the ground. The work was carried out by the unemployed. The Town Council sensibly decreed that all coping and dressed stones were to be carefully preserved, 'with a view to being utilised in any housing schemes which the Council may in future undertake'.

The First World War had provided a use for the East Poorhouse site, and the Cleansing Department was ensconced in Advocates Road, but that apart, one gets the impression that for a time the Council was not quite sure what to do with this considerable area. Educationists, however, were now embracing a philosophy of light, fresh air, pleasant surroundings, the pursuit of sunshine, green grass, the need for playing fields and for open spaces, particularly in heavily built-up areas. These ideas were in vogue as early as 1906 when Sunnybank School was built. And so, during the 1920s and 1930s, over five acres of the site was used for outdoor games for schoolchildren, complete with a pavilion at Nelson Street, under the auspices of the city's education department.

A new school building for St Peter's Roman Catholic School was also erected, perhaps rashly, by the City's education authority on the Nelson Street site exactly where the front range of the Poorhouse had stood. Even before it was built, a note of caution had been sounded at a Town Council meeting in 1934:

The ground already acquired for school purposes is largely of a made-up nature. The levels are bad and good foundations for buildings would be hard to get.

The original school, founded in 1833, had stood in Constitution Street. In time, the building, one of John Smith's finest works, had, become outdated. (It subsequently served as a school for Polish soldiers, housed the Shiprow Tavern, then suffered neglect. It still stands at time of writing, but only just). The new school opened in August 1937 and His Majesty's Inspector subsequently wrote: 'It is a credit to the Education Authority. The admirably planned premises are well equipped for instruction in art, science and practical subjects, and adequate provision has been made for physical education'. Woodwork, in fact, was taught along the way at Causewayend School and some pupils had a delightful new experience, being able to buy Bendelow's famous pies at breaktime. Mr John Brady, headmaster for thirty-four years had just retired, and St Peter's had a new head as well as a new building, the kindly Andrew Durnin, who remained at the helm for the next twenty years.

Just west of the Poorhouse site, the Mounthooly Ropeworks had carried on for a few years after Stephen Goodbrand's death in 1904. But it ceased trading at the time of the First World War, though the other family business of wholesale hosiers, manufacturers and warehousemen contin- ued in Broad Street until modern times. The long sheds of the ropewalk, stretching east towards the Central Auction Mart were demolished to provide more space for the playing fields which could now stretch unhin- dered from Nelson Street across to King's Crescent, almost as far north as the Bower & Florence tenements. The Ropeworks' main building, now owned by the Town Council and numbered 8, 10 and 12 King's Crescent remained and was put to other uses. The 1935-36 valuation roll for example - the numbers are slightly different - gives No 10 King's Crescent as: Dance Hall - occupant Mrs Helen McGill of 22 Great Western Place. A few people

74

'The curving crescent of tenements...' with the Spital beyond.

still remember it. No 8 was occupied by W M B Troup, cycle and radio dealer, and No 6 by James Lyon, butcher.

The curving crescent of tenements, put up by Bower & Florence in 1875 passed into the ownership of James H Bower's trustees after his death, and in the 1930s were still occupied by many granite workers, but not exclusively. Carters, combmakers, trawlfishermen and horse dealers were to be found there as well.

To the east, the City Auction Mart, as the Cattle Market had become, continued to do good business, long after its neighbour, the Poorhouse had gone. Early in the twentieth century it became a private company, John Duncan and Son Ltd, the son in question being the second born, John W Duncan who had gone into the business at an early age. John Duncan himself died in 1915 at Zetland House, by then No 403 King Street, 'one of the oldest, best known, and most popular of livestock salesmen in Scotland' the *Aberdeen Journal* reported. 'Quiet and unassuming, perhaps one of his most striking characteristics was his generous and sympathetic heart, absolutely free from ostentation of any kind'. John W Duncan, 'brusque, straight and honourable,' succeeded his father and like him, was an unerring judge of fat stock and a skilled auctioneer. The Christmas sale held annually at the Mart during the inter-war years was the most outstanding of its kind in Britain. Edward VII and George V continued the tradition of

75

sending in their best cattle and pigs from Abergeldie Mains to these Christmas sales. Leading meat purveyors from London and all over Britain came to buy and paid phenomenally high prices for the Royal livestock.

If the East Poorhouse had gone west, its inmates' vegetable garden, over three acres of it between the Cattle Mart and Advocates Road, had been relinquished by the Cleansing Department and gone to the dogs - and to the football. That was after the First World War. During the war it became a playground for local children and elderly folk can still remember the cinders and the humps and bumps in the ground. After the war, the Council laid it out as Advocates Park Football Ground. It opened in November, 1921 at first with a cinder pitch, but was later grassed over. Mr George Tait, now living in Buckie recalls it as 'a football ground of fond and revered memory.' Hawthorn F C had come into its own at last, sharing the tenancy with East End F C . They jointly owned the pavilion and ground stand, but many teams played there. George Tait recalls Hall Russell's, Bank o Dee, Stonehaven, Parkvale, Mugiemoss, and Inverurie Loco Works, - 'a really excellent team'.

An East End and Hawthorn FC select at Advocates Park. East End, Aberdeen's oldest Junior Football Club won the Figaro Cup, first presented by the 'Northern Figaro' magazine in 1889, so often that they were allowed to keep it. It is still on display at their clubroom at New Advocates Park, Golf Road. Courtesy, East End FC.

76

Advocates Park was a great favourite with spectators and on 28 April, 1923 folk turned out in their thousands to witness, the final stage there of the first official marathon held in Scotland. It was won by Dunky Wright, one of Scotland's greatest cross country and marathon runners, with Jim Ronaldson, the local favourite, second. But it was as *the* venue for junior games, and major schools matches that Advocates Park is remembered. The entrance fee for important games was a penny or halfpenny, but in a time of unemployment and poverty that was too much for many families. A number of unofficial ways of getting into the ground are still vividly remembered and Mr Felix Graham recalls how as a lad he and his chums would sneak in through barbed wire. The officials were aware of this ploy. 'A wee man known as "the Weasel" was posted to cover these loopholes. We kept a lookout and if he was spotted, a shout would go up, "the Weasel, the Weasel". You'd find yourself stuck half way up the barbed wire and your clothes could get badly torn as you tried to scramble down.' George Keith, whose boyhood was spent in College Bounds remembers: 'To get in free we either climbed in from the adjacent granite yard or climbed over from the Nelson Street playfield. One other trick was to swick in between two grown men as they were paying at the gate.'

And the dogs? Next door to Advocates Park was the Excelsior Track, and Mr Tommy Donaldson recalls whippets being raced here in the 1920s. You entered from the cul-de-sac at the King's Crescent end, beside the old Mounthooly Ropeworks, and the track lay just beyond the Crown Granite works. George Tait recalls from his young days, one method of getting in without paying. Owners of competing dogs were sometimes accompanied by their sons who were admitted free. Young loons would take up their position at the entrance to the track and ask unaccompanied owners as they arrived, 'Hey, mister, kin a' tak yer dog in?', often with successful results. He continues:

The dog-racing facilities were primitive indeed. The track was simply a straight run of about 100 yards The dogs were held by handlers while the owners were stationed at the other end. At a signal, the dogs were released and ran towards their owners who waved hankies and shouted encouragement. The disputes regarding the results were numerous and acrimonious.

Later, 'high technology' took over. At the finishing line a bicycle was upended, George Tait remembers, and a length of string, equal to the length of the track was secured to the rim of the rear wheel, and a rabbit skin was attached to the other end. At the 'off' the pedals of the bicycle were turned furiously by hand and the 'rabbit' was wheeled in with the dogs in hot pursuit. This, he recalls was often a total shambles, with the dogs overtaking the 'rabbit' - or the string breaking. Great entertainment! The track was separated from Advocates Park by a 6ft wooden fence, and football matches and dog racing often took place simultaneously. When a shout arose at the start of a race, a line of faces would appear at the top of the fence, as the some of the football crowd hoisted themselves up to watch the race. Typical Aberdonians, George Tait says, getting two events for the price of one.

This area too, was briefly the venue of the boxing booths, which were run by John Stewart from Edinburgh. His booth later moved to Kittybrewster, opposite the Northern Hotel, then the Beach, where Codona's is now to be found. Felix Graham recalls that he had the finest boxers, and George Gordon remembers Stewart announcing £1 prize for any one who could last three rounds against his team, 'a small group of tough-looking young men. There would be a period of silence as the crowd looked around to see who was brave enough to accept the challenge. Eventually some half-tipsy farm servant might step forward. Few lasted the pace.'

Across on the residential side of King's Crescent a major change had occurred at Viewton Place that would have been unthinkable in John Sutherland's time. The house had remained in the Goodbrand family after Stephen's death, and in 1911 his daughter Janet, who was involved in running the hosiery business, feued off a piece of ground to the north where a 'wing', a complete tenement in the style of those in Wallfield Crescent, was

Viewton Place and north 'wing'. Courtesy, R and H Leith.

added to the original house by a local builder. A major excavation was necessary to remove the steep approach to Viewton Place and to expose the basement level which then became the ground floor and a strong retaining wall was built between the 'wing', and No 37, King's Crescent, Viewton Cottage. The 'wing', now No 35, and Viewton Place, which had become No 33, were neatly joined up with the help of a new mansard roof. Viewton Place was 'flatted' at this time. By 1912, Nos 33 and 35 had numerous tenants and Miss Janet Goodbrand had gone off to live in Desswood Place. The family continued to own these properties, as landlords, until 1935.

Roseacre, No 31, next door, once had been the home of the granite merchant, John Florence, and before that, in the early 1870s, of James White, a true Victorian self-made man, in the John Sutherland mould. As a lad he came in from Daviot to work with John Bisset, grocers, Queen Street. He later became manager of the Northern Co-operative Society, then returned to his old firm as partner. He did so well that he was able to retire when he was around fifty, and bought two country estates. The Milne family followed James White at No 31 and stayed there from 1910 until 1952, while at No 27, Mrs Morrison who lived there with her husband Charlie, was an even longer resident in the district. No 27 had earlier been the home of the granite merchant, George Stott, who had his yard in Merkland Road East. George Gordon remembers Miss Emma, the last of the Stotts, by then living at No 29. 'This delightful old lady who might - judging by the antique but immaculate style of her dress - have been taken for the last of the Victorians, died in 1952'.

Moving down towards Mounthooly, James Rae boss of the Crown Granite Works, lived at No 23, the most southerly of the two mirror image houses on the Jute Street corner, from 1904 until 1939. The next owner was Tommy Begg, a well known and popular figure in the Scottish boxing world. Tommy had begun boxing in 1912 when he was fourteen, and became undefeated champion of the North of Scotland both at flyweight and bantamweight. In 1920 he founded the Aberdeen Amateur Boxing Club on the corner of Mealmarket Street and West North Street. Felix Graham, a Territorial Army finalist in the 1930s who still trains young boxers, remembers the club: 'Poverty was the common denominator in those days, and the club was somewhere to go. Many promising boys went there, including the Kemps, a famous local boxing family. The club was half way up the stairs, and when boxing matches were on, we sometimes got in free at half time when some of the spectators came down to 'Brownie's' Bar. If they didn't want to see the remaining bouts, kids would beg the other half of the ticket.' He remembers too that at the boxing tournaments at the Aberdeen Lads' Club in the Gallowgate, 500 members would enter. 'It took

79

three months from start to finish to reach the finals in that club, and this happened twice a year.

'Tommy Begg,' he recalls, 'always fought as an amateur. He was very dapper, about 5ft 4 ins and fought at around eight stone seven.'

George Gordon who used to train at the Empire Club in the early 1930s, remembers Tommy well, and recalls him coming over to the Empire to discuss forthcoming bouts with the manager there, Doddie Shepherd, 'smallish, quiet-spoken, extremely nice.' The Empire was based in a former fire station in Frederick Street where snow blew through the broken glass panes; but the lads training there, local professionals like the bantam-weight Jimmy Knowles and the middleweight, Frank McCall, brother of Steve, who once fought Len Harvey, were working too hard to feel the cold. Mr Gordon recalls Tommy as 'an

*Tommy Begg,
courtesy, John Gillan.*

active sparrow of a man, not the kind to pick a quarrel with.' He helped to stage district and youth championships every year in the Music Hall, served on the Scottish Amateur Boxing Association Council for over twenty years, and several times managed Scotland's Boxing Team. He was delighted when two of his protégés, John Gillan and Tony Kerr, were chosen to represent their country. For a number of years he organised matches between boys from Glasgow boxing clubs and the Oakbank Boys which were attended by staff, their families and friends, as well as the whole school. I can still recall him, slipping nimbly through the ropes to announce a bout, his horn-rimmed spectacles making him look more like a business man than a boxer - in fact he ran a rag and scrap metal business in Commerce Street. He moved from King's Crescent to Forbesfield Road in 1948 where he lived until his death at seventy-four in 1972. His son, Dr Thomas Begg, was Medical Officer of Health for Liverpool.

Across Jute Street were Daniel Macandrew's concrete houses. The corner one, Crescent Villa, No 1 Street, Macandrew's own residence, was subsequently occupied by a shipmaster, James Scott, and in the 1920s and 1930s by William Watson a reporter with the *Press & Journal* who later became the *Scotsman's* man in Aberdeen. Another occupant was the Jute

80

No 1 Jute Street.

Street ghost. According to previous occupants, a piano was heard playing in the house, and a broomstick seen moving from upstairs to downstairs, and a seated, hooded figure was also observed seated in the background. Deeds relating to this area make reference to the old leper territory which, as already noted, appears to have straddled the road, so one never knows...

Mr Norman Smith, a delivery boy for the butchery department at the Co-op in the late 1930s also recalls an uncanny feeling when he made weekly deliveries to Mrs Fisher at No 19 King's Crescent, the widow of Pat Fisher, a *Press & Journal* reporter. 'She always sat in the same room, where the table was always laid out in the same way and nothing ever changed.' A previous tenant - the houses were long owned by Macandrew's trustees - had been another local reporter, William C McDonald. Sandy Mitchell, who became the *Press & Journal's* man in London in the 1960s, and a theatre and literary critic, also lived in King's Crescent. These houses were handily placed for a stroll up the Gallowgate to the Journal's offices in Broad Street, hence the popularity of the area with the press.

The row of cottages nearest Mounthooly, Nos 3 to 15, were of an earlier vintage than the concrete houses. Those nearest Canal Street were pulled down at the time of the mid-1970s demolitions, among them No 7 which, during the 1920s was the home of Arthur Fraser Macintosh, one of the most colourful personalities on Aberdeen Town Council. In fact 'Fraser Mac' was a household name in Aberdeen. He served for twenty-eight years, figured in many a stormy debate and was forcibly expelled from the council chamber three times. This must have taken some doing for he had been an outstanding athlete in his younger day. Like Tommy Begg, who was twenty years his junior, Fraser Mac was a keen boxer, and had fought the

famous 'Gunner' Moir in the old Palace Theatre. He organised big boxing events in the city, was much in demand as referee and MC and ran a boxing booth for many years.

He had first entered local politics in 1919 representing Torry, as a 'Bolshevik', but resigned two years later. He was back in 1925 as a labour candidate, winning Greyfriars Ward, which he continued to represent for the next thirty-six years. He was a member of the Independent Labour Partly (ILP), and close to its leading lights including John Maxton, the most famous of the Red Clydesiders. Controversial he may have been, but Fraser Mac was the most energetic of councillors, and single-handed undertook work which nowadays would demand the deployment of a team of personnel. He organised the annual athletic gathering during the Aberdeen Trades Week, as well as as outings for the elderly and crippled, with whose welfare he was much concerned. He was a member of the Northern Co-operative Society Board for over twenty years, and towards the end of his

Fraser Mac, right, at an ILP sale at the Music Hall, Aberdeen. Guest of honour, centre is the legendary Red Clydesider, James Maxton. Courtesy, George Gordon.

82

time on the Council, Convener of Links and Parks. Fortunately, his job as an insurance agent permitted him flexible hours .

In 1996, Ex-Lord Provost Alexander Collie remembered Fraser Mac 'at the end of his career in local politics as I now am.' He was someone Alex Collie came to respect, and he carried a wreath at his funeral. 'He had a great reputation and there was nothing pretentious about him. What a noise he made when he was drinking his tea!' He was a renowned open air orator, and he didn't just talk politics at the Castlegate. Alex Collie remembers him selling little bits of granite from a box there for a penny. 'No need to buy toothpaste,' he would say, 'just use the granite to clean your teeth.' Fraser Mac died in 1952 at seventy-five, the year after he retired from local politics having been 'father' of the Town Council. Maxton had predeceased him but old comrades, Sir Patrick Dollan, John Rankin, Lord Kirkwood, John McGovern and Neil McLean sent him a telegram on his resignation. It read: 'Hail to the Chief of Socialism in Scotland and its No 1 Champion of goodwill and friendship.'

Chapter 5

Modern Times

The Committee resolve to recommend that from 1st January 1956, the Corporation stop up permanently... Advocates Road.
Aberdeen Town Council Minutes, 5 Sept, 1955.

We left the city's transport department in 1932 at last in sole command of the former Militia Barracks, and determined to keep pace with the transport demands of the new housing schemes. Work went ahead to extend the Barracks, or, more correctly, the Corporation Tramway Depôt much as Pilcher had envisaged. The previous year, however, trams on the difficult and dangerous Torry and Ferryhill routes had been replaced by buses, (a cloud the size of a man's hand as far as tramway enthusiasts were concerned), and the transport department urgently required space for a new omnibus depôt. Acquisitive glances were cast across Advocates Road to Advocates Park. It seemed just the ticket.

As soon as the transport committee's plans to take over the Park became public, controversy raged. A legion of local footballers and their supporters were determined that it should remain as a soccer ground. At this time, however, sports facilities, 'particularly football pitches' were being laid out at the new Linksfield ground, and those councillors supporting the transport takeover could argue that they were replacing kind with kind. As 1936 drew to a close, two opposing roles for Advocates Park were debated in the Council chambers. One was its future as bus depôt, the other, its development as a public park, taking in the area to the south, towards Nelson Street as well. At a meeting of the Links and Parks committee of December 7 1936, the public park proposal was defeated. An amendment 'that the ground

84

known as Advocates Park be reserved for transport purposes', was carried by five votes to three with two abstentions, which effectively sealed its fate. Further meetings of the joint Finance, Links and Parks, Town Planning and Transport committees on Hogmanay, 1936 and of the full Council on18 January, 1937, delivered further *coups de grâce*. At this latter meeting Fraser Mac unsuccessfully moved an amendment to keep Advocates Park open for the public 'especially for the younger people'. He was so incensed at the transfer of the Park, not now for vague 'transport purposes' as in the original amendment, but 'for erecting thereon a Central Transport Depôt', that he registered his dissent in the Council minutes, and presumably made one of his stormy scenes.

In a propitiatory gesture, the Council voted additionally 'that the ground between Advocates' Park and the Roman Catholic School (be transferred) to the Education Department for sports purposes'. There had earlier been concern in the Council in general and the schools sports sub-committee in particular, that this, the Nelson Street playfield which, 'played an important part in the curriculum of physical instruction in the schools', was for a number of reasons, under used. The council expressed keenness to have the field fully 'utilised for the purpose of the physical instruction of school children'. So began the transformation of the old playing area into a sports field for local schools which provided a welcome green oasis in a heavily industrialised area. The decision to convert Advocates Park into a bus depôt, was however, greeted with anger and regret by its aficionados who will tell you that the grounds which replaced it, particularly Linksfield, for long something of a Cinderella ground, but now upgraded as the Chris Anderson Stadium, just did not have the same atmosphere.

Advocates Park eventually closed in April 1940. It lay empty during the war, home only to a huge water reservoir, on standby in the event of air raids. John Gordon can remember local loons digging for clay on what had once been the pitch, to make model aeroplanes. A finger still bears a scar to remind him of those days. Sandy Argo, Head of Marketing at John Fyfe Ltd, who was brought up across the way at Seaforth Road, recalls finding lumps of a chalky substance there which came in handy for making out 'beddies' on the pavements, and generally chalking on walls in the area. After the war, Codona's carnival came to Advocates Park on a number of occasions, and it was not until June, 1951 that Council workmen started to level the ground for transport department use. A T.2 RAF hangar had been purchased, transported north from its Greenock base and was now re-erected at the Park, complete with heating, lighting, examination pits, and everything else necessary 'for the proper maintenance and servicing of transport bus services', at a total cost of £28,532. 'Bus' was the operative word, for at the meeting of 6 June 1949, at which the Council had originally

The former Advocates Park in 1996, the 'Hangar' to the rear.

decided to purchase the hangar, a proposal from the transport committee - 'scrapping of tramway system and sustituting a more modern and mobile system' - was deferred for future consideration. The cloud was growing bigger. As it was, the building to the west of the car shed, the barracks that seemed to have become a hospital, had already been transformed into an omnibus repair depôt.

When the fate of Advocates Park was sealed, the closure of Advocates Road, taken over by the Town Council back in 1922 went onto the agenda.

The small section of Advocates Road which has not yet been enclosed, at its junction with King's Crescent. The hospital building looms to the left.

After the 1939-45 war, such a closure, allowing flexible movement around the Depôt, was discussed on and off in tandem with the creation of a new link road between King Street and King's Crescent. It was even suggested that this link road might be diverted to the south, to Mounthooly, to form part of a proposed route from Hutcheon Street to the seafront. This vision of a sweeping highway came to naught, and in 1951, the Director of Town Planning, not satisfied that the new link road was a 'must', given the existence of St Peter Street and Nelson Street, omitted it from the next twenty year plan. Advocates Road was not closed off until 1956, some twenty years after it was first mooted, while the new link road did not materialise until 1995.

Trams were increasingly stood down during the 1950s. The Bridges route in 1958 was the last to go and the familiar 'swish' and 'clank' clank' as they turned from King Street into St Peter Street and the old car sheds was heard no more. Many recall the funeral pyre at the Beach on 3 May of that year, when forty trams were torched - none were preserved - an act of civic vandalism which caused tram buffs all over Britain to regard Aberdeen with a mixture of horror and amazement. The King Street headquarters was further extended and was now given over entirely to the care of the Corporation fleet of 230 buses. 'The old Baths' - the Beach depôt - could at last be pensioned off (though its buildings remain in use), along with depôts at Queen's Cross, Woodside, Mannofield, Canal Road and Torry.

With the creation of the two-tier system of local government, the new Grampian Regional Council became the transport authority. Ownership of 'the buses' was transferred, and Aberdeen Corporation Transport became Grampian Regional Transport, the formal date of the change of ownership being 16 August, 1975. The old hangar continued to soldier on and in the early 1980s, was updated at a cost of £390,000. Following deregulation in 1986, Grampian Regional Transport added Ltd to its title, and in 1987 acquired the private hire firm of Mairs Coaches.

Captain Beaton too has soldiered on through these upheavals. Indeed he has abandoned his khaki for full regimental dress, and has continued to haunt the front range of the old Barracks. Over the years transport staff have confirmed that they have seen or sensed him, so much so that they became reluctant to enter certain areas of the building; the canteen became a no-go area and was relocated. There were other incidents; lights were tampered with, drivers tripped up by an invisible presence and some areas became deathly cold for no apparent reason, except perhaps that the Captain was passing by. The last reported sighting was October 1988, at the time of the employee buyout which was completed in January 1989. Perhaps as an officer he disapproved of such a move.

At this time, a new holding company, GRT Holdings plc was set up

Advocates Road from inside the depôt, looking towards King's Crescent.

with Grampian Regional Transport Ltd and GE Mair Hire Services Ltd (Mairs Coaches) as subsidiaries, and with Mr Moir Lochhead as chairman and chief executive. Other acquisitions have followed including Kirkpatrick of Deeside, Autotruck, which for a time was based in St Peter Street, and Midland Bluebird and a number of innovations have been introduced including the operation of continental tours. Grampian Transport is now a subsidiary of FirstBus plc, which in 1996 became Britain's largest bus and coach operator.

Of the original four-sided Militia Depôt, the front range, complete with turrets and the north, St Peter Street, range remain in use, for offices and storage, and have been listed by the Secretary of State as being of architectural or historic importance. Although the west range has gone, the building behind it, once a military hospital, still survives and is used now as a store. Stuart Pilcher's original car sheds, neatly confined within the barracks' square are still there complete with tramrails. The sheds now give access to the body shop and the electricians' maintenance area. From the old Barracks a staff of over 150 tend on a fleet of 200 buses which are repaired, painted, fuelled, cleaned, and serviced on site. The greater part of Advocates Road still lies inside the depôt, and one can stand in what was once Advocates Park, and much earlier, the old Lepers' Croft, amidst fleets of colourful buses - Stagecoach rent space there, adding to the variety - and almost reach out to the Gallowhills on the other side of King Street.

The front, King Street, range today, from the former Barracks Square. The plaque on the left is to Colonel Henry Knight Erskine, on the right to Colonel Archibald Keen.

Interior of the former hospital at the west end of the depôt. It is now used for storage.

Inside the former car shed. The tram rails are still visible.

Lines of buses stand on the former site of the Lepers' Croft - and Advocates Park. The link road, centre, cuts through the heart of ancient leper territory.

At the Spital Granite Works of Bower & Florence to the west of the old Barracks, it was Ian McLaren who got the yard on its feet again in the post-war period after the death of his father. The granite trade had gradually gone down a slippery slope since the late nineteenth century, and more noticeably in the inter-war period. There were, however, periods of remission, and in the early post-war period things went reasonably well. Supplies were becoming available again and the firm got the contract to supply the granite for the new Head Offices of the Bank of England, the Aberdeen granite industry's largest contract at that time. There were changes for the better. Tea-breaks became official, working hours shorter and holidays longer. Dust extraction plant was developed to eradicate silicosis, the respiratory disease that for so long had plagued granite workers. Tungsten tipped masons' tools were developed which required only minimal sharpening, but that was a double-edged sword which made the blacksmith redundant. McLaren rented his smithy to Charlie McKenzie, one of the Aberdeen's few remaining independent smiths, and he worked from Advocates Road for some years.

However the decline that had begun in the inter-war year brought about by loss of exports, increasing imports, and a preference for the all grass cemeteries and for cremation accelerated. Too many small firms were fighting for survival, and little was done to restructure the industry. Ian McLaren noted that as early as 27 Decenber, 1917, a granite merchant had written in the *Aberdeen Free Press* complaining that the trade was bedevilled by manufacturers, struggling on their own and always suspicious of others. 'It was only after the 1939-45 war that some limited co-operation between the firms took place, principally to secure contracts too large for any one yard to produce', McLaren wrote. He continued:

The industry was becoming age heavy. It was increasingly difficult to attract apprentices. Granite yards were still dirty, dusty, wet and uncomfortable workplaces. Boys were interested in cleaner trades with more interesting work such as electricians, engineers or joiners, rather than 'chappin at steens' with hammer and chisel which was still the prevailing picture of the granite yard mason to the outside world.

In 1914 there had been ninety granite yards; by 1962 there were twenty-three; among the many casualties were James Rae's Crown Granite works in the cul-de-sac which closed in 1956; a saw-maker, George Reid, worked from the yard for a time. After 1957, the hooter was heard no more from A A Brown's St Nicholas Granite Works in Advocates Road, though the derelict office building survived until 1995 when it was demolished to provide more space for Grampian Transport's buses. Only a part of the

A A Brown's office building prior to demolition in 1995.

street wall, made from granites of many hues, remains. At Bower &
Florence, many of the workforce who had been with the company since the
1920s, were, like the industry, dying off, and the firm amalgamated with
Stewart & Co. at the latter's Fraser Road premises in 1964, though the
merger was shorted-lived owing to Henry Stewart's fatal illness a few years
later. Bower & Florence had survived longer than most, thanks to the wide
range of specialisms it offered. One was turning huge granite rollers, which
would then be cored and taken to Bell & Robertson, the Spring Garden
electricians, and wired for use in the paper mills. And Mr Donny Harper,
now a divisional officer with Grampian Fire Brigade, but a former mason
with John Fyffe Ltd. in Seaforth Road, recalls that one of his tasks as an
apprentice at was to trundle blocks of granite across King Street to Bower
& Florence who had the equipment to punch in the hole for the vase. Their
Spital Granite Yard, subsequently acquired by Aberdeen Dictrict Council,
stood deserted for some years. George Gordon recalls:

It was not levelled until September 1974 and the former office, a handsome
bow-fronted granite building which had been erected in 1873 and which occupied
the corner of Advocates Road and King's Crescent, also disappeared in 1974, on a
dull, misty October day.

The yard, was being made ready for its future role, a car park for

92

The Grampian Transport car-park, formerly the Bower & Florence granite yard. The buildings to the rear from left to right are, the former Viewton Place, Viewton Cottage, St Margaret's Brae and the Convent Chapel.

Grampian Transport staff. Apart from the A A Brown's colourful wall and some large polished granite pieces in the old Bower & Florence wall, only one memento of the King's Crescent granite yards remains, and it is a curious one. Half-hidden in the wall of the former Viewton Place is a representation of the head of Christ, beautifully etched in black granite.

Across at the south end of the quadrangle, St Peter's RC School in Nelson Street, so vulnerably sited only sixteen years earlier, was sinking as rapidly as the granite industry. By 1953 the centre frontage of the school had to be rebuilt. One suspects that the School had been subsiding since Day One since building embargoes would have inhibited any major damage limitation attempts during the war years. In spite of this quite literal facelift, problems of subsidence continued, and now the roll as well as the school was falling, thanks to the Mounthooly clearances, aimed at removing slums, and permitting road-widening schemes

A memento of the granite yards of King's Crescent in the wall of the former Viewton Place. A head of Christ is finely etched in granite.

93

of which the infamous Roundabout was a part. With many families now dispersed to new council schemes, primary numbers were also declining, while the junior secondary department closed down altogether in 1975. A reverse situation prevailed at the Bridge of Don and rather to their surprise, pupils found themselves being bussed to Nelson Street where they were taught in the vacated wing of St Peter's while the new Bridge of Don Academy was being built.

The education department decided to cut its losses as far as Nelson Street was concerned and elected to refurbish the King Street building of Old Aberdeen School whither St Peter's, flitted in 1983. Accompanying the pupils was the peripatetic statue of the founder, Priest Gordon, which had been designed back in 1855 by the Footdee sculptor Alexander Brodie and fashioned almost next door to the old school in the Constitution Street granite yard of Alexander Macdonald & Field. In 1937, Priest Gordon had exchanged his niche in Constitution Street for one at the new school in Nelson Street, and latterly, as the school subsided, passers-by anxiously noted the good priest leaning forward, ever more precariously from his niche. It seems, however, that the lesson of subsidence had been learnt and the police extension, due to be located in that area, was sited further to the north-east, nearer the former City Mart.

The Mart itself had been sold in 1944, after the sudden death that

The City Auction Mart in 1984, prior to demolition. Courtesy, Hugh Duncan.

The Nelson Court flats, King Street, built on the site of the Mart. Part of the Pittodrie Bar is glimpsed extreme left. Courtesy, Hugh Duncan.

January of John W Duncan in his seventieth year, after fifty years in the business. The last auction was held on April 17 and the goodwill of the business was acquired by Messrs Reith & Anderson and the Central & Northern Marts Ltd. The Mart buildings were purchased by the haulage contractor, John C Fiddes, for £8,600, and later became a Scottish Parcels Services Depot. They were eventually demolished in September 1984, to make way for Wimpey Homes' Nelson Court Development.

It was not until the post-war period that steps were taken to upgrade the playfield behind St Peter's School in Nelson Street, on the old Poorhouse grounds. Though such a move had first been discussed as the time of the closure of Advocates Park, the Council noted in the 1950s that the area was still 'unsightly', and work went ahead to create something better. The welcome 'green emerald' became the official sports field for the children of St Peter's RC, Causewayend and other neighbouring schools. In 1954 the main building of the old Ropeworks was pulled down to make more room for the playing field. The nearby house of Friendly Bank, No 2 King's Crescent, which had survived so many changes, was by this time Council-owned and occupied by a number of tenants. The latter were rehoused in the 1970s, and Friendly Bank, a handsome building in its day,

Friendly Bank, prior to demolition.
Courtesy R and H Leith.

was boarded up and eventually demolished in 1977, again to create a more spacious field.

The question of the King's Crescent-King Street link road which had been proposed some forty years earlier, now came off the back burner. Grampian Regional Council made an application to construct it with the aim of proving relief for the side streets running between King Street and Powis Place-West North Street. Aberdeen District Council's Archaeological Section now took the opportunity to carry out the King's Crescent dig mentioned in Chapter One. The road, completed in 1995, cuts across a section of the old Lepers' Croft that had never been built on. This new link road runs from just opposite Nos 9-11 King's Crescent to exit in King Street, north of the Nelson Court flats. This frighteningly fast road had altered the ancient line of the Old Aberdeen highway as our illustrations opposite show. Unwary motorists, aiming for the Aulton, can now find themselves at the Bridge of Don before they know it.

On the residential front, the Bower & Florence tenements were, acquired by Aberdeen Town Council around 1965, at much the same time as they purchased the site of the granite yard. Until the early 1990s, many of

96

The photograph above, dated 1971 shows Mount Pleasant, Canal Street, prior to demolition and the sweeping curve of King's Crescent, en route to Old Aberdeen, courtesy George Gordon.

Right: The road layout since 1995 shows how the unsuspecting driver, heading for the Aulton, may find himself unexpectedly in King Street as the new link road takes a right hand bend.

the tenants were elderly folk who had lived in the area all their lives, children of the granite workers for whom they were originally built. That pattern has now changed. Of the two corner shops guarding the cul-de-sac, the former Co-op bakery at No 44 King's Crescent is to let at time of writing, while the licensed grocer at No 46 had several occupants, including E J B Skidgmore, wine and spirit merchant who was there for a number of years. It now houses a welding shop, Grampian Electrodes. On the other side of the road, there were few changes, apart from a development at Nos 33-35 King's Crescent, the former Viewton Place. In the 1980s, the forty foot gap between No 31, Roseacre and 'Viewton' was spotted by developers. George Gordon takes up the tale:

Inevitably the developers found their way to King's Crescent - to the vacant gap at No 33 - and despite many objections succeeded in gaining permission to erect a building of four flats hard against the south gable of No 31. With that task completed in April 1985, they departed to wreak havoc somewhere else!

Thus did the once solitary outpost, Viewton Place become a small terrace of tenements. Unlike the north 'wing' of 1911, the builders of the new south 'wing', made little attempt to match up with the lines of Nos 33 and 35 as shown in our photograph. Fortunately the original central block

'Viewton Place became a small terrace of tenements'. The courses of the south 'wing', to the left, do not match those of the older buildings.

98

retains gracious windows and well-proportioned rooms. One who would have known more about the Viewton Place buildings than most was Mrs Veitch who lived at No 33 for many years. Neighbours still recall her as a charming elderly lady who wore a black velvet ribbon round her neck. Born in 1892, she died in March 1996.

George Gordon, himself an authority on the history of the area has lived at Roseacre since 1952. Born in the parish of Glass, he served for a time with the Derbyshire Police and during the Second World War saw active service with the First Battalion the London Scottish (the Gordon Highlanders) in Iraq and the Middle East and took part in the famous push through Sicily and Italy. He had joined the Shore Porters in 1938, and was Transport Manager from 1953 until his retirement in 1975. He has written a history of this enduring firm, *Prying with the Pynours 1498-1978*, and also of *The Last Dukes of Gordon and their Consorts.*

George Gordon.

Ronald and Helen Leith are also well known in the area and both have contributed to many aspects of the city's life. Ronald is organist at St Mary's Cathedral, Huntly Street, as well as being a noted recitalist and teacher of music. As Carilloneur to the City of Aberdeen, a post he has held since 1978, it is he who is responsible for gladdening the heart as the mighty carillon of St Nicholas Kirk, rings out across the city, throughout the year. The peal, with forty-eight bells, is one of the largest in the UK and one of the finest in Europe. Ronald Leith is also a founder member of the Aberdeen and North-East Scotland Family History Society. North-east exiles and descendants come in their thousands from all corners of the worlds to visit the Society's centre in King Street to trace their family trees. The Society also publishes an excellent series of local data drawn from a range of sources from censuses to graveyards. Helen has given much time and energy both to Aberdeen Civic Society, having served on the Executive Committee for over ten years, and to the Old Aberdeen Residents Heritage Society, of which she was a founder member. This is one of the most strongly supported and most active heritage groups in the North-east, which works hard to preserve the unique, but fragile qualities of the Aulton, so often under threat in recent years.

The story of this fascinating quadrangle now draws to a close with the saga of the King's Crescent Fire Station. The tale begins in King Street where the fire station, built to prize-winning designs by A H L Mackinnon in 1897, had, by the mid-1980s, been pronounced 'old'. In the next decade it was variously reported as 'deteriorating rapidly', 'crumbling', 'dangerous' and 'decaying'. Problems had arisen when the multi-storey St Clement's Court was built to the rear of the fire station in 1985, affecting the stability of the station and resulting in some subsidence. Structural repairs were carried out and granite buttresses erected. But it was the doors of the station, designed for the days of horse-drawn fire engines, that posed perhaps a more difficult problem. With no apron to allow manoeuvrability, vehicles, or at least their drivers, were having to cope with a tricky exit directly on to King Street, before they could turn right or left. Restructuring the doors and installing an emergency traffic control system seem not to have been options, and a search got underway to find a site for a new fire station.

The Nelson Street playing fields were one of a number of possibilities under consideration, but given the proximity of the police extension, the chief constable objected, worried that 'in the event of a strike (of firemen) policing could be put in jeopardy because of picketing'. Further exploration revealed ultimately thirteen possible sites including the Mounthooly Roundabout (one of the dafter ideas), and a good central site, the area between Frederick Street and East North Street. The playing fields were also back in contention, the Fire Brigade Union, arguing that was the only

Sports Day at the King's Crescent playing field site, July 1992. The police building is left, rear. Courtesy R and H Leith.

100

The King's Crescent playing field site, July 1996. The fire station is under construction.

site which firemen could reach city and harbour fires within the maximum response times. (Later, correspondence in the press would maintain that other sites were available but the choice of the playing fields was influenced by the fact that Grampian Region already owned the land and no demolitions or purchases were necessary). To avert the chief constable's fears that policemen might be subverted by striking firemen, the positioning of the complex was shifted away from the police building, towards King's Crescent. And so in June 1991 Grampian Region's public protection committee, under whose auspices the fire service came, applied to Aberdeen District Council for outline planning permission to build a new fire station complex on the King's Crescent site.

Locals such as Mrs Jane McGloy, resident in the area for over thirty years, had only just been made aware of the switch from the Nelson Street to King's Crescent side and were stung by the lack of public consultation. They quickly organised a campaign against the siting of the station, on grounds of road safety, traffic congestion, pollution and loss of open space, and petitioned Grampian Regional Council. At this point it was difficult to envisage how large the complex would be, though the city's planning officer subsequently stated that the fire station would be two storeys high, with a three-storey training block, to the rear, and a two-storey L-shaped headquarters with ninety car parking spaces on the north side of the link road, adjacent in fact to the most southerly of the Bower & Florence tenements. Loss of the playing fields would be compensated for by a pavilion, multi-use courts and a football pitch, facilities to be shared by policemen, firemen, schoolchildren and the public.

The local regional councillor supported the King's Crescent move, so Ronald Leith offered to express the concerns of over 300 local residents. That August he made his first presentation, to the education committee who owned the land. Apart from traffic concerns, he stressed that the decision to site the fire station complex on the playing fields was contrary to the new city wide local plan and in breach of planning conditions relating to the police extension building in Nelson Street. These stated that the remaining ground would be left as recreational open space. Now that space was being halved again.

The education committee passed the making of the decision to the policy and resources committee which was also addressed by Mr Leith. Policy and resources in turn made no decision and referred the matter to the transportation and roads committee, and to the public protection committee. In October, Ronald Leith addressed to the public protection committee who then invited the director of property to report on 'traffic aspects, response times, other sites and a detailed planning application for members' consideration', which sounded rather like 'back to square one'. The decision was subsequently passed again to the education committee who decided to refer the matter to the full council for a final decision. In fact, the education committee never did vote to release its land for purposes of building a fire station. On 8 November, 1991, the full Regional Council finally decided in principle to make the land available for the building of the complex. Reassurances were given to residents that the King Street entrance of the link road would be used by fire engines on call, unless the actual fire was in King's Crescent. Eventually, in December 1992, after several earlier withdrawals, the planning application made it to the planning committee of Aberdeen District Council who decided by nineteen votes to eighteen 'to express a willingness to approve the fire station in principle'. Thus closed a chapter in the saga, and left local government watchers with much to ponder on; the committee system; consultation or *fait accompli?* the role of the local councillor; the problems posed by two-tier local government; the value, if any, of grandiose blueprints such as city wide local plans. Those who remembered the Advocates Park had a feeling of deja vu.

Span Construction had been appointed the main contractor, and the cutting of the first turf was carried out with little ceremony in case of disruption by residents. Though the conflict over the acquisition of the site had ended in favour of the local authorities, it now began to resemble a Pyrrhic victory. It was discovered that the ground was spongy - construction, was, after all, taking place on the old Lepers' Marsh. To prevent subsidence, a firm of specialists had to be brought in to compact the soil. Then there was a setback of a different nature for Grampian Regional Council in April 1995. The region stated it had over-estimated to the size of the pavilion and proposed reducing it from seventeen to ten metres. This the city planners would not swallow. The pavilion was intended partly to compensate for loss of open space, and agreeing to the request would also reduce the available recreation space. Worse followed. In July 1995, Span Construction collapsed with very considerable debts. Work came to a standstill and the site took on a *Marie Celeste*-like aspect. Months passed. Then another building firm, Mowlem (Scotland) Ltd took over and inspections soon revealed that some of the recently completed structures were in a poor state. Much remedial work required to be done on the site, including the demolition and rebuilding of the training block. At the time of writing a shortfall in funding of nearly £750,000 delays the completion of the King's Crescent Fire Station. Through the troubled years, the King Street Station has soldiered on and will achieve its century. And the Howe o Spital, which a century and a half ago was dominated by the Barracks at one end and the East Poorhouse at the other, with the huge green swathe of the old Lepers' Croft in the centre, is now covered over with institutional buildings of another sort.

Chapter 6

From Love Lane to St Peter Street

The committee had before it a letter from certain proprietors in Love Lane suggesting the name should be changed and resolved to recommend that (it) should be changed to St Peter's Street.

Aberdeen Town Council Minutes, 1888

Before starting off up the Spital itself, a word, first, about St Peter Street, or Love Lane, as it was long known, at the junction of King's Crescent and the Spital. Indeed it was considered part of the Spital, and for much of the nineteenth century was referred to as 'Love-lane, Spittal'. To the modern passer-by, looking towards the King Street end, it may seem that its plainness is relieved only by a glimpse of a corbie-stepped gable of the former Militia Barracks. But in earlier times, as we know, it marked northern boundary of Aberdeen, or at least a part of it that was readily identifiable, and derived a little importance from being at the 'frontier'.

Before Love Lane came into existence, the ancient march 'dividing the lands within the freedom and jurisdiction of the burgh from the county-lands' was marked by a little burn, long vanished, but which flowed eastwards towards the Links where it became the Banstickle Burn. Taylor's Plan of 1773 shows a line of trees and a dyke beside which the burn would have flowed, just north of the Sickhouse field. In September 1790, a committee of gentlemen, including Captain George Taylor himself, riding the marches on behalf of the Town Council, examined this boundary where it carried on towards the Links, and gave it the thumbs-up. 'The march is clear by the key-stones along the south dike dividing Scotstown's property from the freedom lands. (Like farmers, lairds were known by the name of

St Peter Street looking east.

their lands and the 'Scotstown' of the day would have been George Moir, fifth of Scotstown and Spital).

Love Lane, the origin of whose name is a mystery, makes its first appearance on Taylor's Plan, (page 138) just to the north of the line of trees, straggling towards the bents and petering out near the present Pittodrie Street. In the early street directories is described as running 'from Spittal to Links', and though it came to be regarded as the city boundary, it is, strictly speaking, just out of bounds. Taylor's Plan also shows at the Spital end of Love Lane, an L-shaped dwelling on the north side, and on the south, a small house in an enclosure. Bar the north range of the Militia Barracks, small clusters of such dwellings at both sides this junction would be the only pattern of development in Love Lane for much of the nineteenth century; Scotstown's fields lay to the north, and to the south, the crofts of the city's inner marches.

In later eighteenth century, a pleasant shrubbery had been planted in the area, and it was here that the exotic if unlikely figure of Mrs Symes appeared, weeping and wringing her hands. She was the widow of a Lieutenant Charles Symes, a veteran of the American War of Independence who, after his return to Britain was posted to Aberdeen. In the winter of 1786 he fell heavily on ice while skating. He died on 26 Decenber. Reflecting on this sad business the *Aberdeen Journal* of April 6 1831 reported that :

his funeral and the regret experienced by all classes at the sudden decease of one so much respected, are quite vividly remembered by the older inhabitants.

There was an irony here, for Symes had survived the Battle of Cowpens where the British army and particularly Symes' regiment, the 7th of Foot, the Royal Fusiliers, had suffered heavy losses. Mrs Symes who was pregnant at the time of her husband's death, gave birth to a son the following May. The baby died within months, and was buried beside his father in St Nicholas Churchyard. (The gravestone, near the Schoolhill side of the graveyard, was broken during the building of the Bon-Accord Centre and replaced with a replica). The *Aberdeen Journal* of April 1831 continued its reminiscences:

After his death the beautiful and accomplished, but disconsolate widow spent many a solitary hour in wandering about the shrubbery which then flourished where Love Lane now is. She was a great favourite from her accomplishments and beauty...

Mrs Symes was certainly a great favourite. Born in India, daughter of a French official, she was first the mistress, then the wife of a English civil servant called Francis Grand. She left him in 1780 for the continent and had several other liaisons before arriving in Aberdeen in 1786 as Mrs Symes, while possibly still Mrs Grand. *Scottish Notes & Queries* of 11 September, 1914 noted that 'the utmost sympathy was extended to her on the death of her husband and his posthumous child', and adds, 'in fact a local Professor narrowly escaped becoming her third husband'. One wonders who that could have been. The main purpose of the *Aberdeen Journal* article of 1831, however, was

Mrs Symes, Mme Grand and Princess Tallyrand? From the drawing by Vestier.

to note that she was now the wife of the famous, nay, infamous, statesman, the Prince de Talleyrand, French Ambassador to Britain at that time.

On leaving Aberdeen and the shrubbery of Love Lane, Mrs Symes had returned to France, and subsequently appeared in society as Madame Grand, moving in the same circles as Talleyrand. She fled the Reign of Terror during the French Revolution, then returned and renewed her acquaintance with Talleyrand with a plea for assistance. He was France's own Vicar of Bray, an amazing survivor, serving Napoleon Bonaparte, the Bourbon monarch Louis XVIII, and the Orléanist king Louis Philippe in succession. Talleyrand and Mme Grand were wed in 1802, though the statesman's associates felt that he had married beneath himself. It was not a successful union for a number of reasons, including perhaps the fact the new Princess de Talleyrand once so seductive, had become fat and forty. It is difficult to reconcile the beautiful, bereaved Mrs Symes, weeping in Love Lane, with the devious courtesan, Madame Grand. She died in December 1835.

By the time Talleyrand was doing his tour of duty at the Court of St James, Love Lane no longer meandered towards the Links, but ran straight and narrow towards King Street, which at that point, the city boundary, became the King Street Road.

In May 1834 the *Aberdeen Journal* was advertising:

To let, the nursery ground near Love Lane lately occupied by Jas Walker. The sale of nursery plants and flowers at the Nursery Ground, Love Lane is still going on at greatly reduced prices. Part of the ground adjacent to the King Street Road may be feued on reasonable terms.

No offers were made and 'the whole stock of trees, fruit trees, roses, plants etc.' were rouped on October 31 and November 1 that year. At this time, Sir Michael Bruce of Stenhouse and his wife Dame Isabella Moir were the lairds of the Spital and we learn from the *Journal* of October 3, 1838 that 'four quarters of new oats grown by Alex Marr tenant of Love Lane Croft, Spital on the lands of Sir Michael Bruce, produced 5 bolls, 1 firlot and 2 stones of meal which was sold at the Aberdeen Meal Market on Thursday 27 September. This was first of the new crop harvest'. A little later, in January 1840 , four Scotch acres 'lately occupied by Alex Anderson was offered for let at Love Lane. A new road made this lot more accessible, though whether or not this was a good thing is debatable. The town had made a dung midden near the site. By the 1850s William McIntosh was the tenant of Love Lane farm, 'part of Spittal Lands'.

The Aberdeen street directory of 1825 notes at No 3 Love Lane James Sheriffs, perhaps the recently retired owner of the Spital Asylum of which more in Chapter Ten. No 3 was possibly was part of a short row of buildings on the south-west corner which, by the time of the 1868 ordnance survey map had become known as Hay's Buildings. One of them was an inn. Alexander Hay, vintner, was mine host there from at least the early 1840s, and other residents included Charles Bruce, a weaver and a Mrs Ewen who kept lodgings. Mrs Hay took over as vintner in 1848, presumably on her husband's death, and the inn is mentioned in a letter published in the *Aberdeen Herald* on December 16 that year, deprecating the noise made by students in the area, perhaps some of Mrs Ewen's clientele. (Students making a din as they walked to and from King's College are no new phenomenon). In 1856 Mrs Hay moved to the Red Lion in the Spital where she remained, as joint vintner with James Ross, until 1863.

The census returns of 1851 for 'Love Lane, Spital' reveal families from Forfar, Banff, Moray and Old Meldrum as well as those locally born living there. Mrs Charles Hutton, a Spital gardener's widow lived at No 1 Love Lane, and the Knox family whose head was a woodsawyer at No 2. The tenant at No 3, 'Love-lane houses' was James Valentine, 'reporter to *Aberdeen Journal*' then aged twenty-nine, with his wife and three of a family. Valentine, along with William Alexander of the *Free Press* and William Carnie of the *Aberdeen Herald* formed a great triumvirate of local reporters. And though Valentine's records of statistics are hardly in the same class as Alexander's *Johnny Gibb of Gushetneuk* or Carnie's *Reporting Reminiscences*, they serve a useful function in advancing our knowledge of Aberdeen in the later nineteenth century. 'There used to be a good-natured joke at the reporters' table in my day over Valentine's head for figures', said Carnie. And according to William Alexander, 'he just ravelled in them'. They were the best comrades 'that ever pointed pencil'.

Other residents of Love Lane in 1851 were something of a mixed bag; a tailor, a dressmaker and a combmaker at No 4, and at other houses, a cooper, a shoemaker, a housekeeper, a pauper, a rope and sailmaker, and William Chalmers, flesher, who employed one man, as well as Mr Knight, an advocate's clerk, and Mary Reid, a schoolmistress from Ballater, who added a touch of class. Later still, two 'paramedics', made their homes there. Peter Joss, machinist and artificial limb maker, and Mrs Bisset, midwife. By the late 1870s, her address changes from No 2 Love Lane to No 1 Spittal - possibly the same place.

By then the character of the street had changed, becoming increasingly industrialised. By 1861 the police commissioners, responsible for cleansing, paving, lighting and water supply rather than policing in the modern sense, had set up a yard in Love Lane, and the following year, the appearance of the north range of the Militia Depôt occupied much of the south side of the street. The invisible boundary of the inner marches ran through the barracks square, which technically speaking left about three-quarters of the

A section of the old boundary wall in the north-west corner of the former Bower & Florence granite yard, now a Grampian Transport car park. Hays Buildings, and the elusive horse bus depôt would have been sited in this area.

Depôt in Aberdeen and one-quarter in 'the county' - at this point, the no man's land of the Spital Road. Around 1881 a horse bus depôt and stable, shades of things to come, were built at the Spital end, near Hay's Buildings, serving the Bridge of Don and Old Aberdeen bus routes. Its existence was fleeting and it was probably sold when the Bridge of Don bus service in closed in 1892. The photograph above possibly includes a part of this site. At the far end of the Lane, James Hutcheon's extensive granite yard, the King Street Cemetery Granite Works, which, as its name indicates, fronted onto King Street, had been established around 1870, perhaps on James Walker's old croft. By the late nineteenth century, two builders' yards, owned respectively by David Porter and Hunter & Coutts, were also in business in Love Lane.

The Town Council was now mindful of widening this narrow little street, a useful link between King's Street and King's Crescent, as the Spital Road had become. There was little option but to widen to the north since the Militia Barracks, to the south, provided a formidable barrier. At the end of 1887, both James Hutcheon and David Porter were agreeable to ceding a part of their property to the Town who then demolished Hutcheon's wall and smithy, and re-erected them for him on the new line of the road, and dealt similarly with Porter. Hutcheon and Porter were doubtless among those Love Lane proprietors who were now of the opinion that their newly

109

widened thoroughfare was too grand to be called a lane. On January 31 1888, they wrote to the Town Council requesting a new name. The Council agreed, and recommended that the name be changed to St Peter's Street It is unclear from the report whether it was the proprietors or the councillors who had suggested for that name. The site of St Peter's Hospital, the inspiration for the choice, was some distance to the north, but it was no doubt felt that such a name would endow the street with a measure of *gravitas.*

Though the new name soon came into formal use - that November approval was granted for alterations to a workshop belonging to John Matheson in the lane 'on the north side of St Peter's Street' - the charming name of Love Lane did not quickly disappear, even in official circles. The description of the Riding of the Marches on 4 September 1889, related in the Council Minutes refers to March Stone No 62: 'On the east side of King's Crescent, near its junction with St Peter's Street (Love Lane)'. The apostrophe was soon dropped. And as with Windy Wynd, elderly people who have lived all their lives in the area, can recall their elders using the old name.

By the end of the nineteenth century, two tenement buildings, Nos 18-20 had made their appearance halfway along the north side, providing a residential oasis in the midst of the miniature industrial complex that had

A residential oasis, Nos 18-20 St Peter Street.

developed along the north side of St Peter Street. Working from the King Street, westwards towards the Spital, the James Hutcheon's granite yard was later occupied by John Gibson & Son Ltd of Leith, who specialised in Leyland vehicles. There is now a block of student flats on this corner. At No 22 was Charlie Michie, the haulage contractor, and the Spital Motor Engineering Works, a site later occupied by George Simpson & Co, builders. In the 1920s, Charles Dorian, granite merchants, set up a little to the west of the tenements at Nos 24 - 30 and remained there for the next fifty years. Roseburn are now to be found in this area. At No 32 was a solitary tenement, also dating from late nineteenth century, now demolished. The old fireplaces still can be made out, a poignant sight.

Beyond the opening to St Peter's Lane, we arrive at the Spital corner where there was once a small shop owned by Charles Taylor. It closed in 1978 and was converted into a house, as shown in the photograph on page 115. Although the Barracks' north range occupied much of the south side of St Peter Street, an old, single-storey cottage, at the Spital end, used as a spare parts store by Corporation Transport, survived well into living memory, and may originally have been part of Hay's Buildings.

We turn now to St Peter's Lane, whose entrance is near the Spital end. For a hundred yards or so the lane continues northwards. The St Peter Street Turnery Works which made cabinets and brushes, and the workshops of J

St Peter Street Lane looking north to Applebank House, Spital

& A Massie, cabinetmakers, whose showroom was in Broad Street were at one time based here. Straight ahead is Mr Dennis Christie's haulage business with the vehicles stabled behind discreet dark blue doors.

The Christie family have long been resident in the area. Dennis Christie's father Mr Dick Christie was in long distance haulage with his premises in Merkland Road, behind his home, Rose Villa. Dennis Christie, on the other hand, is in the tipper business, and he and Mrs Christie live in an quaint white cottage which is also in Merkland Road but opposite Rose Villa overlooking St Peter's Lane. One access to the haulage depôt in the lane is via the old world back garden, a very pleasant way of arriving at work.

The Christie's old world garden lies between their house in Merkland Road and the haulage depôt in St Peter's Lane. Making use of the lie of the land, the house has an extra storey to the rear.

The lane now turns east to run parallel to St Peter Street. A blacksmith was still working there in 1996, but Toffolo Jackson's Terrazzo Works had closed. At the far, King Street, end there stands deserted what seems to be an old barn and loft, perhaps a survivor from the days when the Love Lane area was farmed. For six months every year the loft was home to the French onion seller, Henri Chapelin, who came over from Roscoff and bothied there. 'He was a lovely man,' says Aberdeen business man Ean Emslie, who

The onion seller's barn, viewed from the students' flats at the King S treet end of St Peter Street.

knew him well, and supplied him with a series of Morris vans over the years. 'He brought over twenty-two tons of onions - an Artic load - every year. He grew five or six tons himself. His wife looked after his small-holding when he was here. I think he grew artichokes as well, though he didn't bring these over.'

Henri Chapelin was the third or fourth generation of the 'onion Johnnies' who came regularly to Aberdeen. They used to live in lofts at the harbour, and later in Virginia Street, always in primitive conditions which had not improved when they rented the loft in St Peter's Lane. Mrs Susan McGowan who lived in the Spital at that time recalls that there were no facilities for preparing food, no heat, no running water. She invited Henri and his assistant across for dinner one freezing New Year's Day. The assistant was an old friend who would help with the gathering of rushes at Ellon, then spent his days in the van, using the rushes to string the onions. Ean remembers calling on the pair one evening to find them sitting round a rickety table in the loft, supping tea from bowls. 'They had a round of regular customers, including some up north.' Henri Chapelin died quite young and that was the end of an old tradition.

Local March Stones

The march stone in Lindsay's Folly, with its key and saucer, is long gone, but its modern replacement, March Stone No 61, sits in the front garden of Viewton Cottage, No 37 King's Crescent. It is one of a number marked both CR for the City Royalty or Regality indicating that it is a march stone of the Inner Marches, and ABD, Aberdeen, indicating the Outer Marches. This is one of the places where the boundaries meet. The long gone incised keys would have indicated that it also marked the boundary of St Peter's parish. On the other side of the road, at the Spital-St Peter Street corner, is March Stone No 62, also an ABD CR, and an addition of the

modern era. It has a twin! John Souter, the City's first Conservation Officer, whose remit included the care of the March Stones, writes:

The change of direction of the Inner Marches near the corner of King's Crescent and St Peter Street is unique in being marked by two march stones of the late eighteenth/early nineteenth century type. When the Town Council resolved to identify the boundaries of the Marches more concisely and clearly with this design of granite monolith, the original No 62 was placed in a recess in the basement retaining wall, a part of the Bower & Florence Spital Granite Yard at No 64 King's Crescent.

At the time the firm was established a condition must have been made by the Council, instructing that ABD 62 CR to be positioned on the west-east line of the Marches. Through time, this stone was lost sight of and after the Second World War, it was decided at the request of James Cruickshank LLD, Convener of Aberdeen County Council, 1945-49, and an authority on the Freedom Lands, to place a duplicate stone on St Peter Street, near its junction with King's Crescent.

After Bower & Florence ceased trading in 1964 and their range of buildings demolished, the original stone was rediscovered. In 1976 the second stone was moved by Aberdeen District Council to the corner of King's Crescent to prevent it being damaged by the formation of a new carpark. Passers-by can now readily see it.

Above, March Stone No 62 that was thought to have gone AWOL. It sits inside a little shelter in the Grampian Transport car park. See also the drawing opposite, courtesy, John Souter.

Right, the replacement March Stone No 62 near the St Peter Street-Spital corner. Beyond is the former corner shop, now a house.

Part Two

The Spital

The Chapel, St Margaret's Convent, the Spital.

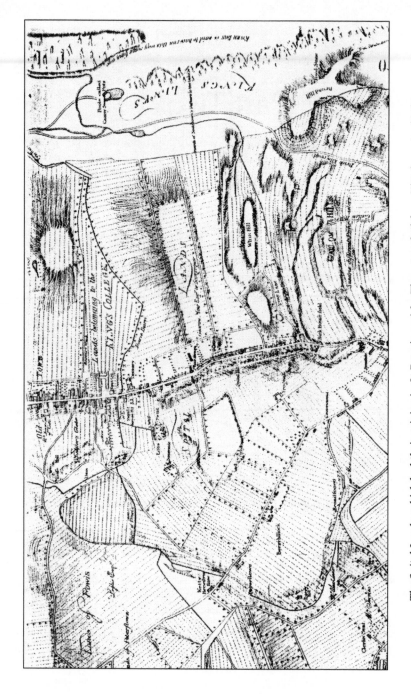

The Spital Lands, which had their origins in St Peter's parish. They stretched from Kittybrewster in the west to the Links in the east. From Taylor's Plan of 1773.

Chapter 7

St Peters: a rather peculiar Parish

A little further on the highway a chapel sacred to Peter was placed...Nothing is
established about the founder.

Gordon: Description of Bothe Touns of Aberdeen. 1661

We now leave the miry Spital howe and head north, tackling the steep
hill that leads to Old Aberdeen. It was at the brow of this hill some time
between 1172 and 1199, that Matthew Kyninmund, Bishop of the fledgling
diocese of Aberdeen, established the Hospital for 'infirm brethren' from
which the Spital would take its name. A new St Machar's Cathedral, seat
of the diocese of Aberdeen, was also being built at this time, predating the
Cathedral we know today by some two and a half centuries, and King's
College by three hundred years. We have truly stepped back into the mists
of time.

The Hospital was more akin to an old folks' home or a hospice than a
hospital in the modern sense. Its foundation charter tells us, in the
conventional wording of such documents, that Bishop Matthew was di-
vinely inspired to establish it in honour of St Peter, the chief of apostles, for
the weal of the soul of the king, William the Lion, a generous benefactor of
St Machar's, his ancestors and successors, and likewise for the soul of
Bishop Matthew himself, his ancestors and successors. The charter was
witnessed by an impressive gathering of local VIPs, among them Maurice,
parson of Tarves, Gilchrist, Earl of Mar, Fergus, Earl of Buchan, Norman,
Constable of Inverurie, Robert of Rayne and William of Slains. Given the
'decayed' state of the residents, it seems odd to have sited the Hospital in
open country on a steep hill and at a fair distance from the Cathedral and

the Chanonry, then at the threshold of development. A clue is provided by the lands with which Bishop Matthew very handsomely endowed the Hospital. These, the future Spital Lands, stretched as far west as the hamlet of Peterstown beside the den of Kittybrewster, as far as the Links to the east, and north to south from the Chanonry port to the Gallowgate port. The lands of 'Ardschelly and Petenderlyn, Carnakerde and Ardonachyn' are mentioned, but where were these tongue-twisters? 'The land we gave to our man Caperon' is specifically excluded and that provides the clue. His 'toun', Caperstown or Caprastoun was the old name for a part of Hilton, so these lands must have lain near that area. 'Hilton of Spital' appears from time to time in various old deeds. St Peter's may have seemed to be planted in the middle of nowhere; in fact it stood at the centre of its substantial lands.

The Bishop also bestowed on the Hospital the teinds, tenth parts of meal, malt, grain, salt, flesh, fish, in fact of all the food intended for his own table. This generosity had perhaps something to do with the fact that in 1170, King William had given Bishop Matthew the whole lands of Brass (the Forest of Birse), whose tenants were charged to convey to the Cathedral, in annual rent, oats, meal, bere, malt, butter, fowl, swine, and much more. The Bishop had plenty to spare. And after 1317 the infirm brethren would find salmon on the menu when Bishop Henry de Cheyne made a grant of a whole net's salmon fishing on the River Don. The Bishop had three nets at Polgouny (Balgownie) and the Hospital was entitled to receive all the fish caught in one net in one season.

The Hospital fell on evil times. In 1427, it came to the attention of Bishop Henry de Lichtoun, that the masters of St Peter's had, for the past forty years and more, not only neglected the Hospital, but appropriated the income. Bishop Henry partially reorganised the original foundation by a charter of 4 February, 1435, founded a chapel and chaplaincy near the Hospital and made a parish around it. The ordnance survey map of 1868 indicates a 'Site of St Peter's Hospital' and nearby, 'St Peter's Church (Remains of)' on whose foundations the Moirs, post-Reformation heritors of the Spital, built a mausoleum. A number of cottages had sprung up around St Peter's, forming a little Kirkton and two chaplains, vicars choral of the Cathedral, were appointed to minister to the Spital folk in the chapel, taking turn about on Sundays. This was in addition to their duties at St Machar's. They had to provide bread and wine for mass, and wax candles for the altar from their own pocket, but were given ten merks annually from the Bishop's revenue and a chamber and garden each, little studio apartments on the east side of the Chanonry. The mediaeval historian, Dr Leslie Macfarlane, has argued that Bishop Henry at that time was anxious to ingather funds to complete the nave of St Machar's Cathedral. The creation of a viable parish in the Spital would be a source of revenue, and such a parish could be one which

The raised rectangle of grass which may mark the foundations of the Spital Kirk. The Moir Mausoleum is at the far end.

future bishops could retain and even extend.

Things changed dramatically after William Elphinstone became Bishop and persuaded King James IV to erect Old Aberdeen as a burgh of barony in 1489. One of Elphinstone's foremost plans was the creation of a new parish which would include both the Aulton and the future King's College. By 1497 Elphinstone had established St Mary's, the Snow Kirk, several hundred yards north of St Peter's, a new parish church for the new parish, a part of whose boundary was defined as going up 'by the old boundaries and divisions between the lands of Seaton and the lands of the hospital of St Peter's'. Folk living on the Spital Brae would belong to this new parish and Elphinstone would be free to redirect the revenues of the now redundant St Peter's. Further evidence of the Bishop's ability to make the best use of available financial resources became clear six years later when he annexed the Snow Kirk and its revenues to King's College, and appointed the University's canonist, the lecturer in canon law, as prebendary of St Mary's. A prebendary was a priest who received a 'prebend', a part of the church's revenues as his stipend. Thus was his college salary taken care of. At this time all masters of King's were in holy orders, so the locals did have a genuine priest. A manse and glebe were now necessary for the new prebendary, and land from St Peter's Hospital was acquired by a charter of May 1503, witnessed by our old friend Master Alexander Galloway, himself a skilled canon lawyer. The charter tells us that 'Mr Patrick Ramsay,

121

presbyter, rector of the Church of Spital, and Mr Matthew Pacock, chaplain, possessor of the said lands, freely conceded the land. This land, in today's terms, was near the University Road-College Bounds junction, but on the west side of the highway. Parson Gordon shows the site of his manse - 'Place wher stood the canonists H(ouse)' - almost as far north as Powis Brig. (The Powis Burn ran from west to east through what is now the grounds of Crombie Hall, across College Bounds, and along University Road).

In 1527, some thirteen years after Elphinstone's death, Bishop Gavin Dunbar promoted the rector of the St Peter's by conferring on him a seat in the Cathedral chapter, with the revenue of that church assigned to him as a prebend. He was also made subchantor, that is assistant choir-master of the Cathedral, and St Peter's, the source of income, was dignified with the title of 'subchantry of St Peter's'.

Master Alexander Kyde was subchantor in the 1540s, and it was he who, with the consent of the bishop, dean and chapter of the Cathedral, began the 'alienation' or the transference of the Spital Lands to lay ownership. In 1544 he feued Peterstown, 'lyand within the boundis of the said Spittall ground on the West siyd of the Spittall Hyll' to George Quhyit (White), burgess of Aberdeen, his wife and eldest son. White was no newcomer to the scene. He was in the words of an earlier deed, 'for many years and at the present time, tenant and farmer on the town lands of Petyristoun of Spitall', both sun syde and shadow half, and there is a description of the 'corne lands and gryss manurit and not manurit with houss and bigging.' This set-up, in the old infield-outfield system, may not have been as cosy as it sounds. White's cottars had an obligation to tend 'twenty heide of scheip' for the benefit of Master Alexander and his successors. And 'the puir folkis and indwelleris of ye Spittall' were to retain their customary right as in 'tymes bygane' to the 'sustentatione of thameselff and ther bestiall'. What with the subchantry sheep, and the poor folk howking up the land and grazing their beasts, though hopefully on the commonty, the attractions of farming Peterstown seem somewhat limited.

William Gordon, last and worst pre-Reformation Bishop of Aberdeen remained in post from 1545 until his death in 1577, surviving the Reformation, which arrived in Aberdeen early in 1560, more or less unscathed. He enjoyed the protection of his brother, the powerful fourth Earl of Huntly, at that time sheriff of Aberdeen and the king's lieutenant of the North. Gordon wrought considerable changes as far as the ownership of the Spital was concerned. As Kennedy grandly puts it: 'the patrimony of the Hospital was dilapidated by Bishop William Gordon who alienated the lands by way of feu to different persons'. One of these 'different persons' was the Bishop's 'bidey-in', Janet Knowles, the daughter of a burgess. On 20 October,1565 with the concurrence of the then subchantor and rector of St Peter's, John Collison, and the rest of the Cathedral chapter, Bishop Gordon conveyed the 'plum' of the Spital Lands, North Spital including Sunnyside, for an annual feu duty of £15 Scots, to Janet in liferent (for her lifetime only), and to George Gordon her son in fee - he was entitled to the property after her death - whom failing, his brothers John and William and to his sisters Elizabeth, Margaret and Mathia successively. The Bishop had a large if unofficial family to support, and he was seeing them all well-provided for. His argument for feuing out church lands seems to have been that things were falling apart, it was all up with the Church of Rome anyway, and 'materials' for improving the ground could not be had. Earlier, Bishop Gordon had feued the sparsely populated South Spital, where the Spital foothills impeded development, and with it, Wester Peter, a part of Froghall, to an Aberdeen burgess, Andrew Brebner. His son, Andrew Jnr went on to consolidate his Spital holdings some time before 1602 by acquiring the toun and lands of Sunnyside and Spittlehill from the Knowles-Gordon ménage which did not retain its property for very long after the Bishop's death.

After the Reformation the revenues from the Spital Lands had reverted to the Crown, but in 1574, during the infancy of King James VI, 'all teinds, rents, revenues, emoluments, buildings, gardens, lands, church manses, glebes and other possessions of the church of St Peter, which is called the church of Spital, or the subchantry of Aberdeen' were granted to King's College, now turned Protestant and very low on funds. This grant of income from 'Petterkirk called Spittell' was confirmed to King's College by the Estates of the Scottish Parliament at least three times during the seventeenth century, but it did not produce great revenues for the hard-pressed academicians. The North Spital brought in an annual 'few meallis' - feu duty - of £15 3s 4d rising to £15 6s 8d during the seventeenth century, a slight increase on the feu duty originally payable by Janet Knowles. South Spital was static at £4 4s per annum, Sunnyside at £8 8s, and Peterstown at £2 10s. The mysterious 'Spittel House' paid a feu duty of 6/8d while the 'Spittel Outfields' brought in three bolls of grain in teind in Martinmas 1685-86.

Meanwhile, in May 1583, a precept that the 'Snaw and Spittal Kirks', which were falling into disrepair, should unite with the parish church of St Machar was issued from Holyroodhouse by the sixteen-year-old James VI. It was pointed out that 'the fructis of the said of the saidis Kirkis of Snaw and Spittall ar not abill to sustane ane minister of Goddis word', Their congregations 'maist convenientlie may resort to the said cathedrall of Machar' - though before the end of the document, this suggestion has changed to, 'be compellit to resort'. Unions of congregations were no more popular in the first flush of the Reformation than they are in these days of declining attendances. The teinds of 'Machar, Snaw and Spittall' were all now paid to King's College, whose masters, as feudal superiors, were instructed:

to dimoleishe and tak doun the ruinous wallis and tymber of the present kirkis of Snaw and Spittall now abusit to superstitioun and idolatrie, and to employ the same for reparation of the said kirk of Machar being utherwyiss a grit and costie work.

This precept, with its admirable rationalisation of church resources, had greater concerns than keeping repair costs at the Cathedral in check, important though that was. 'Abusit to superstition and idolatry' was the code for covert Catholicism, obnoxious to St Machar's, which after the Reformation had become a Protestant parish kirk. There was another problem that caused fulmination in the St Machar kirk session during the seventeenth century and beyond. Spital folk showed a preference for being laid to rest in the graveyards of the Snow or Spital Kirks to that of St Machar's. It may that they opted, quite naturally, for a local graveyard compared with one which would at that time have been distant and unfamiliar. It was also a means of avoiding the burial dues demanded by St Machar's, which, in all fairness, were required for the daunting task of maintaining the fabric of the Cathedral. The kirk session complained about this on a number of occasions to the masters of King's College since 'the said Spittel kirk yeard doth properly belong to the said College'. The masters promised, in vain, one suspects, 'to do ther endeavour to restrain persons from burying ther'.

We left Andrew Brebner Jnr in 1602 with his recently acquired lands of Spital and Sunnyside. Attempts to farm them would be dogged by problems. 'Materials' for improving the ground, as Bishop Gordon had delicately called them, continued to be in scarce supply and that April, Brebner, and Patrick Cheyne, who owned Ferryhill, had a row with the magistrates of Aberdeen. The two landowners protested, in vain, against an ordinance prohibiting the transport of fulzie (dung) for the guiding (fertilising) of lands outwith the freedom of the burgh, as the Spital and Ferryhill most certainly were. An appeal to the traditions of 'tymes bygane' cut no ice and Brebner's lands were destined to remain 'non manurit' for the time being. A few months later, 'Johne Kid, Indwellar in Auld Aberdene' was indicted for stealing 'ane yow' from Brebner's 'toune of Sunnysyde, about Bartholl Day last', that is St Bartholomew's Day, 24 August. Kid had headed north with his quarry in an attempt to sneak her into the Aulton, but was foiled. 'Andrew Wentoun & ane uther of his nichtbours hard hir bleit cumand in at the Chanrie port'.

These reverses however, were small beer compared with Brebner's financial difficulties. By November he had entered into a contract of wadset with a man of some importance, William Moir, MA, burgess and Treasurer of Aberdeen, a role now undertaken by the city's Finance Department. This contract involved Brebner having to put up the 'toun and lands callit the Sonny Syde, Spittelhill and others lying within the Regalitie of the College of Auld Abd.' as a security for a loan of 800 merks. As creditor, Moir took over the management, and by 1604, the possession of Sunnyside and Spital since Brebner was unable to make repayment. A similar fate had attended Lindsay's property down in the Mardyke, so it was a case of history repeating itself. Thus the Moirs, who owned the estate of Scotstown beyond the Brig o Balgownie, first came into possession of the Spital Lands which were to remain in their family for nearly three hundred years.

Parson Gordon shows the 'Ruins of the Spithill Kirk' in an enclosure, the kernel of the future St Peter's Cemetery. The kirk, with its bell tower sits behind the rigs of a row of cottages, apparently at a lower level than the road. It looks not in the least ruinous. Gordon was probably using his standard chapel symbol, for he produced a similar sketch for the ruinous Snaw Kirk, at the foot of the hill. His accompanying *Description of Bothe Touns of Aberdeen*, tells us little. He writes that a little beyond the ruins of the former Snow Kirk (this was on the way back to Aberdeen), a church sacred to Peter was once situated. And it seems that Gordon did not overburden himself with research. His epitaph for Matthew Kyninmund, is, in the

Looking up from the site of the Spital Kirk to the higher levels of St Peter's Gate and the Spital.

Latin of the original, something of a put-down. He writes: *Nihil de fundatore constat* - 'Nothing is established about the founder'.

THE MOIRS OF SCOTSTOWN AND SPITAL (1)

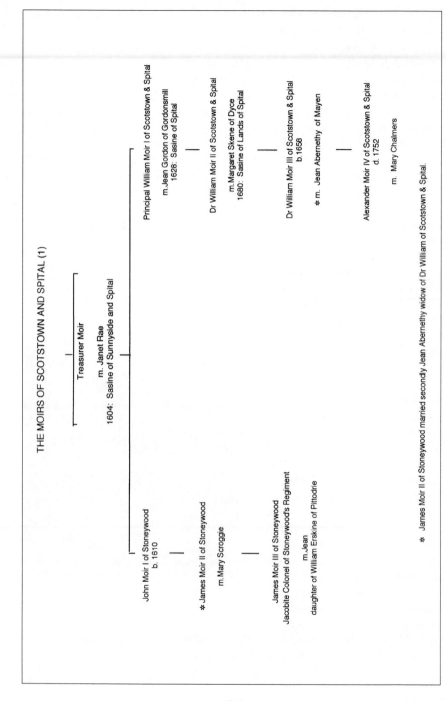

Treasurer Moir

m. Janet Rae
1604: Sasine of Sunnyside and Spital

John Moir I of Stoneywood
b. 1610

* James Moir II of Stoneywood

m.Mary Scroggie

James Moir III of Stoneywood
Jacobite Colonel of Stoneywood's Regiment
m.Jean
daughter of William Erskine of Pittodrie

Principal William Moir I of Scotstown & Spital

m.Jean Gordon of Gordonsmill
1626: Sasine of Spital

Dr William Moir II of Scotstown & Spital

m.Margaret Skene of Dyce
1680: Sasine of Lands of Spital

Dr William Moir III of Scotstown & Spital
b.1658

* m. Jean Abernethy of Mayen

Alexander Moir IV of Scotstown & Spital
d. 1752

m. Mary Chalmers

* James Moir II of Stoneywood married secondly Jean Abernethy widow of Dr William of Scotstown & Spital.

Chapter 8

A Multitude of Moirs

One Scottish Christian Moir can kill three pagan Moors.
Moir family legend.

There are multitudes of Moirs with genealogies galore, but available knowledge of the Moirs of Scotstown who became heritors of the Spital is limited. Their charter chest has been reported missing and we have to glean what we can from vicarious glimpses, names which appear in feu charters or feature in local and national affairs. They are not the same people as the Moirs of Stoneywood though the families were closely linked. William Moir, the Treasurer of Aberdeen, had acquired the Spital and Sunnyside in 1604 after Alexander Brebner foundered. The Treasurer's second surviving son, also William and a baillie of Aberdeen became the first Moir of Scotstown and Spital, taking sasine or legal possession of the Lands of Spital from his father in 1628. It was the Treasurer's eldest son, John, who bought Stoneywood in 1671 - he had already acquired other estates - and so became the first Moir of Stoneywood.

We know a little about William Moir, first laird of Scotstown and a fervent Covenanter, for he was prominent in civic and academic circles. He contributed handsomely to the restoration fund when the east quarter of Marischal College 'was all burnt to nought' in 1639 and two years later was appointed to the Chair of Mathematics there, events which are not necessarily linked. Moir is credited with a treatise on 'Geometry and the Mechanical Part of Mathematics'. But he was wearing his baillie's bunnet when he rode to Edinburgh on 19 March, 1644, to complain to a Committee of the Estates about the 'disaster and injurie' carried out in Aberdeen that dawn. The perpetrators were the Lairds of Haddo and Drum 'and their associats

...accompanied with ane hundredth horsemen, by footemen armed with swords, pistols, hagbuts...' The mob had carried off the provost of Aberdeen and some colleagues and would keep them captive for five weeks, all part of an ongoing feud between the two factions. It was fortunate that Moir was available to undertake the mission the very day the outrage had been committed, but then he had no lectures to give that day or any other. His Professorship was a sinecure. When Moir eventually returned from Edinburgh - he had to hole-up at Dunnottar Castle until the Covenanting army marched into Aberdeen a few weeks later and it was safe to return - the Council pronounced itself 'weill pleased with his report' and gave him two hundred merks. At least there had been no disruption of classes.

When he became Principal of Marischal College in 1649 he combined that office with his professorship and his baillieship, the Council throwing out regulations against such pluralities 'all in ane voice'. Nine years later he gave 'Twentie Pounds Scottis', the minimum donation for inclusion on a list of benefactors contributing to 'the New Building reared up at the north-east corner of (King's) Colledge' - the Cromwell Tower as we know it today. (General Monck, Cromwell's man in Scotland donated £120 Scots and his officers gave generously, hence the name). Principal Moir was deposed from office in 1661 at the time of the Restoration and fined £2400 Scots. His son, Dr William Moir, second of Scotstown and Spital, took possession of the Lands and Barony of Spital in 1680. A few years later the second laird was succeeded by his son, yet another Dr William Moir.

How did the Spital look in those days? The southern territory, between Aberdeen's boundary at Love Lane, almost to the brow of the Spital Hill had the disadvantages of hilly ground to the west and marshy ground to the east. Parson Gordon depicts only a couple of dwellings in this area, standing together, just beyond the 'Ruins of the Sickhouse'. Moving northwards, St Peter's at the top of the hill, would have acted as a magnet, and Gordon shows a Kirkton of around two dozen thatched cottages, some perched at the top of the Spital Hill, with long rigs running east to the kirk and others with orchards, descending north to the Powis Burn. These cottages, the original heart of the Spital were considered part of Old Aberdeen which, for civic, military, legal and religious purposes was divided into a number of natural sections, though in a variety of permutations and combinations. In August 1636, for example, according to the Burgh Records, the north entry to Old Aberdeen and the Loch Wynd were much in need of repair - 'the access in winter (is) so difficult that men and horse are both in danger'. It was agreed 'with uniform consent of the haill indwellers of the Spittell, Chanrie and Middel Toune, the latter the future High Street area, that these two areas would be calsayed before winter. No

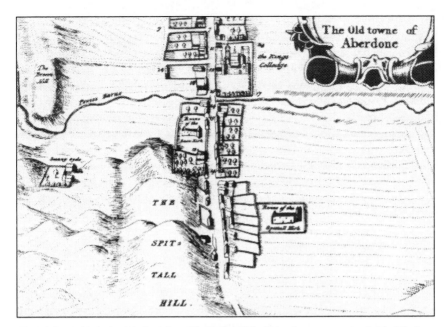

The Kirkton of Spital, with the ruins of the Spital Kirk sitting in open country behind the long rigs of cottages on the east side. The Spital foothills prevent cultivation to the west, but beyond the hills, the sizable farm toun of Sunnyside looks prosperous. Note the 'Ruins of the Snow Kirk', centre. The canonist's house sits in an enclosure with two trees just to its north. The North Spital descends to the brig over the Powis Burn. On the other side of the burn, the mediciner's house is the low building opposite 'the Kings Colledge'. From Parson Gordon's Plan, 1661.

murmur of complaint came from Spital folk, it seems, even though they were at the opposite end of town.

The Spital men were hopefully better at road-mending than they were at fighting. In March 1639, at the time of the covenanting troubles, the men of Spital Bounds, (sometimes written as Hospital Bounds), Oldtown and Seaton were mustered for the Marquis of Huntly, the king's lieutenant; 'waik, febill and unarmed bodeis' for the most part, as the chronicler Spalding unflatteringly presents them in his *Memorialls of the Trubles, 1624-45*. Huntly armed them with three-score muskets, staves, powder, lead and match and told them to join him at Inverurie. 'They obeyit', wrote Spalding:

and went out of the Oldtown, Spittell, and Seatoun, about 200 men ... Thus wes the countrie people drawin to sic extremetie, that they knew not whome to obey, whidder the Kingis proclamatiouns and his lieutennandis charges, or the covenanteris commandment.

At the end of the day, the Spital men and their comrades obeyed no one. Dismayed at the news that a covenanting army headed by Montrose and the Earl Marischal was approaching Aberdeen, they upped sticks and vanished. Possibly a more warlike spirit prevailed in September 1644 when the Aulton was divided into three sections and Spital men and the other indwellers joined the Home Guard, marching out in arms headed by their baillies for drill every Monday, Wednesday and Friday 'at ten ilk day, wind and wadder servand'. The first section was the Chanonry, the second from the Cross (in front of the Town House) to the College on the east side under John Forbes; the third was the corresponding area on the west side under Mr John Lundie, the College's humanist and master of the Grammar School - he taught Latin grammar. 'The Spitel boundis' was to be divided between Forbes and Lundie, though the latter declined the honour, arguing that university lecturers were exempt - though he found plenty of time for university politics.

A neat definition of the boundaries of the Aulton is contained in the punishment meted out to Margaret Strachan, 'ane notorious thiefe' in 1652. She was sentenced to be scourged by James Andersoune, hangman, through 'the haill toune of Old Aberdeen betwix the churche (St Machar's) and the Spittal Hill', with the threat of an instant watery grave - 'drunit without doom or law' - if she ever returned. Margaret had a weakness for stealing clothes and I wonder if it was she who, some five years earlier, had stolen '4 paire of hewed plaides' from the loom of 'George Glennie, distressed webster (weaver) in the Spittall'. Hopefully George was consoled by the nine merks and seven shillings collected for him on the instructions of the Kirk Session. A different division of Old Aberdeen was made in June 1695. Elders nominated by the kirk session to keep an eye untoward on-goings included James Thomson who took the area 'from the Cross, the east side of the toun, Colledge bound and Spittell to John Seatons dwelling' - which at that time marked the southern boundary of the Aulton - while William Smith undertook the corresponding west side, which included 'Sunnieside' as well.

An interesting picture of the families who lived in the Spital emerges from a census taken in May 1636 of the 'haill inhabitantis of the Auld toune, Chanrie and Spittell, their bairnes and servandis'. The aim of the exercise was to winkle out 'all infamous persons, all ydleris (idlers) and those that hes no certaine calling to live by, and wer not provided of kaill and fewall (fuel) and other necessaries of good neighbourheid'; and to uncover those who were giving refuge to such potential spongers. What seems to the modern reader to be Gestapo-like activities were undertaken with good reason. Folk in Old Aberdeen, like the rest of Scotland in those days, lived near subsistence level and the town's modest resources had to be carefully husbanded. St Machar's kirk, responsible for the poor of its parish, could not afford to sustain incomers with no means of support. But the kirk session records show that genuine cases of hardship, both local and further afield were supported sympathetically. In 1624, for example, the baillies of Old Aberdeen travelled through 'the Toun and Spittell and Colledge, to tak in sic volontaire contributions as may be had to the support of Dumfermling' - which had been totally destroyed by fire.

The results of the census of May 1636 were to be assessed by a jury 'of the most honest and aged persons of the Toun'. The Spital's good and great were William Troup 'in Spittell', implying a tenant of some consequence. Troup has long been a Spital name. He was joined by Andrew Youngson, a webster, John Anderson a tailor, and James Innes. The census shows that the Spital had a population of 140 spread over twenty-eight families, though two were away at the time. That ties in with the number of cottages between the Spital Hill and the Powis Burn on Parson Gordon's Plan. Seventeen families had young children, a total of fifty-one bairns all told. William Troup had most with eight, six families had four, the next highest number, while three families had but 'ane bairne'. Parents and children, two generations, was the most common family unit, but John Cow lived with his wife, four bairns and Marjorie Wood, his gude sister (sister-in-law), while James Innes's family consisted of his wife, his mother and 'ane bairn', plus three male and two female servants. Three families were just man and wife. One of these was 'James Skedway, wobster', who sounds like an incomer, 'and his wyff onlie', while another was that of Hendrie Annand, (another Spital surname), his wife and 'ane servant lase'. Thomas Elmslie lived alone with his grown-up daughter, and Alexander Volume (a well known Old Aberdeen surname) had only his servant, Agnes Kellie, for company.

There were four tailors, two wrights, one cordiner - a shoemaker or leather worker - and one cooper, Robert Barnet, 'subtennent to George Halden', an unauthorised set-up as it transpired. It was the websters however, eight of them all told, who formed the largest group of artisans. But there was no blacksmith and no one was providing bread, meat or ale. For such necessaries, Spital folk would have to cross the Powis Brig and make for the heartlands of Old Aberdeen where smiths, bakers, butchers and brewers, as well as purveyors of comestibles such as kail, dulse, and black puddings were to be found.

Dr William Gordon, who lived with his wife, three bairns and four servants, was the Spital's most distinguished resident at that time. He was the King's College mediciner, and held the Chair of Medicine from 1632 until 1640. The mediciner's house was opposite King's College and appears

Dr William Gordon, courtesy, Aberdeen University.

to have been still extant at this time. If Dr Gordon actually lived there, Spital Bounds and College Bounds must have been virtually synonymous. Gordon has the reputation of an able doctor, but with no students, no classes, and no teaching duties he was able to devote time to university politics, and to his other official post, common procurator, concerned with the financial administration of the university. In February 1633 when 'ane gryt storme of snaw with horribill heiche wyndis' toppled the Crown from the Chapel it was the versatile Gordon who designed the new Crown, set up a national fund-raising campaign, and saw to it that its replacement, the Crown we see today, 'was biggit up little inferior to the first'. It was he who had organised the road mending programme already noted.

A fair number of servants appear in the census, twenty-one male, and ten female, spread over thirteen families. James Innes, with five had most, and several other families had four. In cases, where the head of the family was an artisan, male servants were likely to be journeymen, but for some, particularly women, being in service amounted to little more than serfdom. However, as the outcome of the 1636 census indicates, going into service, finding a place in a household, was an alternative to being forced to leave the burgh.

'Elspet Troup and three bairnes in the canonists hous extravagentes' as they are described, is one of the curiosities of the census. 'Extravagentes' implies that Elspet and the bairns were vagrants rather than spendthrifts in the modern sense, and the canonist's house, indicated merely as a site by Gordon's Plan - surveyed some years before its publication in 1661 - was likely to have been in a poor state in 1636. Given that Troup is a Spital name, there is a mystery as to why this all female household was squatting in a ruinous house. Then there is the case of Peter Barnet, whose trade is not given, but who had the company of his wife and 'thrie uther strang (stranger) women'.

Those exposed by the census as being without 'ane testimoniall', the equivalent of illegal immigrant, were expelled, though a few were given the

132

option of finding work as servants. Spital indwellers who had transgressed by sheltering some unauthorised person were to be 'amerciat' or fined. Among them was George Halden who had taken in the cooper, Robert Barnet, and his family. Barnet's fate is unclear, but at least, he had a trade to offer. Later that year, at a Martinmas court, two of the Spital men who supervised the May census, John Wylie, elder, and Andrew Youngson, whom one might have expected to be beyond reproach, were both fined £4 Scots - subsequently 'migitat' to 40s and 20s respectively - 'anent resetting of strange beggaris'. These and similar infringements indicate that Aulton folk were far from heartless. And by imposing the occasional fine, the lean coffers of the Aulton treasury were usefully replenished.

Spital indwellers might have been glad to see the back of one of their own number. In March 1642, Margaret Walls, 'spous to William Gray in Spittill', and something of a housewife from hell, was accused of 'swearing and blasphemeing of the lords name and scolding against her nightboirs'. A repetition of such behaviour, the kirk session pronounced:

will be punished in sackcloth, barefoote & bare leggit before the pulpit and thereafter to be put in the govis or joggs (pillories), and to pay sic penaltie as the Judges sall injoyne her.

But the majority of Spital folk appear to have been hard-working and respectable. From their numbers, a wright, a merchant, a maltman, a blacksmith, and a gardener were admitted as Merchant or Trade Burgesses of Old Aberdeen during the seventeenth and eighteenth centuries. Among the weavers admitted was John Crevey, in 1674, 'brother to the minister of Newhills', and in 1679, William Strachan, 'chapman and residenter in the Spittall Bounds'. As the century progressed, the cordiners and shoemakers overtook the weavers as the most numerous trade in the Spital. In 1649, George Allane, a Spital cordiner, was admitted a trade burgess along with his son, and in 1662, he and his neighbours had their 'dask' a desk or pew at St Machar's allocated, a sign of the trade's increasing importance. The Dollas or Dallas family were also prominent shoemakers or cordiners - like the Allanes they used the terms interchangeably. In June 1695, 'John Dollas in Spittill' became an elder of St Machar's. The following year, The List of Pollable Persons within the Shire of Aberdeen divided the Spital into the east side where there were fourteen shoemakers and the less populous west side where there were four. There were by then only four weavers on the east side, and one on the west compared with a total of eight in the 1636 census. The Spital had also lost two of its four tailors, but gained a flesher, a blacksmith, a mason, James Baverlay, and two gunsmiths.

The Spital was expanding southwards at this time, encroaching on the exclusiveness of Aberdeen's liberty, the area over which privileges of the burgh extended. The magistrates complained of 'great prejudice our traidsmen susteines by the Spittell and other contrie men working upon ther liberties.' An Act of the Scottish Parliament of 1592 prohibited the exercise of crafts within the suburbs of royal burghs but it was highly questionable if the Spital lay within the suburbs of Aberdeen. The Town Council had been given advice in 1670 which was unsatisfactory :

ye have brought us home ane informatione of the advocats which...mentions nothing what ane suburb may be, or how far distant from the burghe nor what the magistrats may do theranent for assistance of ther freemen'.

Nor did everyone agree that John Seaton's house 'in the Spithill' was the marker that denoted the end of the Spital and the end of the 'freedom' of Old Aberdeen. In 1699 the Parliamentary Commissioners who regulated trade between royal burghs and burghs of barony were not impressed by arguments to that effect; 'the Commissioners doe not find that the Toun of Old Aberdeen hes a privilege or jurisdiction over the Spithill. The offer of tuelfe pennies Scots is too mean and very far below the extent of their trade'. The implication was the Spital was doing rather better than Old Aberdeen and the Commissioners were able to tax it separately.

The Commissioners note that the Spital 'pertained to James Moir of Stoneywood', who was member of Parliament for Aberdeenshire at that time. This has created the impression that the Stoneywood Moirs owned the Spital. The laird was Alexander Moir, fourth of Scotstown, who was but a bairn at that time. He did not attend Marischal College until 1703, at a time when the average entry age was twelve. The explanation is simple; his widowed mother had married James Moir, second of Stoneywood, who under Scots law would have acted as Alexander's 'tutor', his legal guardian.

Alexander had an interesting life. At the time of the Jacobite Rising in 1715, he rode into Aberdeen with the Earl Marischal's supporters, attended the Proclamation of the 'Old Pretender' as James VIII and III, attended the meeting of Stuart supporters at Mistress Hepburn's Tavern, helped to appropriate the town's store of ammunition laid in by William Lindsay, insulted the Hanoverian magistrates and, with his stepfather, was elected one of the Jacobite councillors. After the debacle of the '15 he fled the country, in the same boat with his stepfather and step-brother, James Moir, third of Stoneywood, and his stepfather's brother, William Moir of Invernetty and about ten other Jacobites. Before returning to Scotland he spent some time in exile in Holland where his heir, George, fifth laird of Scotstown and Spital was born.

The Moir Coat of Arms

Legend has it that the Moir coat-of-arms originated with Kenneth Moir who accompanied Lord James Douglas, 'the good Sir James', into Spain with the heart of Robert the Bruce in the year 1330. When they landed they entered into an agreement with Alonzo XI of Spain to fight on the Christian side against the pagan Moors. Lord James was killed in attempting to rescue Sir William St Clair of Roslyn; but in the charge, and before this happened, Kenneth Moir slew three Moors and cut off their heads. One of the Scottish soldiers is reputed to have shouted, 'One Scottish Christian Moir can kill three pagan Moors'.

This is said to be the origin of the heraldic pun depicted on the Moir coat-of-arms - three Moors heads with blood dripping from the neck.

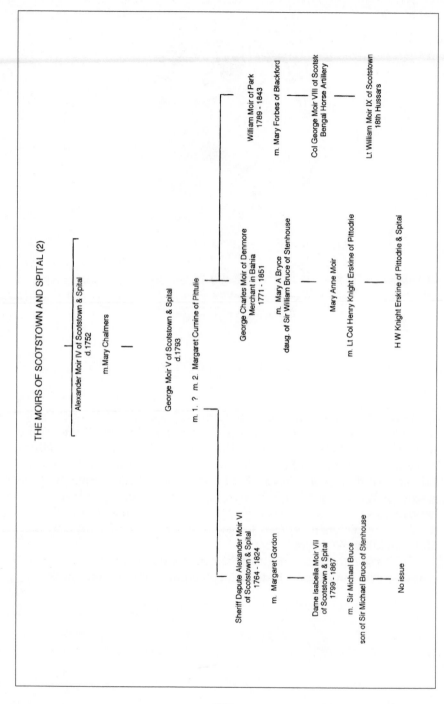

THE MOIRS OF SCOTSTOWN AND SPITAL (2)

Alexander Moir IV of Scotstown & Spital
d.1752

m. Mary Chalmers

George Moir V of Scotstown & Spital
d.1793

m. 1. ? m. 2. Margaret Cumine of Pittulie

Sheriff Depute Alexander Moir VI
of Scotstown & Spital
1764 - 1824

m. Margaret Gordon

Dame Isabella Moir VII
of Scotstown & Spital
1799 - 1867

m. Sir Michael Bruce
son of Sir Michael Bruce of Stenhouse

No issue

George Charles Moir of Denmore
Merchant in Bahia
1771 - 1851

m. Mary A Bryce
daug. of Sir William Bruce of Stenhouse

Mary Anne Moir

m. Lt Col Henry Knight Erskine of Pittodrie

H W Knight Erskine of Pittodrie & Spital

William Moir of Park
1789 - 1843

m. Mary Forbes of Blackford

Col George Moir VIII of Scotstc
Bengal Horse Artillery

Lt William Moir IX of Scotstown
18th Hussars

Chapter 9

Lairds and ither Folk

The lands on each side of the village called the Spital between New and Old Aberdeen, have been considerably improved of late by George Mair (sic) Esq, of Scotstown, the proprietor.

Francis Douglas: Description of the East Coast of Scotland, 1782

George was one of the few Moirs of Scotstown to leave his mark on the Spital Lands. He succeeded to the family estates as fifth laird after the death of his father Alexander in 1752 and no harm at all was done by his Jacobite heritage and his continental upbringing. In the Spital itself he set the scene for the creation of a thriving village. During the latter half of the eighteenth century he feued numerous plots of land on both sides of the Old Aberdeen highway, mainly to artisans. One of them was a relatively rare breed. On 11 September, 1759 the *Aberdeen Journal* ran an advertisement:

George Alexander, glover and breeches maker in the Spital 'twixt New and Old Aberdeen. Maker of buck and doeskin breeches as good as from the best of London glove and breech makers.

Taylor's Plan of 1773 shows how the Spital village looked during this era. On the east side a row of houses ran from just north of Love Lane in a continuous line to the Powis Burn. Several houses stood on their own, others formed little terraces. They were the successors of those in Parson Gordon's time; perhaps in some cases, the originals. A rectangle encompassed the east side of the village with the Old Aberdeen Road forming the long west side. Parallel to it the East Back Road formed the eastern side.

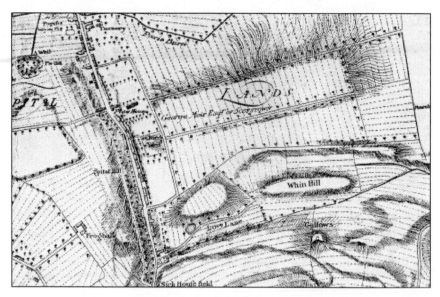

Taylor's Plan of 1773. Note Love Lane, the Play House, Church Yard, (St Peter's), the rectangle on the east side of the Spital, and the loanings beyond.

Merkland Place and Orchard Place mark the south and north ends respectively of this back road, but the middle section was obliterated when St Peter's Cemetery expanded. It would have run along what is now the boundary between the higher, older portion of the graveyard and the newer, lower section. The short south end of the rectangle has become that section of Merkland Road between the Spital and Merkland Place; the north end is now Orchard Walk. In Taylor's time, the Spital Kirkyard lay roughly in the centre of this rectangle, and the 'Play House' of which more anon, just to the north of it.

Beyond the Churchyard, two loanings (on either side of 'Lands - George Moir Esqr of Scotstown', above) led off to the Links. Pittodrie Place and Linksfield Road are laid out along their line. Baillie Logie indicates these on his Plan as 'Scotstown's Inclosures'. An improving laird, Moir brought considerable tracts of the Spital Lands under cultivation. Francis Douglas, traveller and agricultural writer, rode past in 1780 and was impressed. He wrote in his *General Description of the East Coast of Scotland:*

> The lands on each side of the village called the Spital, between New and Old Aberdeen, have been considerably improved of late, by George Mair (sic) esq, of Scotstown, the proprietor, who has gained a great deal of ground from the links, or

138

benty sands, towards the sea. The upper parts of them … consist of little hills or rising grounds, of a light sandy soil, which when cleared of weeds, and sufficiently manured, are found to produce good crops of grain, and sown grass.

Not everyone approved of George Moir gaining ground from the Links. The Town Council 'were continually resisting encroachments by Mr Moir' into the Town's Links. The two parties were at variance over a 'grey' area which ran lengthways 'from the Tyle Burn by the Links of Seaton southward to a stank (pool) or strype of water at the foot of the Broadhill', and in breadth from 'the laboured (cultivated) lands of Spittal on the west to the sea on the east'. The dispute was resolved by the Contract of Marches in 1759, with the division between 'Scotstown's land' and the Town's lands marked by a row of civic saucer stones and duly enshrined by Captain Taylor as 'March of Scotstown's Pasture in the Links' in his Plan of 1773. (See page118). An area of pasture 'remaining forever unlaboured' was defined as common to both parties. George Moir had the right to pasture 'not exceeding twenty black cattle, whether oxen or cows, and eight horses, but no sheep. The Contract continued:

> The Inhabitants of the Town of Aberdeen shall have the right to pasture thereon such cows and horses as belong to them whatever their number but no sheep; on the understanding that no common Carrier or Drivers horses be included in this privilege.

The hilly terrain of the west side of the Spital made development more difficult. There is no terrace of cottages here though three or four separate groups of dwellings can be made out on Taylor's Plan. Some of the houses in the two larger groups are probably still with us. Behind them, a track runs along the edge of the Spital foothills, probably the same one that the goldsmith William Lindsay had to promise not level in 1715. This 'west back road' is probably represented in modern times by the short cut through the Froghall plotties to Sunnybank, now Froghall View, and further north, by the Firhill Road. Opposite the 'Play House' a track, the future Firhill Place, led westwards to Sunnyside Farm.

To help fund the improvement of his lands, George Moir borrowed from James Beattie, renowned poet and Professor of Moral Philosophy at Marischal College at a time when that subject was Queen in Academia. Beattie was a leading member of the Aberdeen Philosophical Circle and friend of the great and the good. In 1774 he noted in his Memoranda: 'Interest of £100 from Mr Moir' - £5. That year the second book of Beattie's great poem *The Minstrel* was published. Sales were excellent and he was well-positioned to oblige his friends. Sometimes the boot was on the other foot. In October 1786, we find Beattie paying £2 6s 10d interest 'of money borrowed from Mr Moir of Scotstown and repayed this day'.

Beattie was a member of the Aberdeen Philosophical Society alias the Wise Club which met regularly at the Red Lion Inn in the Spital between 1758 and 1773. It formed the ideal halfway house between King's and Marischal Colleges, not then united. Another leading member was one of the great philosophers of the age, Thomas Reid, first Regent, then Professor of Moral Philosophy at King's between 1751 and 1764. He set off for Glasgow University in that latter year to succeed Adam Smith in the Chair of Moral Philosophy there.

One wonders if the learned philosophers saw any of the theatricals that took place in the Spital. In allowing these performances, George Moir and his father before him, had cocked a snook at city's authorities. At that time, actors, or 'comedians' as they were called, were *persona non grata* as far as Aberdeen's tight-laced magistrates and clergy were concerned. A troupe had performed in Edinburgh in the face of official opposition in 1750, then came north to try their luck in Aberdeen. Their performances were banned in the city so the actors resourcefully built a playhouse at the south side of the Spital, 'near the extremity of the town', presumably just north of Love Lane, outwith the magistrates' jurisdiction and with 'Scotstown's' blessing. They planned to return for a second season, but the magistrates were ready for them. The Council Register of 15 December, 1751 recorded:

The said Day the Council being informed that the players from Edinburgh that acted in the Spiytal last autumn had taken a Tack of a piece of ground in the Spittel from Scotstown in order to erect a Playhouse to act in the spring and autumn seasons yearly which would tend greatly to debauch the morals of Children and Young People and cause them make Bad Shifts.

As the Spital was deemed 'within the County' of Aberdeen, the councillors pressed for a meeting with the relevant authorities, the Justices of the Peace, to 'entreat them to prevent (the players) acting within the county'. Whether or not the Justices found 'some Effectual Method' to ban the actors, the latter did not, as Kennedy reports in his *Annals* 'meet with all the encouragement which they expected from the people, and took their departure at the close of a short season'. But the following year, 1752, the *Aberdeen Journal* was advertising a performance 'at the Great Barn, in the Spital betwixt New and Old Aberdeen this present Evening, June 16th'. What was on offer sounded more like circus acts than 'straight' theatre:

140

Some curious Performances by the celebrated Company of ROPE DANCERS and TUMBLERS from Edinburgh, Mons. DOMINIQUE, Mris GARMAN, Mr. FRANCISCO, Miss ALICE, a Child of six Years of Age, and others. With several surprising Balances on the SLACKWIRE, by Mr. BARBAROUSE, such as were never done before by any but himself; and several curious EQUILIBRUMS on the TABLE and CHAIR, by the famous RUSSIAN BOY. The above surprising Performances, as particularly mentioned in the daily Bills have given great Satisfaction in Edinburgh, Glasgow, in this Place, and wherever he exhibited. Price, One Shilling and sixpence each Person. Mr Dominique (as his Stay is but short) intends to perform every lawful Day, (Saturdays excepted)

The magistrates continued to show concern about the effect of theatrical exhibitions on public morality. Early in 1773 they sought guidance from the city's legal advisers, Edinburgh advocates Alexander Gordon, and Henry Dundas, the future Viscount Melville who would later become Scotland's most powerful politician. The magistrates wished to know if they had the authority to lock up the actors. The gist of the advocates' reply was that if the worst came to the worst, they could. But they concluded cheerfully: 'we can suppose many of these public shows to be innocent'. In spite of such reassuring advice, the Aberdeen authorities banned the actor West Digges Esq, then 'in the zenith of his popularity in Edinburgh', that same year. 'Digges', Kennedy tells us, responded by erecting 'a very neat play-house in the north end of the Spital, where the Edinburgh company performed for several seasons, successfully and with much éclat'. Taylor's Plan shows this 'very neat play-house' at what would now be the west end of Orchard Street, further from Aberdeen than its predecessors. Though attendances were good, the theatre, was 'exceedingly inconvenient for those who frequented it, on account of its great distance from the town'. After a year or two, however, the magistrates became more liberal in outlook and Mr Digges and his company were at last permitted to play in Aberdeen.

George Moir did not live in the Spital himself. While there may well have been a plain, old-fashioned residence at Scotstown, something of Moir's personal style is reflected in the simple but stylish townhouse that he built in 1778, in Belmont Street, some four years after the street was laid out to link Schoolhill and the Green. This was a daring move for this new street was on the very edge of the town. The hub of the city was still in the Castlegate and Broad Street. The move west had not yet begun and Union Street was almost thirty years in the future.

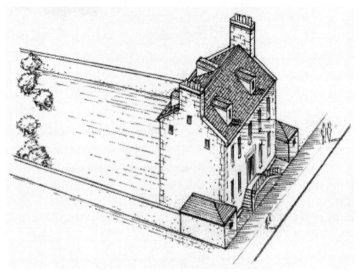

George Moir's townhouse at Belmont Street, based on a sketch by James Forbes Beattie, surveyor, dated 1869.

This rectangular house with its distinctive quoins, flanked by two miniature pavilions, was built of surface gatherings of granite, squared and dressed. On the ground floor, were the dining-room, sitting-room and parlour where a french casement opened out onto a long garden sloping down to the Denburn. An open-well staircase with a fine handrail and hand-carved balusters of two alternating designs gave access to the first floor where drawing room, boudoir, powder room and library were to be found. One can almost hear the harpsichord tinkling, and the swish of satin - though it would have been very much a male household. George Moir had three sons, Alexander, his heir, by his first wife, and George Charles and William by his second wife, Margaret Cumine. The spacious attics housed the bedrooms and closets while scullery, wine-cellar and servants' hall were in the basement.

142

Sheriff-depute Alexander Moir.

George Moir's eldest son, Alexander, born in 1764, was destined for the Scottish Bar. He was educated at Marischal College where Beattie's course in Moral Philosophy included legal principles. He then studied law in Edinburgh, a requirement at that time for prospective advocates. On his father's death in 1793, he became sixth laird of Scotstown and Spital but seems to have been more of a public man than his father, dividing his time between his legal practice in Edinburgh and his Aberdeenshire estates. He was a keen part-time soldier and in 1794 was appointed major-commandant of the new 'Gentlemen Volunteers' of Aberdeen, formed to counteract the current war scare. Moir's special interest was coastal defence which was just as well for that year the French revolutionary army, having successfully invaded the Netherlands, was making threatening noises.

In 1796, he resigned his commission on becoming sheriff-depute of Aberdeenshire. These deputes - the modern equivalent is sheriff principal - were in the enviable position of combining advocacy with a spot of judging, occasionally hearing cases on appeal from the sheriff-substitute (now simply the sheriff) while continuing their careers at the Edinburgh bar. That same year as his shrieval appointment, Marischal College conferred the honorary degree of Doctor of Laws on Moir. He was still only thirty-two and it is said that both distinctions came about as a result of Professor Beattie's influence.

In the years that followed, Alexander's two younger half-brothers would also do well for themselves. George Charles Moir born in 1771, became a successful merchant in Bahia in Brazil, while William, born in 1789, when his father must have been a fair age, became the laird of Park on Deeside. In 1806, Moir sold the family home in Belmont Street. It had become 'surplus to requirements'. The buyer was John, the last Menzies laird of Pitfodels.

Like his father, Alexander made more land available in the Spital, and the Commutation Books for 1811-12 list some 144 householders. There were many weavers and shoemakers, as well as a chapman, a blind fiddler, William Hogg, and a gravedigger, Robert Leslie who perhaps had the sad task of preparing the laird's lair in the Spital Kirkyard. Alexander had resigned as sheriff-depute in 1822 when only fifty-eight and died two years later. The appointment had been *ad vitam aut culpam*, the incumbent removable only by death or default. He was well thought of by the Society of Advocates in Aberdeen, so it seems that he must have been a victim of ill health. (There is a portrait of him on the ground floor of Advocates' Hall in Concert Court, an advocate in Edinburgh amidst the advocates in Aberdeen). On news of his death, the Society met 'to consider the propriety of showing some mark of respect to his Remains.' Having paid tribute to his 'Integrity and Talents as a Judge and his virtues as a Gentleman', the members decided:

> to assemble in a Body in full Mourning and join the Funeral Procession opposite to King's College and accompany it from, thence to St Peter's Churchyard, the Place of Interment.

The cortège, starting out from Scotstown, would have negotiated the Brig o Balgownie, then the Seatongait. A large gathering of lawyers in deepest black, awaiting the procession as it came slowly along the High Street, attended by a train of respectful tenantry, must have been a memorable sight. Burials were no longer taboo in the kirkyard, now St Peter's it seems rather than the Spital graveyard. It had been acquired from King's College by the Moirs some time after 1727, and here the family mausoleum was built not long after Alexander's death. He was the first Moir to be commemorated there.

The seventh laird of Scotstown and Spital was Alexander's only child, Lady Bruce or Dame Isabella as she was generally known, wife of Sir Michael Bruce of Stenhouse, who traced his descent from Robert the Bruce. Over fifty years would pass before legislation would permit women rights over their own property so Dame Isabella, perforce, always had Sir Michael in tow regarding everything she did in the Spital. Indeed Sir Michael more often than not appears as the laird. In 1826, for example when the Spital, with a valued rent of £200, was 'cessed' at £2 for land tax purposes, Mr Bruce - he did not succeed to the baronetcy until 1827 - is shown as the sole heritor. Similarly, in the valuation rolls Sir Michael is shown as owner of numerous properties within the Spital Lands, including twenty-five farms, at Canalside, Sunnybank, Love Lane, King Street, Howie Park, the large farms of Sunnyside and Froghall, and one on the 'Spittalhill' itself. The aggregate yearly rent was £828 3s 1d, a tidy sum in those days.

'Scotstown' was 'every inch a gentleman', maintained William Carnie of Sir Michael in his *Reporting Reminiscences.* As chairman of the Oldmachar Parochial Board, 'he could speak well and kept the business firmly in hand'. In November 1838, he survived the fifty-three toasts proposed at a notably gargantuan annual dinner of the Society of Advocates, though fortunately his involvement was fairly early in the toast list. He was the subject of Toast No 10, 'Sir Michael Bruce and the Baronets of Scotland', and proposed Toast No 17, 'the New Treasurer of the Society'.

Dame Isabella was a Catholic and was the principal lady guest at the festivities held in the School Buildings in Constitution Street in 1845 to mark the fiftieth year of Priest Gordon's ministry in Aberdeen. Of a Sunday she would be dropped off at St Peter's Roman Catholic Church at the Castlegate while the carriage then took Sir Michael round to the fashionable St Paul's Episcopal Church in the Gallowgate. In spite of agreeing to differ over religion, a cosy set-up existed between the Bruce and the Moir families. In 1828, six years after Sir Michael and Dame Isabella were married, Mary Agnew Bruce, Michael's sister, then twenty-five, married George Charles Moir, Isabella's uncle, or, strictly speaking, half-uncle, in his late fifties by this time and back from Bahia, no doubt having made his pile. He was able to buy the Denmore estate, handily sited just south east of Scotstown. A daughter, Mary Anne Moir, was born of this union.

A few Spital dwellers appear in the first Aberdeen Directory of 1828 offering literary and educational services, but it is not always easy to pinpoint exactly where they lived. Spital house numbers were changed twice, and the early versions, where they existed at all, were idiosyncratic enough to make strong men weep. George Annand of the Royal Artillery was at No 13, and William Munro, dealer in books, at No 50 with his house at No 51. This was on the west side, below the future Hillhead Terrace, which, like the east side used odd and even numbers in sequence. The house address of an Upperkirkgate bookseller, William Gordon, is given merely as Spital, though one suspects it might be Gordon Cottage of which more anon. James Edward, teacher of English and Stenography was further north, at No 72, next door to the old Red Lion. Those gentlemen do not appear to be among the dozen or so who had registered themselves as eligible to vote following the passage of the 1832 Reform Act, indicating that they owned or tenanted property valued at £10 or more per annum. Among the latter were Ninian Kynoch, merchant, a licensed grocer who was also clerk to St Peter's Churchyard and lived at No 64, one of the cottages fronting the graveyard. His family were still there in the early twentieth century. There was also James Mitchell, a stocking manufacturer, Robert Leys, an iron-turner, William Hunter late of the excise, a blacksmith, several weavers, a farmer, a tailor, and a gardener. These men of property, in those days before the secret ballot, would have found it imprudent to do other than to vote for Sir Michael, who represented the Whig-Liberal interest for the county of Aberdeen in the first post-Reform Act election. To no avail;

the Tory candidate was successful. Suffrage was still far from universal and to give Sir Michael his due, he was the favourite candidate. His supporters cheered him in defeat with a set of silver plate, while the non-electors held a penny subscription and presented him with two handsome cups.

During the Bruce years, the Spital became ever more densely populated with an increasingly wide mix of residents, enjoying a more thrifty lifestyle than obtainable in Aberdeen. In the 1840s, for example, there were a handful of farmers and gardeners, the inevitable shoemakers, four grocers, two of whom were licensed, and an enclave of fleshers. There was a tailor, a dressmaker, and Miss Gray, a straw hat maker at No 68. There were two carters, one of whom, Charles Downie was the Old Aberdeen carrier. There were also two manufacturers who may have been in the cloth industry. One of them, William Deans, was also keeper of the Trades Mort Cloth. Near the Old Aberdeen end was John Torrie, teacher of French, and it is not surprising to note that by the end of the decade, he had retired. He appears in the Old Aberdeen Valuation Roll of 1796 and the following year taught John, the eldest son of Hugh Leslie of Powis. He fell on hard times for in 1799 he and 'his family in distress' received charity from Hugh Leslie, and again 1801. Nevertheless he must have survived to a good old age.

Early street directories reveal principally the genteel and those with a service to sell. Valuation rolls and census returns record things as they were, and the earliest, those of the 1850s and 1860s show a crowded Spital whose inhabitants undertook a wide range of occupations including farming, handcrafting, manufacturing, clerical and retail work, the service industries and public protection. As with Causewayend, there was a fair proportion of 'immigrants' from many parts of the North East and some from further afield. There is a bread and provision shopkeeper from Ripon, Yorkshire, a soap manufacturer from Germany, now naturalised, and in a back house on the east side - the future Merkland Place - Daniel Breslin, a fish cadger from Ireland. There were several granite masons including one whose previous place of abode is given as 'America, Canada'. There are a number of Chelsea pensioners, not at that time required to board at the Royal Hospital. There were laundresses, blacksmiths, ironmongers, brassmoulders, combmakers, envelope folders, bandbox makers, handloom weavers, wool rug weavers and many workers in the flax trade.

There was a stone dyker, a salmon fisher, a salmon net maker, and a crofter - Robert Sutherland farmed four acres - perhaps this was the Spital farm. A haberdasher had joined the ranks of the shopkeepers. There was a furnace manager at the gas works, two female bookbinders, merchants, mariners, a railway clerk, a shipping clerk, a ship's steward and stewardess, a night constable, a fireman and Alexander Ogilvie, hat manufacturer, at No 42. Of the family groups, William Watson, a road contractor from Elgin,

146

employed four of his sons. Ludovic Sandison, fishing rod and golf club maker, lived over the shop in one of the little cottages that formed part of Spital Terrace and had his thirteen-year-old son working with him. Joseph Massie, a policeman from Ellon, had a son who was a teacher, and a Spital carter had one son who was a coachmaker, and another who was a farm servant. The requirement for students to live in residence was abandoned by King's College in 1825, and eleven sets of lodgings in the Spital are given in the street directory for 1849-50. There were likely to have been more. The census returns of 1851 show Mrs Hector at No 79 with five students from Ross, Sutherland, Banff and Clackmanan. There were four at No 60 where Margaret Gale (or Gill) was landlady. Two of the personalities in Neil Maclean's autobiographical *Life at a Northern University*, Peter Fendour and Grigor Allan, lodged there in the mid 1850s. Maclean himself studied at King's from 1853-57 and had digs in the Spital during his final year.

The Red Lion Inn where the Wise Club once met was originally located nearer Old Aberdeen than nowadays, and on the west side. On 7 February, 1810 the *Aberdeen Journal* had advertised: 'that house in the Spital called the Red Lion to be let as a tavern'. This curiously worded notice probably indicates that the tavern had always been located in a house. Later, it may have been replaced by a custom-built inn with a public room. Nor were its clientele always tipplers. On 1 February 1845 the *Aberdeen Journal* reported that:

On the evening of Tuesday 21st January, the friends of the College Bounds Sabbath Evening School held a tea meeting in the Hall of the Red Lion Tavern, Spital. Tribute was paid to the late Mr G Hunter, coal broker who had been up to the time of his death in 1844 connected with the Church for over 30 years.

In 1851 Thomas McFarlane was mine host, followed by the Ross family and Mrs Hay from Love Lane. At this time the inn had a capacious signboard on which was painted the Latin motto *Serva Jugum* which students inevitably translated as 'Hand round the jug'. It was a favourite houff and features in one of the most notorious incidents in *Life at a Northern University*, when after a tumbler of toddy in the Cafe Royal in town, Maclean, Fendour, and others wander up the Spital, bent on mischief. They halt outside the Red Lion, then decide to head for Old Aberdeen, where they 'pin a cart' successfully, removing the wheels and sending them to the four corners. On the way back, one of their number for no reason assaults an old man who happened to be passing, something the worse of drink. A shoemaker rushes from his shop, strikes one of the students in retaliation, and in a moment a brawl breaks out. Locals spill from their homes to join in and the students flee back up the Spital, outnumbered and somewhat the worse of wear:

When we got to the middle of the hill, instead of mounting it, made a rush for the Red Lion, and bursting into a room, ordered a round, and proceeded to inspect the disasters of the evening.

The Spital's most famous student was the Huntly-born novelist, George Macdonald, who 'lodged in a small house of two floors and a garret at the top of the Spital Brae', the modern No 37 at the junction with Froghall Terrace. He studied at King's from 1840-45, dropping out for the 1842-43 session when his father, a meal miller, did not have the funds to keep him at university.

George Macdonald's digs at No 37 the Spital. His room was in the garret, top right. Note the two separate entrances and the old building at the top of Froghall Lane (Terrace).

He contrived, nevertheless, to be something of a dandy, with a tartan coat 'the most dazzling affair in dress I ever saw a student wear', according to a contemporary, while his 'fine velvet coat' brought fellow students to their windows to catch a glimpse of it. He graduated MA in 1845, studied divinity in London, made his living by lecturing, preaching and writing. For many years he and his family over-wintered in the Italian resort of Bordighera near the French Riviera. Macdonald's ashes are interred there. This is a far cry for from the setting of his North East novels among them *Alec Forbes of Howglen* and *Robert Falconer* where his use of Doric dumfounded

148

the critics. His children's stories, including *The Princess and the Goblin*, and *At the Back of the North Wind* influenced Tolkin and C S Lewis and have long been classics, while his 'strange and disturbing' adult fantasy novels, *Phantases* and particularly *Lilith* have made him a cult figure in recent years.

Another remarkable Spital personality was John Ross, whose signboard at No 62 proclaimed him as 'teacher of the fiddle and player'. Like the earlier fiddler, William Hogg, Ross 'than who no better ever drew a bow' was blind, the outcome of smallpox in childhood. Nevertheless he knew every corner of Aberdeen and the Aulton 'and found his way without difficulty, with the help of his stick, generally carrying his fiddle at his back inside his coat' as the author of *Aberdeen and its Folk* tells us. He had devised an ingenious method of noting music, a type of Braille involving a board and wooden pins, 'notched to represent the positions of the stave and the value of different notes'. Ross was an ardent florist and cultivated a small garden attached to his house with great success

Life at a Northern University gives an account of a meeting of 'The Lobby' an all male student society for the dancing of reels, to counteract 'the evils produced by prolonged sedentary habits'. It met in the abandoned residential attics of the south wing of King's Quadrangle (demolished, with its remarkable piazza, in the 1860s). There is an atmosphere of a wild, if teetotal bacchanal, Ross controlling events by the brilliance of his fiddling. Reel after reel is danced, and between dances, his 'intermediate pieces' hold the students in thrall. Then came the summons for departure. 'After a reel danced with the most tremendous noise and fiendish yelling, the 'Lobby' closed, the greater part bursting pell-mell from the room, making their way downstairs, laughing, knocking, tumbling over each other... Carefully led by some Magistrands, (fourth year students) John Ross was helped down the stairs and conducted to his home'.

Reels, if there were any, would have been danced in a more decorous fashion at the wedding of Mary Anne Moir. Her father, the Bahia merchant, had died in 1851, and the honour of giving her away fell to her uncle, Sir Michael Bruce. We have already met the bridegroom, Major (as he then was) Henry Knight Erskine of the Royal Aberdeenshire Highlanders, the future commanding officer of the Militia Barracks and laird of the fine estate of Pittodrie near Chapel of Garioch. The reception, a very grand affair attended by the County, was held, not at the bride's home of Denmore where there was a fine country house, but at Scotstown, affording the Bruces the opportunity of showing off their own imposing mansion. Built in 1845 in the classical style, to designs by Archibald Simpson, the façade with its Ionic portico was reminiscent of the Assembly Rooms (later the Music Hall) which Simpson had designed over twenty years earlier.

Scotstown House.

Scotstown, with its fluted columns, magnificent bows and clear cut pediments, was perhaps even grander. Inside there was much that was architecturally remarkable, including a colonnaded entrance hall, which vied with that of the Assembly Rooms in splendour. The Bruces, after twenty-three years of marriage, were childless and the house seems to have been built as a status symbol rather than to accommodate a large and growing family. The family mausoleum in the Spital Kirkyard, a Greek temple in miniature, was erected in the 1840s and it is feasible that Archibald Simpson threw in its design along with that of the mansion.

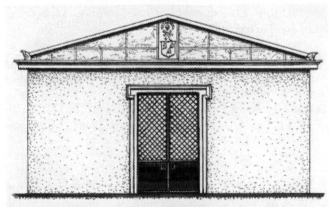

The Moir family mausoleum at St Peter's Churchyard, as it would have looked, with harled walls. The insignia on the pediment, now removed, showed the family motto, 'non sibi sed cunctis' - not for oneself but for all people - encircling a skull and crossbones, with the three Moors' heads below.

150

Left: The interior of the mausoleum is dominated by a tablet 'sacred to the memory of Alexander Moir Esquire of Scotstoun, Sheriff of Aberdeenshire' and to his only daughter, Isabella Moir, wife of Sir Michael Bruce of Stenhouse, who lies below, in the stone 'coffin'. The family coat of arms has again been removed, this time from the interior pediment. Below: Moir memorials on the west wall of the mausoleum. The shield, top left is in memory of George Moir of Scotstown, Colonel of the Royal Bengal Horse Artillery, 1820-1870. The dark tablet, extreme right, to the memory of Jean Margery May Moir (1910-1960) marks the last family interment.

Chapter 10

The Asylum, the Penitentiary and the Primrose School

The locality itself is a bad one
Annual Report, Aberdeen Female Penitentiary, 24 December, 1849

Glimpses have come down to us of three institutions which were set up in the Spital during the nineteenth century. The earliest of these was the Spital Asylum. On 4 August, 1813, the *Aberdeen Journal* announced:

Mr James Sheriffs late keeper of the Lunatic Asylum of Aberdeen has now opened for the reception of lunatics, a small private establishment of the same nature on his own property in a healthy and airy situation in the Spittal.

The interests of the asylum were looked after by a committee of the scholarly, the saintly and the worldly, and things got off to a good start. Of the eight patients that had been admitted in its first year, only two were considered incurable and remained in the house. One was removed by his friends, and three were dismissed, completely restored to the use of reason 'and are now following their usual occupation'. Those who remained were under the care of two highly reputable physicians, Drs Dyce and Brown. William Dyce was an MD of King's College, where his lectures in Midwifery would presumably have been enriched by his practical experience. His wife had been brought to bed of eleven children. One son, Robert, followed in his father's footsteps and became Professor of Midwifery at Aberdeen University and another, also William, is among the greatest of the North

East's artists. There were two Dr Browns in practice at this time, Muckle and Little and I suspect it was Muckle, who lived in King Street. Little Dr Brown was more of a Gilcomston man, and founded the forerunner of Skene Square School.

James Sheriffs, whose surname enjoyed a variety of spellings, was at pains to stress lack of coercion at the asylum.

Any patient may be removed when the relatives by whose desire that patient was admitted shall demand their release and none shall be held on any account even though the relatives themselves desire it, if the Physicians shall deem them capable of caring for themselves.

This was no place for paupers. Before being admitted the patient or his friends had to furnish bed and bedclothes, and board per patient was from 6/- to one guinea per week. Road Commutation Rate Books for Oldmachar parish show that at the relevant time a Mr Shirrefs owned a building on the east side of the Spital possibly just north of St Peter's Gate. It had a very high rateable value of £12, indicating a property of some substance. A neighbouring house with a rateable value of 10/- owned by James Shirrefs probably formed part of the asylum complex. By 1824, the first Aberdeen Directory had appeared and we find James Sheriffs, Lunatic Asylum, Spittal, noted for the first and last time. On 11 May 1825 'that centrical premises in the Spital belonging to James Shirreffs and partly occupied as a private asylum' was offered for sale in the *Aberdeen Journal.* It consisted of four dwelling houses and had a large garden.

Things were not going well, it seems. On 25 January 1826, the *Aberdeen Journal* printed a notice which requested 'claims against the estate of James Shirreffs late Keeper of the Lunatic Asylum, Old Aberdeen, indicating bankruptcy rather than death. In 1825 the Aberdeen Directory listed a James Sheriffs at No 3 Love Lane. (Incidentally, though the origins of Love Lane are unknown, it is written as 'Love's Lane' in older documents, indicating, perhaps, a bye-gone resident of that name). Three years later, on May 6 1829 the *Journal* was advertising the 'Farm of Sunnyside of Spital possessed by William Campbell and James Sheriffs' to let for eleven years'. Perhaps Sheriffs, after the stress of sequestration and of tending on the mentally ill for twelve years, had sought, for a time, the solace and hard work of an open air life at Sunnyside. But that is just speculation.

The Aberdeen Female Penitentiary came on the scene some years after the asylum went out of business, and lasted longer, from 1842 until 1859. Its managers, like James Sheriffs, may have been attracted to the Spital as a less expensive place in which to run such an establishment compared with the

The former Penitentiary, now No 45 the Spital.

royal burgh of Aberdeen. If the site of the asylum is unknown, that of the penitentiary is not, but there is some confusion over the actual address. The 1851 census gives it as No 27 Spital while in the 1855-56 valuation roll it becomes No 29. The address, however, appears consistently in the street directories and in its own advertisements (washing and sewing were taken in) as No 28. The confusion may have been caused by the fact that there was more than one house in the complex, and almost certainly a small forehouse in the front yard of No 28.

This place was not a prison but a House of Correction where young women could apply for admission. Their true nature is revealed in the Minute of Seventh Annual Meeting of Subscribers held at the Mechanics Institute on 22 January, 1849. During a prayer from Professor Martin - he lived near the Spital and was probably batty enough to have qualified for admission to the previous establishment - reference was made to reclaiming 'the unhappy victims of vice'. The girls were impelled 'to an immoral course of life by the pressure of the times and especially by the stoppage of the manufactories'. Grandholm had crashed in 1848, and Woodside Works, already on short time, would go in 1850, swelling the ranks of the destitute. A high moralistic and religious tone pervades the minutes which note, with a measure of sympathy, that the girls, in 'one or two cases, in consequence of early religious education, endured protracted suffering before they yielded to temptation'.

The 1849 minutes reveal that of the sixty-seven young women admitted to the penitentiary in the previous year, twenty-two were still there, seven were reconciled with friends, five were provided with situations, three went to the House of Refuge, seven deserted, while six were dismissed for improper conduct. Those were probably the girls who had 'returned to their former evil ways', the reason given was that they, 'experienced the discipline of the penitentiary for too short a time'. Seventeen had 'declined to continue', and the directors turned what was apparently an increase in

154

such numbers to their own advantage. This, they felt, was a sufficient response to allegations of coercion, which they stressed was not employed. On the credit side, since the institution opened, a total of forty girls were now 'reconciled and respectable'.

Problems which we associate with modern times dogged the institution. The building was unprotected and 'great annoyance and evil consequences' resulted 'from intrusion of improper characters', presumably the girls' pimps if they had any, or would-be customers. And there was a scam which greatly annoyed the management. This was to apply for admission, then a few days later, run off with everything on which one could lay one's hands. 'In every case of desertion, the Institute was more or less robbed of its property. The last two who ran off carried articles of clothing to the value of several pounds and left town immediately'. The penitentiary took in washing or sewing, but clearly housewives handed items in at their peril.

PRICES OF WORK

AT THE

ABERDEEN FEMALE PENITENTIARY,

28, SPITTAL.

	MAKING.	WASHING.		MAKING.	WASHING.
Shirts	1s to 2s	2d to 3d	Barries	8d to 1s	
Boys' Shirts	9d „ 18d	1d „ 2d	Pelches	2d „ 3d	
Night Shirts	1s „ 15d	1d „ 2d	Trousers or Drawers	3d „ 1s	1d to 3d
Shifts	9d „ 18d	1d „ 2d	Stockings ⅌ cut	2d „ 3d	½d „ 1d*
Girls' Shifts	8d „ 1s	1d	Sheets ⅌ pair	6d „ 18d	3d „ 4d
Night Gowns	1s „ 2s	1d „ 3d	Tablecloths	3d „ 6d	2d „ 4d
Night Caps	6d „ 1s	½d „ 2d	Table Napkins ⅌ doz	1s „ 18d	4d „ 6d
Long Dressing Gowns	18d „ 3s	1d „ 3d	Pillow-cases ⅌ pair	1d „ 3d	1d „ 2d
Short do.	6d „ 1s	1d „ 2d	Bolster-slips	1d „ 2d	1d
Slips	9d „ 18d	1d „ 2d	Towels ⅌ doz.	6d „ 1s	4d „ 6d
Petticoats	4d „ 1s	1d „ 2d	Blankets ⅌ pair		4d „ 8d
Flannel Petticoats	3d „ 6d	1d „ 2d	Quilts		2d „ 6d
Handkerchiefs ⅌ doz	6d „ 1s	4d „ 6d	Small Articles ⅌ doz.		5d „ 10d
Pinafores	2d „ 6d	½d „ 1d		* ⅌ pair.	

Family Washing taken on reasonable terms, by the Month, Quarter, or Year.

PRICES FOR GLAZING.

Chintzes, Printed Calicos, &c. Glazed		at 1d ⅌ Sq. Yard.	
Do.	do.	Starched and Glazed	„ 1½d „
Do.	do.	Washed, Starched, and Glazed	„ 2d „
Small Articles			⅌ Piece.

Orders received by the MATRON, at the Institution, and at Mr. SUTHERLAND'S, Druggist, 34, St. Nicholas St.
Articles to be Made, Glazed, or Washed, will be sent for and sent home.

Penitentiary Price List, courtesy, Aberdeen University Library.

It was not all physical drudgery. Much emphasis was placed on teaching and learning. In an examination on religious knowledge, the reading and answering of eight or nine girls was 'respectable', sufficient to show 'the great care bestowed on them by their matron and teacher'. Mrs

Jean Anderson the matron 'conducted herself with zeal and discretion', taking 'an untiring interest in everything to do with the Penitentiary'. Approval is also expressed of Mrs Simpson, the teacher, a newcomer in 1848 for in the minutes she is described approvingly as an 'acquisition'.

The building was owned by John Webster, Advocate, who owned the estate of Edgehill, Milltimber and was a director of shipping, gas and insurance companies. He was Provost from 1856-69 and subsequently Liberal Member of Parliament for Aberdeen. The directors of the penitentiary were the usual assortment of the great and the good, among them Alexander Webster, brother of John, and the brothers Francis and James Edmond, all of them Advocates in Aberdeen; Captain Fordyce RN, MP for Aberdeen, the Reverend Dr Pirie, Provost George Thompson Jnr of the White Star Line who was Lord Provost at this time and Joseph Rowell, whom we met in *Round About Mounthooly*. The penitentiary was supported by Visiting Committees of Ladies and various Ministers who provided religious services during the year.

Unlike the residents of the Asylum, the inmates were unable to pay their way, and the institution was dependent on the generosity of subscribers, of whom there were 432 in 1848. That year's list reveals a wide and interesting section of North East people who were willing to put their hands in their pockets to help fallen women. Contributions from the better off were usually between one guinea and 10/6, with a sliding scale down to 1/ - for others. Among the gentry subscribing were the Duchess of Gordon, Bannerman of Crimonmogate, Davidson of Inchmarlo, Fordyce of Brucklay, Forbes of Migvie, Lumsden of Balmedie, Mrs Nicolson of Glenbervie, Miss Burnett of Kemnay, and Miss Paton of Grandhome then in residence with kinswomen at Sunnybank House from which she would have had a good view of the rear of the penitentiary.

Many doctors, ministers, gentlefolk, businessmen, industrialists and tradesmen subscribed; cabinetmakers, candlemakers, painters, carvers, ironmongers, tobacconists, druggists, dyers, insurance brokers and bankers; the iron-founding Abernethy family of Ferryhill, Alexander Brown, bookseller, George Cornwall, printer; William Duthie, Walter Hood and James Hall, all shipbuilders, Mrs Gibb, Willowbank, widow of the great harbour engineer; Alex Mackie of Mackie Place, James and William Henderson, builders, Daniel Macandrew, builder, George Jamieson, jeweller, Francis Muil, baker, John Marr pianoforte maker; McKinnon & Co. of Spring Garden, ironfounders, George Pegler, fruiterer, Charles Playfair gunsmith, and Pratt and Keith, drapers who had the ground floor of the Palace Hotel. The directors nevertheless complained that the amount of contributions was too small to fund the establishment, and were again having to fall back on the munificence of Mr W Harvey of Beedlieston, who made up any shortfall. The 1848 subscription list does not include any contribution from Dame Isabella Bruce who owned the Spital at this time, though it does show 'MB - 2/6'. Perhaps Sir Michael slipped Provost Thompson half-a-crown when Dame Isabella wasn't looking.

The Report tells us that the daily cost of running the establishment was 9d while the average period of residence ninety-six days. The costs for 1848 were £282 7s 3 d and for 1849, £224 17.2d. The premises were far from ideal:-

The house, or rather houses, though not so bad inside, are not fit for the purpose intended. There is little accommodation either inside or outside. The locality itself is a bad one.

The directors were on the outlook for something bigger, more suitable, but by 1851 nothing had changed. The census returns for that year show fifteen inmates, aged between sixteen and twenty, from Aberdeenshire, Banffshire, Forfarshire and Belfast, who were still sewing and washing, with many more washing than sewing. In the Aberdeen Directory, Mrs Anderson is noted as superintendent between 1849 and 1858. In 1858/59, the last year, Mrs Simpson the teacher, takes over as superintendent. After that, the penitentiary vanishes. The building remains, now No 45, a good-looking house that is still very much with us. And perhaps Mrs Anderson did come back for a time.

One of the subscribers to the Penitentiary was Mrs Primrose of Old Aberdeen, and around the time when that establishment was nearing the end of its day, she set up a school a little to the north which would educate the children of the Spital for the next half century. The actual date of its foundation is not known, but Mrs Primrose's name is associated with the property in the 1855 Valuation Roll.

The obituary to her daughter Margaret, her successor as benefactress, published in the *In Memoriam* of 1897, casts a little more light on the Primrose family. 'Mrs Primerose (their spelling) was the founder of the Spital School (that district being counted no man's land then), assisted by the late Mrs Anderson, Gymnasium, and Mrs Allan'. Both these ladies lived in the Chanonry, the former being the wife of the famous 'Govey', the Reverend Alexander Anderson, head of the renowned Chanonry school, the 'Gym'. Mrs Primrose herself was the widow of 'George Primrose Esq sometime proprietor of Raemoir', near Banchory who was made an honorary burgess of Old Aberdeen in 1818. He lived in Don Street in the 1820s and 1830s and Mrs Primrose continued there, at No 61, after his death. She died in 1857 and her daughter carried on as patroness, assisted by Miss Buchan

The former Primrose School, now Primrose House.

of Auchmacoy, whose family had a town house at No 16 Chanonry.

The school was likely to have been set up in one of a group of eighteenth century houses on the west side of the Spital, of which the penitentiary was one. But Margaret Primrose was a lady of independent means, and perhaps not as concerned about shortfall in subscriptions as were the directors of the penitentiary - though her school too was maintained by contributions. In 1863 she built a new school out of her own pocket, a plain, sturdy building on the site of the old, which was straightaway called the New Schoolhouse. The headmistress, Miss Mary Ann Milne, was resident there throughout her long career.

The 1872 Education Act made education compulsory for five to thirteen-year-olds and established School Boards throughout Scotland, empowering them, among other things, to acquire the better voluntary schools. The Spital School was taken over by the Oldmachar School Board to whom Miss Primrose transferred the building free of charge. To show appreciation of this, and of her work with the school, the Board renamed it Primrose School in her honour. Miss Mary Ann Milne continued at the helm under the Board, with two youthful assistants, Sarah Anderson and Jessie Forsyth, while the Misses Primrose and Buchan kept up their interest in the school. That first year of the new regime, a half-holiday was declared 'for a Picnic given by Miss Primerose and Miss Buchan of Auchmacoy to the children'. In February 1876 'a fête was given by Miss Primerose and Miss Buchan for

158

the scholars', while in April 1878, the log reported that 'Miss Primerose, late patroness, came on Friday afternoon and gave cakes and sweets to the children - all were highly pleased'.

It was not all cakes and sweets. That first year under the Old Machar Board, attendance was very variable, and absentees, those who would not have gone voluntarily to school under the old system, were rounded up by the Oldmachar School Board tak-a', Sergeant William Robb, whose home was handily situated next door to Primrose School at 2 Hillhead Terrace. The

Miss Buchan's garden at the Chanonry where Primrose School children enjoyed picnics. Courtesy Susan McGowan.

erstwhile truants made their displeasure felt by causing a great deal of noise in the school. Boys were punished for lying that year, and 'arithmetic required more attention'. Apart from the latter comment, the first report from Her Majesty's Inspectorate was good: 'This School is taught with much fidelity and with fairly successful results on a first inspection'; a later one is even more charming: 'The school is taught with care and faithfulness and the teacher's heart is in her work'. An evening school was held for working scholars, and though it was, not surprisingly, less advanced than the day school, it improved with time.

There were visits from the local minister, in this case the Reverend Jamieson of St Machar's, and half holidays for the Aulton Market and Timmer Market, and on 27 September 1883, a holiday for the opening of the Duthie Park. Though there was no half holiday for the Aberdeen Races in September 1885, that did not deter scholars from a day at the races. Only thirteen turned up at school that afternoon. Assorted epidemics of fevers, measles and whooping cough were attended by the school medical officers, Dr Polson and Dr James Gordon, both well known Old Aberdeen GPs.

School tended to be either 'thin' or 'wonderfully full'. There were occasional closures because of bad weather, Christmas was a sometimes a school day, sometimes a holiday, but there were always holidays at New Year. Subject lessons were a feature of Miss Milne's teaching programme; the lead pencil, the clock, house-cleaning, thunder, cruelty to animals, the sponge; taste - sweet and sour, salt and bitter; the Chinese, the Cow, the Tiger, the Leaf, parts of the body; and the Railway and the Canal, an apt lesson at a time when the former was replacing the latter down at Mounthooly.

There were other, long-forgotten wee schools in the area. In November 1876 the log reports: 'School very full this week owing to the shutting up of a small private school nearby'. In 1879 HMI reported; 'younger children very noisy and difficult to control and inattentive during the course of their lessons'. He requested that 'slates should be suitably ruled and pencils sharpened'. By 1880 a new blackboard had been procured though the following year, the Inspectorate found desk accommodation inadequate and unsuitable.

In June 1881 the log reported that at the Whitsunday 'term'- Primrose, in common with other North-East schools closed to facilitate the twice-yearly flitting - many of the best scholars were removing to town. Those who had the means were leaving for better conditions, for an improved 'quality of life' in Aberdeen. However there was hope for better things when the Spital became part of Aberdeen in 1884. In parallel with this move, the Scotch Education Department as it then was, ordered the transferral of 'this suburban fringe', (which also included Ruthrieston), from the Old Machar to the Aberdeen School Board. This mightily pleased Thomas Hector, clerk and treasurer to the ASB. Beyond maintaining Primrose and Ruthrieston Schools, the Old Machar Board had had no outlays for schooling in the area now annexed by Aberdeen, 'for the simple reason that the children belonging to it were for the most part already attending schools within the city'; And he continued:

> The task of the old Machar Board being confined, therefore, to drawing the rates of the productive properties lying inside the extended area, while the City Board educated the children. As might be expected, the anomalous nature of this arrangement was defended and its removal objected to by the Parish School Board, but without avail.

In April 1886, the name changed officially to Aberdeen Primrose Public School. Conditions, however, did not improve and overcrowding, a problem from the early days, now featured regularly in HM Inspector's

160

reports. Batches of children were already being turned away turned away, twelve, then thirty-one, then all the Standard III girls to make way for infants coming in. Parents were not pleased, but the business of the School carried on. Mary Anne Milne retired in 1890 and was succeeded by Miss Jessie Sheriffs as acting head. She seems not to have lived- in for Primrose School now had a caretaker, Eliza Ross who with her son Mansfield, a plumber, and daughters, Nellie, a milliner, Lizzie a printer's assistant and Bella, a scholar, squeezed into Miss Milne's former rooms.

A Penny Savings Bank opened in 1894. Four years later, the Inspectorate noted: 'this small school continues to be carried on with vigour and success', but warned the Board that it was insufficient for the number of children in attendance. The roll was little short of a hundred. There were other problems. 'The back playground has standing water and should be levelled and the offices (toilets) must be put right as there is only one for both boys and girls'. In December 1898, following lack of response to these reports, the Scotch Education Department deducted a tenth of the grant to Primrose School. In the new century, the Inspectorate continued to complain. 'It will be well for the sake of seemliness to obscure in some suitable fashion, the lower part of the window that commands a too near and clear view of the offices'. The porch was too small for hats and coats and the playground was too steep. Aberdeen School Board continued on its merry way, ignoring the cries of the Inspectorate. It was too busy building magnificent new schools to level the Primrose playground, which did involve tackling the western slopes of the Spital Hill. But in 1898, one man, Dr Mitchell of Old Aberdeen, had been concerned enough about the situation at Primrose School to initiate the movement to build a new and spacious successor at Sunnybank.

The proposal to discontinue Primrose School was announced in 1898. Nevertheless the school soldiered on for a few years. In 1899 morning classes were delayed until 10.30 am to let the children see Barnum & Bailey's procession. That year the log recorded: 'one child has been removed by death'. Standard I and II were sent away to other schools prevent overcrowding. The tak-a' had to ensure that those turned away turned up elsewhere.

A holiday to celebrate the end of the Boer War was the last school treat. On 6 June 1902 it was announced that Primrose School would close permanently at the end of that session. Scholars had been continually dispersed to other schools over the past few years, and now only nineteen pupils were left to perform the obsequies. They were subsequently admitted to King Street and Causewayend Schools. Spital children continued to be taught elsewhere, in overcrowded conditions for the next four years. When Sunnybank School opened at last in 1906, local bairns were back on

Spital children at Douglas Park, Old Aberdeen, with the parkie.
Courtesy, May Forrest.

home ground being educated in the most modern conditions.

Miss Primrose did not live to see the closure of her school. She had died in 1897 at the age of eighty-eight at No 333 Holburn Street, a peripatetic figure for years, a lodger at many different addresses. Had she overreached herself in building the new Primrose School? No sooner had the school was closed, than the building became a dwelling house. By the time of the First World War the name Primrose House was in use, retaining a connection with the past that could so easily have been forgotten. Having been No 38, then No 41, it is now flatted and numbered No 65 and 67 the Spital.

Chapter 11

Anschluss with Aberdeen:
Sewage Wars and other Municipal Matters

The district is one that, if annexed, will require much improvement.
Aberdeen Journal, 20 July, 1878.

The Spital has been considered something of a no man's land between Aberdeen and Old Aberdeen. However Old Aberdeen Burgh Records spanning the seventeenth and eighteenth centuries tell a different story. They defined 'Spittell' along with 'Colledge Boundis', 'Chanrie' and 'Seatoune' as 'places about Auld Abirdene'. 'Auld Abirdene' itself was little more than the High Street and the wee wynds leading to the back gates (roads), and as far as the running of the burgh was concerned, what applied to 'Auld Abirdene' also applied to the 'places about Auld Abirdene'.

Though the cost of living was lower in Old Aberdeen than in the royal burgh - hence its attraction to so many shoemakers and weavers - Spital residents with property worthy of assessment were liable for the appropriate fiscal dues. The Commutation Rate Books of Old Machar Parish of the 1820s divided the Spital into east side, west side, south side (which included John Duncan, flesher and George Kidd, weaver), and north side (with William Massie and William Munro, booksellers) as well as 'College to Spittal' and 'Spittal to College Bounds' - a fairly comprehensive network - and assessed qualifying property owners and tenants at 2d in the £.

Turning from the parish to the burgh, the Old Aberdeen Police Assessment Rolls - policing in the sense of cleansing, paving and water supply - noted in the 1830s, thirty-three Spital residents the value of whose properties qualified them for assessment. Alex Littlejohn, John Smith, John Wilson and Duncan Grant who kept lodgings for many years at No 97 Spital (old numbering), on the west side beyond Firhill Place were top of the list. Each paid a police rate of 1/-. This Roll divided Spital dwellers into proprietors and tenants. In 1843-44 for example, six proprietors and fourteen tenants were assessed on the east side and on the west side, four proprietors, and six tenants. In 1845-46, Thomas Yeats is among east side tenants assessed. By 1847-48 the distinction between east and west side is dropped. That year twenty-nine residents are assessed. Two of the dwellings most highly assessed are those of Duncan Grant and Captain Stephen, who lived at Orchard House, at that time included in the Spital.

Of course there could be no taxation without representation and in the 1850s, the interests of Spital folk were represented, *ex officio*, by police commissioners Alexander Clark, sexton to St Peter's Cemetery - he lived on the Spital side of the graveyard before the King Street Lodge was built - and William Gibb, a shoemaker in College Bounds, and a little later, by Dr William Gordon, one of the most prominent of the Old Aberdeen baillies. There certainly was dialogue between Spital residents and commissioners, though about what is not always clear. In 1850, a letter from Spital proprietors and feuars was 'laid on the table' by the police commissioners, always the code for 'we don't like it and we aren't going to do anything about it'. Disobligingly, the minute -taker does not reveal the contents. On a brighter note, we find Dr Gordon dealing with 'Cash for Spital Gas Lamps' in the early 1850s, while in 1858, a policeman was appointed for the Spital, though by the Town Council. At that time Old Aberdeen was governed by a cosy diarchy of town councillors and police commissioners.

Things changed in 1860. Old Aberdeen became an official police burgh under the Rutherford Act of 1852, constituted by the sheriff, and taking policing powers for the improvement of the Aulton. One statutory requirement was a clear definition of the boundaries and these were fixed on 30 March, 1860. From the south-west end of College Bounds they fanned out west then north and east, returning to College Bounds via 'the garden of Orchard House, along the south boundary of said garden to the street and across the street to the point of commencement', encompassing the important Orchard Well, and excluding the Spital.

One outcome of the defining of boundaries was bad blood between Lady Bruce and the Aulton police commissioners. Dame Isabella 's Spital Lands went as far north as the Powis Burn, her march was a straight line 'from the north corner of the parapet of the bridge over the Powis Burn at the Turnpike (the King Street-University Road junction) to the north east corner of the garden wall of the house in College Bounds immediately South

The boundary between the Spital and Old Aberdeen as drawn in 1860.

of University Road'. A tenant of the Bruce's farmed in this area, and in February 1862, Dame Isabella was on the warpath over lack of fencing and the exposed condition of her tenant's land. She argued it was up to the commissioners to do something about it. 'Lady Bruce called here yesterday and complained of the delay', her lawyers wrote to the commissioners. One can imagine her legal team at Lumsden and Robertson contemplating the scene with a degree of apprehension as the Bruce carriage drew up outside their offices at No 3 Union Terrace and Dame Isabella descended. 'Her tenant will soon be cropping the ground and he has long enough already been exposed to the inroads of the public'.

Though they were technically beyond the pale, Spital residents were by no means excluded from Old Aberdeen services. In July 1861 Dr Gordon reported to the police commissioners that he and Mr Alexander Clark:

had called on proprietors of Houses lining the Spittal beyond the boundary of the burgh who draw water from the commissioners wells and that they are quite willing to pay for the same at the rate of sixpence per pound per annum of rental on their respective properties and also to grant Bond for regular payment of the same.

One clause indemnified the commissioners 'in consequence of any deficiency of water', a wise move, for water shortage was a very real problem. Those signing on for a water supply at that time were Janet Robie who made a mark, Elizabeth Smith, George Moir, Margaret Leask, George Gill, William Aitken, John Robertson, on behalf of Lady Bruce, and James Anderson for George Donald. The thanks of the commissioners were unanimously recorded to Dr Gordon and Mr Alexander Clark 'for the great trouble they have had in connection with this matter' so one appreciates that there had been a bit of an argy-bargy. The recalcitrant Duncan Grant would not sign or pay the rate but nevertheless went using the commissioners' water. He possibly felt he had already been stented enough. The commissioners set about interdicting him from 'using water from any of the wells under the charge of the commissioners'. It seems that water pipes from Aberdeen came as far north as the Red Lion Inn which explains why only a small, number of consumers at the north end of the Spital found it necessary to sign up for the Aulton wells.

During the 1860s, there was prolonged discussion between the police commissioners of Old Aberdeen and their opposite numbers in the city over the provision of water. When the Cairnton supply from the Dee came on stream in 1866, providing five millions gallons daily, Aberdeen agreed to be make water available to Old Aberdeen by meter and at favourable rates, a situation compounded on occasion by the Spital feuars who in 1867, for example ' would not allow this burgh (Old Aberdeen) the use of their pipe under a compensation of £25'. But even with one reservoir built at Mannofield to hold the Cairnton water, there still was not enough to supply the Aberdeen's expanding population, and Old Aberdeen suffered accordingly.

The supply of gas for lighting does not seem to have been fraught with so many difficulties. The Police Accounts to May 1861 show that 'the Assessment for Lighting Spital per Dr Gordon' was 3/11, and that various Spital properties were assessed by agreement. The Spital had its own Lighting Committee during these years, as well as a Spital Feuars Committee. The secretary to both was Hugh McLennan, advocate in Aberdeen who lived at Applebank, a couple of hundred yards north of St Peter Street, and who would have kept an eye on the interests of Spital dwellers on the south side of the hill.

A priority of the new police commissioners was to improve drainage and sewerage in the Aulton and in December 1860, they sought donations from local heritors to this end. Hugh Fraser Leslie wrote them a charming letter from Powis House concluding: 'I shall cheerfully contribute £50 to an object so desirable'. When it came to Dame Isabella's response, it was with a hint of embarrassment, that Messrs Lumsden and Robertson, advised the commissioners:

> We have just received a note in which Lady Bruce says that as Sir Michael and herself do not think they have any concern with the Drainage of Old Aberdeen, they beg to decline interfering in the matter.

This was not accurate, for sewage on the north side of the Spital naturally flowed down the hill to Old Aberdeen and was carried off in the Powis Burn.

In February 1861 the Old Aberdeen commissioners announced 'that is their intention to make new sewers in...High Street, Chanonry, Don Street, University Road, and through the King Street Turnpike Road', commencing in College Bounds. The Spital was not cut off as might seem. The Old Aberdeen Roll for Police Assessment for 1881-1882 shows that fifteen Spital residents paid a separate sewer rate of tuppence halfpenny on the rentals of their houses. Those included were Dr Macquibban at Nos 100-102 at the north end, and as far southwards as Benjamin McDonald, stonecutter, and Alex Harvey, engineer, both in Hillhead Terrace and George Troup in Boa Vista Place, these terraces being newly built at that time and Alexander Farquharson the grocer, whose shop was at No 59 (No 113 in modern numbering). One resident round the corner in Sunnybank was also assessed. The Loch Street builder Daniel Macandrew who had recently rebuilt houses at Firhill Place had the most highly valued property at £87, playing a sewer rate of 18/1.

The conclusion to be drawn is that in spite of the exclusion of the Spital from the police burgh of Old Aberdeen, Spital residents whose property sloped down the northern flank of the Spital Hill to Old Aberdeen, could, if they wished and had the money, come to an arrangement with the Aulton police commissioners for the supply of light, water and sewerage based on the rateable value of their property. Nor did development stagnate altogether. As hinted at above, a number of Spital building projects had been undertaken in the 1870s.

Not everyone in the Spital was connected with the Aulton mains by any means as an intrepid reporter from the *Aberdeen Journal* discovered when he sallied forth to investigate conditions there. In Love Lane he found a large brander under a ground floor window, choked with refuse from which a most disagreeable stench arose, 'the location of which could be unerringly determined by the cloud of flies which hung over the decaying heap'. He presses on, into the Spital, narrowly avoiding further dunghills then goes down into Froghall Lane (now Terrace) to be brought to a standstill by an overpowering stench. An inky black stream issues from a wall and flows into the middle of the lane. 'Holding my handkerchief to my nostrils I approach the wall to look over and am almost choked by the offensively smelling steam ascending from an ashpit and privy'. A 'tidy-looking housewife' tells him that the lassies from the Jute Work sometimes 'bock at the stink when they're gaun by.'

Back in the Spital he turns down a lane leading towards the King Street Road, the future Merkland Road, then turns left to walk towards the cemetery along the future Merkland Place. Here he comes on pigsties:

> after running gauntlet of the disagreeable stench attendant upon the culture of these porkers, I finally make a spurt and succeed in getting to windward of a small pond of black water skilfully dammed by a low dyke of manure.

He presses on, only to be sickened by the smell of horns, decaying matter, more dunghills and is eventually seen off by a large black dog. A local takes him inside the cemetery to point out where he interred the body of a friend while the sewage flowed into the grave. Back to the Spital, and turning down one of the numerous closes on the east side he finds an uncovered ashpit 'so close to dwelling-houses that you could lean out of one of the windows and throw a shovelful of ashes into the midden with great ease'. And so it goes on, dunghill after dunghill, midden after midden, though it must be said that contemporary reports reveal Old Aberdeen itself to be far from squeaky clean; middens were too near the houses, ash pits were 'liquid' and closets were filthy. Meanwhile an unhappy local was telling the reporter; 'We are in neutral territory, and nobody looks after us. The sheriff tries crimes that are committed in the Spital but otherwise we are not recognised by the county. We pay the city for our water which at times is very deficient and we also pay for the maintenance of the municipal buildings - that's all'.

The reporter's exposé, published on 20 July, 1878 had been prompted by Aberdeen Town Council's thoughts on annexing the Spital, and other locales similarly outside the city boundary. The reporter rounds off his article with the unsurprising conclusion: 'The district, if annexed, will require much improvement'. Annexation was achieved by the Aberdeen Extension and Improvement Act of 1883, and in the following year, the Spital, along with the lands westwards to Kittybrewster, and along the King Street Road to the Lady Mill and other areas, became part of Aberdeen. Towards the end of 1882 there was a move to unite 'the burgh of Old Aberdeen with new Aberdeen under the proposed legislation' but it proved abortive. It was not until 1891 that the Aulton made reluctant *anschluss* with Aberdeen.

The city began to crack down on Spital nuisances. It was Alexander Wilson, horn merchant, who was responsible not only for the unpleasant smelling horns, but for the 'porkers' as well which had so offended the *Journal* reporter. He continued in business for some years, regardless of the strictures of the press and apparently running his piggery as a side-line. In June 1885 the Town's sanitary inspector caught up with him, reported on the insanitary condition of his 'pigsty and store yard at East Back Road, Spital' (Merkland Place) and instructed him to remove it within fourteen days. Wilson's home address was given as 37 Spital, (old numbering), the same address as the well known Duncan family of fleshers and cattle dealers. Later, the number changed to No 52, and it is possible to locate these premises, one of the row of cottages which backed onto Merkland Place. The 1868 ordnance survey reveals a long, rig-like back area with a number of byres and sheds where the Duncan's would have carried out their slaughtering, and where Wilson would have stockpiled the horns from the carcasses. By the late 1880s, he had retired from dealing in horns and in the directories is noted respectably at No 1 Merkland Road as 'feuar'.

With plans for an improved water supply underway - the city supply was boosted to eight million gallons a day in 1885 and a second reservoir built at Mannofield - Aberdeen Town Council could pencil in improvements for the Spital and the other new territories. A new five inch water main was planned to run from Love Lane to the city boundary at College Bounds, and in April 1884, Hugh McLennan successfully claimed compensation on behalf of the Spital feuars for the redundant water main in the Spital, a three inch cast iron pipe of 550 yard long, valued at £27. He had been less successful that February when, as secretary of the Spital Lighting Committee, he wrote to Aberdeen Town Council proposing to hand over the Spital street lamps at valuation. This offer was sniffily declined 'as the lamps were old and not of the pattern now in use throughout the city'. (City lamps terminated in an elegant thistle finial). McLennan ate humble pie and that April wrote again stating that his committee would hand over the street lamps to the Town Council of Aberdeen free of cost. This was more to the councillors' liking. They resolved to accept them, 'and instructed the Inspector to have them removed', thus putting the Spital folk's gas down to a peep, but hopefully, only metaphorically speaking.

Finally, to sewage. In January 1885, Aberdeen Town Council decided on a new drainage scheme for the Spital. It was clear that the burgh surveyor,

William Boulton CE, one of the city's most outstanding servants, had nothing but scorn for the existing system and was determined to kick off with a *tabula rasa:*

There are in the main street or road from King's Crescent to Old Aberdeen several old-built drains or sewers which are in such a dilapidated condition and so shallow as to be of little or no use for draining any part of the Spital. I would therefore propose to treat the whole of this district as if such sewers did not exist.

There was no problem with the southern area, where the new drains would have an outfall into the existing Aberdeen sewers in Love Lane, King Street and King's Crescent. As far as the northern drains, were concerned, an arrangement would have to be made with the Old Aberdeen Police commissioners, 'for admission into their outfall sewer.' By April the necessary sums had been done. Three main and three branch sewers would serve the needs of the Spital and district, the total cost, including linkage with Old Aberdeen system, coming to just under £600. The police commissioners had driven a good bargain. Aberdeen would foot the bill, take responsibility for any damage, make connections 'free of rate to any tenements within the burgh of Old Aberdeen...through which the pipes pass' and pay the police commissioners £30 an annum for their trouble. Alas, it all went down the drain. The new arrangement was to hold good during the pleasure of the police commissioners, said the police commissioners. No, replied Aberdeen's magistrates; 'it shall be in the power of the Town Council to terminate the (arrangement) after three month's notice in writing to the commissioners'.

Prolonged discussion resulted in impasse and in June 1885, Aberdeen Town Council abandoned the scheme. There followed an outbreak of sewage wars with the Aulton commissioners, firing the first salvo. 'After 15th May, 1886,' they trumpeted, 'no sewerage from Aberdeen will be allowed to pass through the commissioners' sewers'. Aberdeen's Town Council's Sewerage Committee let this letter lie on the table and told Boulton to come up with a new scheme. This he did. Sewerage from the north end of the Spital would now be drained eastward to the Links, wend its way past the eastern base of the Broad Hill and eventually discharge - along with sewage from other areas flowing in *en route* - into the harbour at Abercrombie Jetty. The estimated cost was £10,500.

By way of a postscript we can briefly follow the fate of the heritors of the Spital. Dame Isabella had died in 1867, surviving Sir Michael by five years. Her property was inherited by the descendants of her father's half-brothers. George Moir, Colonel of the Bengal Horse Artillery, son of William Moir of

Park, became eight laird of Scotstown while the Spital went to George Charles Moir of Denmore's daughter, Mary Anne Moir, wife of Lieutenant Colonel Knight Erskine of Pittodrie. Mary Anne later attempted to sell the Spital superiorites without success, while her son, Henry W Knight Erskine of Pittodrie and Spital, the last laird, offered the Spital Estate of 140 acres for sale on 10 August 1882. The upset price was £61,000, but no bids were offered and there was no sale. Later, for a time, he became much involved in creating streets out of the Spital Lands at Sunnybank and around King Street.

Scotstown House was demolished in the 1930s and great trees now grow amidst its gaunt ruins. George Moir's Belmont Street townhouse, subsequently No 37, saw service as the Deaf and Dumb Institute from 1848 until 1901 when it was acquired by Colonel Innes, and became the Gordon Highlanders Memorial Institute. (see pages 59 and 142). It lost its double forestairs and miniature pavilions, and after purchase in 1927 by A G Nicol Smith & Coy, scientific instrument makers, a shop front was added. Such sacrilege was greeted by a furore, but, 'Colonel Nicol Smith's word was law,' as a long-standing employee, Mr William McLaughlin remarked. The old-established firm of Lizars, Opticians, are now based there. Happily, at the end of 1996, a more elegant frontage was installed.

Chapter 12

South Spital
St Peter Street to Merkland Road

Aberdeen was the first of the four Scottish Universities to have a residence of the
kind and (it) has been attended with great success.

Aberdeen Journal, 28 March, 1902

A walking tour of the Spital will reveal a little history, several architectural gems, some interesting developments, three possible ghosts and a
wealth of memories.

Our journey begins at the Aberdeen end, with an exploration of the east
side of the south Spital. We start at the St Peter Street corner, where there
was once a wee shop. There soon looms up part of the south block of the
former High School for Girls (Harlaw Academy) which has somehow made
its way there. At least that's what it looks like! The architecture is of the
same mid-1930s style, strong and robust though a trifle institutional. The
lintel over the door of this block, Nos 6-10, bears an interesting legend,
shown opposite. This block of tenements was not a school extension, but
'Welfare Houses' as they became known, funded by Aberdeen Voluntary
Housing Trust to help relieve the city's desperate housing problems. A site
was found, the lower part of Applebank's garden - that is the next house on
the brae - and the foundation stone was laid on 10 October, 1934. The
concept of a voluntary association providing housing for the underprivi-
leged was an innovatory one and to mark the occasion, the laying of the
foundation stone was carried out with due ceremony. The honour went to

The foundation stone remains in its original setting.

Mrs George Garden of Jute Street, a member of the Aberdeen Mother and Child Welfare Association which had voted the first £100 towards the project. The vote of thanks was proposed by the local MP, J G Burnett Esq of Powis.

The architect, John G Marr, top man at A Marshall Mackenzie & Sons, had abutted the Welfare Houses neatly onto the tenement on the St Peter Street corner. The building boasted a novelty, balconies at the rear, 'streets in the sky', thirty years ahead of their time, giving access to the open air. Twelve tenants were to be selected 'from deserving people who would take care of a good house'. The layout of most of the 'houses', as flats were then called, was: living-room, scullery, larder, bedroom, bathroom and coal cellar. The rent was 5/- weekly. These days one bedroom sounds inadequate for a mother and child, but three of the houses had an extra bedroom at 7/6 weekly. The slopping ground permitted the excavation of a large basement which all too soon would serve as an air raid shelter.

Sixty years on and the Welfare Houses had become rundown. The building was made the subject of a local authority disrepair notice, which brings with it the incentive of a maximum improvement grant. The building was acquired and completely refurbished by the award-winning architect, Alexander Reith. By 1995 he had reconstructed the interior to provide eleven one and two-bedroom flats for private purchasers. The balconies, formerly in a very poor state, have been reconstructed, and the

The former Welfare Houses have been handsomely refurbished. The back gate to Applebank is left foreground.

windows, all now identical, provide one of the building's most striking features.

Beyond the former Welfare Houses the road narrows and we come to the fascinating Applebank which has its origins in a plain old rectangular house, sitting east to west, its gable end to the Spital and the front of the house facing south. In old deeds, the land on which the house was built is described as extending between the Spital Road and the lands sometime belonging to Alexander Moir of Scotstown; on the south at one time was the feu of James Walker who by the 1830s was seeking to dispose of his well-stocked nursery in Love Lane (St Peter Street). The entrance to Applebank from the Spital was via a circular carriage drive, surrounded by trees. It terminated in front of a walled terrace - the sloping terrain probably created difficulties for horses and carriage - and a flight of steps gave access to the terrace and the house. South of the carriage drive was the orchard, banked against the slope that gave the house its name. By the 1860s, the occupants would have had fine view of the volunteers drilling in the Militia Barracks below.

The owner in 1868 was a Captain Gilbert Henderson, shipowner, and one might be forgiven for thinking that it was he who built the distinctive bow-shaped wing which now forms the main section of Applebank. But

174

Applebank around 1902, showing the wing of 1890 and the original, plain house gable-end to the Spital. Courtesy, City of Aberdeen Libraries.

Henderson had no young family to occupy such a large house, and besides, had other ploys. Because of its hilly nature, the south-west side of the Spital was the last part to be built up. Opposite Applebank were slopes covered with gorse and rough grass, part of those 'croftlands outwith the burgh', which provided a tenant with no more than rough grazing. After scrambling up these slopes on a fine day, the Captain would have enjoyed the view across to Aberdeen Bay, putting him in mind of his seafaring days. And so he acquired a few acres opposite Applebank and built Bay View, a little terrace of two cottages, one for himself, one for a colleague who, so the story goes, was soon to leave the sea. The original path up to Bay View starts directly across from Applebank and one can imagine Captain Henderson strolling across every day to see how the work on this dour terrain was progressing. By 1869, the cottages were ready and Applebank sold. The name of the new owner, John McLennan, appears in the 1869-70 directory, while the census returns of 1871 show Gilbert Henderson, retired shipmaster aged 45, now living across at Bay View with his wife and servant.

John McLennan and his wife Agnes had a family of three daughters and a son, Hugh, an advocate in Aberdeen. John McLennan was tacksman for the Bridge of Don and Kittybrewster tolls. This was an early form of privatisation, in which the tacksman paid a sum to the Town for the privilege of collecting the tolls, with the expectation of making a profit. McLennan must have got the price right, for he is shown in the 1891 census returns as 'living on private means', just like John Sutherland in Viewton Place. The year before, he had added a splendid wing to the house, running north to south over the erstwhile carriage drive, though the orchard to the south remained intact. The new wing terminated in handsome bay windows which were carried up from the basement kitchen through the ground floor dining-room to the first floor drawing-room, and were surmounted by a crown of iron brattishing. This, unusually for the Spital, was a thorough-going Victorian extension. The hall tiling, the drawing-room coving, the design of the balusters and banisters were similar to those of new houses going up in the west end of Aberdeen. But Applebank also boasted something rather special on the first floor landing, a splendid stained glass window by Daniel Cottier. If the sketch on page 175 is accurate, McLennan, or at least

The stained glass window by Cottier.

his architects, Messrs Jenkins & Marr, also added west facing bay windows and a conservatory at this time. These have now gone, and a simple plaque near the entrance gives the date of the extension, '1890'.

The son, Hugh McLennan was in practice on his own account, and as we have already seen, looked after the interests of the Spital feuars. He was also clerk and treasurer to the Old Machar School Board and on one occasion was required to draw to the attention of the Old Aberdeen police commissioners, the case of two children, one from Orchard Court, one from College Bounds 'whose condition from a sanitary point of view is such that they cannot be sent to school (yet) are allowed to run about the streets and mix with other children'. Conditions in some houses were indeed grim. Dr Gordon was aware of the situation, but the commissioners felt that they could do nothing about it.

John McLennan died in 1893 and a few years later Hugh bought the estate of Springhill and went to live there with his sisters. In 1900 the family sold Applebank, though not before they had whisked the gasoliers and gas brackets and the lamp in the hall off to Springhill. The purchasers were the Aberdeen Committee of the Board for the Initiation and Development at University Seats of Institutes for Pastoral Training, later, thankfully abbreviated to the Church of Scotland Institute for Pastoral Training. The aim was to provide a residence specifically for theological students and with the purchase of Applebank, Aberdeen became the first Scottish University to have one. Closely associated with the Institute was D M M Milligan, advocate, a partner in Messrs Davidson and Garden where Hugh McLennan had served his apprenticeship. When the question of finding a suitable residence had first been mooted, David Milligan would have known the very chap with an ideal place for sale, near King's College. Milligan had a personal interest for his father was Professor of Biblical Criticism; his sister was the renowned Mrs Katherine Trail, author of two memorable vignettes of Old Aberdeen.

Initially the Institute for Pastoral Training was somewhat strapped for cash and had to raise a bond on part of the £800 purchase. To the rescue there came, in 1902, a bequest of £5000 an immense sum in those days, from the estate of the late Mrs Stephen Wilson. In 1916 her generosity paid for a major reconstruction of 'The Residence', as Applebank was now known. The plain, original house was stripped down and reconstructed in sneck-coursed granite rubble, with large bay windows to allow plenty of light and high chimney stacks, though the original gable end to the Spital was retained. A new wing, in tenemental style, running eastwards and not visible from the Spital, was also added to provide addition accommodation.

Applebank today showing the plain house as rebuilt around 1916, but retaining its original gable-end to the Spital.

177

Applebank from the south, with its bay windows rising to three storeys, and its tenemental east wing. In the foreground are the balconies of the Welfare Houses prior to restoration.

Alas, the way north was barred by two old houses, and 'The Residence' was only able to form three legs of a crucifix.

In 1931 'The Residence', by now No 24 the Spital, changed its name again, and became St Katherine's Hostel for Girls. Two years later the owners, the Trustees of St Katherine's Club, were able to boost their funds by selling the southern, orchard, half of the garden to the Voluntary Housing Trust as a site for the Welfare Houses. In 1957 there was another change of name when the building was acquired by the YWCA. Hazel Melvin (Mrs Smith) boarded there at that time and still remembers the scratchy blankets, the linoleum and the food, 'dreadful - the thinnest slices of ham, beetroot and a small bowl of potatoes of Tuesdays and Thursdays.' Rent, she remembers was £2 10s weekly. No male visitors were permitted after 7pm but a late pass was valid until 10pm. Two or three girls usually shared a room but a particularly large room in the basement accommodated five young ladies. It was they who obligingly pulled in those night birds who had exceeded the curfew. Once, having entered by these unorthodox means Hazel was startled to see a dark figure sitting silently at a window. A Spital ghost? She remembers two old ladies, Agnes and Mina, who had been there for years, and must have remained behind after the St Katherine's era.

In 1975 Patrick and Jacinta Birchley bought Applebank and over recent years have devoted much time and energy to restoring the Victorian ambience of the main wing. Countless layers of paint have been removed to reveal the original handsome woodwork and rich velvet curtains, scatterings of sofas, huge mirrors and chandeliers adorn the drawing-room and dining-room. Students are again in residence in the cosy study-bedrooms, and the Birchleys are creating pockets of old world gardens to the east and west of the long wing. Indoors the dumb waiter which used to serve the dining-room has survived since 1890 and so has a more recent relic, the pediment over the gatepost which once proclaimed the YWCA. A new plaque now announces Applebank House, for the Birchleys have reintroduced this pleasant old name.

Titles deeds reveal that immediately north of Applebank in the time of George Moir of Scotstown and his son Alexander, there had existed three dwelling houses 'sometime possessed by John Gavin', and 'at the back thereof of the same breadth with the said houses' a new house erected by Alexander Abernathie, turner in Aberdeen. It was bounded on the north 'by the passage betwixt it and the new house built by James Garden'. Two of these houses survived to become Nos 26 and 28 the Spital, and the close where they stood was known locally as 'Flechy Den'. The most easterly, No 26 was a plain old house, its gable-end crammed on to the street while No 28, which had forestairs, was a back house, gained by going right through the close. Behind that, again, there would have been other houses which have not survived into modern times. Mr Gordon Cardno, who has lived in the Spital for eighty years remembers the houses of 'Flechy Den' as 'damp, dismal and down and out'. Alex Slessor recalls many families living there, poor people, and in particular, one boy with rickets. 'He still managed a paper round on his bike'. By the 1950s these houses had been boarded up and after buying Applebank, the Birchleys acquired them, hoping some day to restore them. Building work further north at Glamis Cottage affected their stability and the two old houses had to be demolished. The land where they stood was sold, and by 1995, two attractive new houses, Nos 26-28, were completed, which with their canted dormers, and corbie stepping have a feel of the past about them.

In 1772 George Moir of Scotstown feued land just north of 'Flechy Den' to James Webster, farmer in the Spital, reserving to himself 'the whole trees', which were not to be cut down, removed or pruned. Here, and perhaps not too long after this time, a roomy east-facing cottage was built with a sloping front garden. Its rear quarters faced the Spital, with trees to north and south. The entrance was by a gate in the Spital, and a path led round to the front. Construction was of rubble, wet harled to dressed granite reveals. On the

The front elevation of Glamis Cottage in 1982, looking eastwards, prior to extension. Courtesy, City of Aberdeen Planning and Strategic Development Department.

north side of the house, a long lane straggled north-eastwards towards the Links. Around 1880 that lane was straightened out and as Merkland Road joined the Spital and King Street.

This substantial dwelling appears as Gordon Cottage in the 1868 (10.56 feet to the mile), ordnance survey but as Glamis Cottage in street directories of that era. Since cottages at that time were often called after their owners, Gordon Cottage might have been the home of William Gordon, bookseller, Spital - no number then - who appears in the first street directory, dated 1828-29. Gordon, whose shop was in the Upperkirkgate, could, of course, have been in residence for some years prior to that date. He had disappeared from the directory by 1831-32, and soon after there was a new entry, Alex Mitchell, stationer and bookseller, shop No 20 Upperkirkgate, house, Spital. Later entries identify Mitchell's house as No 20 Spital, Glamis Cottage, the same place as Gordon Cottage. Mitchell may have been Gordon's successor, perhaps even his son-in-law. From 1840 we find Mitchell sharing No 20 with John Duncan, flesher, who had a business nearby at No 19. The bookseller and the butcher seems an unlikely duo, though by the late 1840s it was the widows, Mrs Mitchell and Mrs Duncan who were living there, both took in lodgers.

By 1865 David Kyd, a writer (solicitor), was in residence, though by 1869 he has become an officer of the mercantile marine. Had been listening to the tales of his neighbour Captain Gilbert Henderson and gone off to sea? Or was he was inspired by the view of Aberdeen Bay from his attic dormers? Kyd was succeeded by a Mrs Pyper and by the turn of the century by John Burnett then by his widow and daughter, Miss Grace Burnett, who was sub-postmistress at the George Street post office. In 1901 John Burnett sold Glamis Cottage to the Town Council for £525, thus becoming one of the city's earlier council tenants, after the fishermen of Fittie and the workmen of Urquhart Road and Park Road; though the reason for the purchase of Glamis Cottage was road-widening, not housing the homeless. The belt of trees at the northern corner had largely been replaced by outhouses, (contrary to the feu charter, as it happened), and they too now went as a strip of 167 square yards was removed to widen Merkland Road. That, and subsequent widenings, have left the cottage with a dockit look, pinned behind its outer wall.

Glamis Cottage was renumbered No 30 the Spital in 1903. Alex Slessor

Glamis Cottage left, with Nos 26-28 the Spital, at right angles.

remembers it as home to Mr Thomas Allison, lay preacher and missionary at the Gallowgate United Free Church, and his large family. Many folk still recall the two Misses Campbell, Jeannie and Ida were there from the 1930s, and took in students. 'They were,' says Gordon Cardno, 'petite ladies of the old school.' One of the sisters was a dressmaker, and clothed a fair number of Spital dwellers. Ronald Leith remembers navy serge scratchy shorts and Elizabeth Weston recalls; 'she made clothes for my mother and some for me as well. I remember the house well because it had gas light long after everyone else had electricity and clothes were pressed with the old-fashioned irons heated in the fire'. The house had a huge basement.

Glamis Cottage, subsequently became a Children's Home and in 1975 was taken over by the Social Work Department of the newly formed Grampian Regional Council. The building was extended in 1983, both to the south, and to the east, where once the front door and the long garden had been. It is now a residential unit for men and women who require care and support on a permanent basis and has been run, since the 1996 reorganisation of local government, by Aberdeen City Council's Social Work Department.

We started off up the south side of the Spital hill at the 'Welfare Houses', originally built as residential units and now converted into private flats; we end at the Merkland Road junction, at Glamis Cottage, built originally as a private home, and now converted into residential units. A curious coincidence.

Chapter 13

South Spital
St Margaret's Convent

The chapel is the power-house through which we get our strength.
Mother Verity Margaret.

If we cross to the west side of the south Spital, directly opposite the Welfare Houses a lofty chapel can be glimpsed amidst the trees, standing guard over a row of cottages. This is St Margaret's' Convent, the first group of buildings on the west side. It was originally 'St Margaret's Convalescent Home and Sisterhood,' Bay View, Spittal, though 'Convalescent Home' was dropped within a few years.

St Margaret's owes its origins to two remarkable men; the Reverend John Comper, Father Comper, as he was known in the Scottish Episcopalian community, and the Anglican clergyman and hymn writer, Dr John Mason Neale. The two had met in 1850, at the consecration of St Ninian's Episcopal Cathedral in Perth and became friends. Neale was the founder of the Society of St Margaret at East Grinstead in Sussex whose sisters tended the poor and sick in their homes and Comper was much impressed by this work. When Neale visited Comper in Aberdeen in 1861, soon after his installation as rector of St John's Episcopal Church, the two men discussed the great need in the city, for a community like that at East Grinstead. Neale arranged for Sister Zillah, one of the most capable and energetic of the East Grinstead sisters, to come north. She arrived in 1862, the first Episcopalian sister to settle in Scotland, and lived with the Comper family for six months. When other sisters joined her, they stayed near St John's, at 2a Affleck Place which became the sisters' first house in Scotland.

St John's Episcopal Church, just off Crown Street, traced its origins to the seventeenth century. It had a fine new church building in a genteel part of town, a middle-class congregation, and a well-run day school which Comper himself had set up. Excellent charge though it was, it did not offer him the challenge he sought. In the memorable words of the church historian, Alexander Gammie: 'His mind and heart now turned steadily towards the poor and outcast in the slums'. By 1864 Comper had set up a mission in the Gallowgate and a benefactor had provided the sisters with a house in Ferguson Court, a little north of the present-day Greyfriars House. 'From this centre', wrote Gammie, 'a vigorous and determined attack was made on the surrounding vice and misery'.

This step marked the foundation of both St Margaret's Episcopal Church in the Gallowgate, and of St Margaret's Convent, which was now granted autonomy by the mother house at East Grinstead. A large room served as both chapel and school but by 1870 great progress had been made. St Margaret's Episcopal Church, built on the Ferguson Court site to designs by the architect James Matthews, was already open for worship, and a new school for boys, girls and infants had been built in the foreground of the church. Father Comper now gave up his charge at St John's, devoting himself heart and soul to the Gallowgate mission.

By 1871 Comper was looking for suitable land or property near the Gallowgate to found a permanent convent for the sisters. That year, Ann Presslie, poultry and gamedealer, sold him several Spital properties at St Peter's Gate, in his capacity as 'incumbent of St Margaret's Mission in connection with the Episcopal Church in Scotland, for behoof of the said mission'. But this site did not offer much scope for expansion, and perhaps the Red Lion Inn was too close for comfort. More like the thing were the twin cottages of Bay View, recently built by Captain Gilbert Henderson late of Applebank, which came on the market in 1874. Nearer the Gallowgate than St Peter's Gate, they stood in spacious grounds on a commanding site on the west side of the Spital Brae. (The illustration on page 57 shows the height of the Spital Hills at this point, before the building of the Convent). For some reason - death perhaps had intervened - Henderson's plans to live side-by-side in retirement with an old colleague had been abandoned and the Bay View cottages were acquired by Father Comper as a base from which a custom-built convent could later be developed. The properties at St Peter's Gate were conveyed back to Ann Presslie in 1876 and any moneys released would had funded developments on the Bay View site.

Over the next few years, a handsome group of buildings began to appear beside the cottages. First, in 1879, John Comper built a family home, St Margaret's Brae, just south of the cottages. Two years later, with the girls

St Margaret's Brae, No 39 King's Crescent, headquarters of the Episcopalian Diocese of Aberdeen and Orkney. (Frank Donnelly)

St Martha's.

from the recently built Froghall Jute Works in mind, the Trustees of St Margaret's commissioned a 'Home for Working Class Girls at Bayview, Spittal' immediately to the north. Possibly because of financial problems, St Martha's - the home was named after the patron saint of cooks - was not completed until 1887, the sisters making do in the interim with a temporary home for the girls at No 17 Jute Street. The architects were Messrs Pirie & Clyne, though the Home's external features bore the hallmarks of J B Pirie's Hamilton Place mode rather than Arthur Clyne's ecclesiastical whimsy. St Martha's, in Pirie's favourite combination of pink and grey granite, rises dramatically, its dominating feature, a lofty gable with a handsome window of Gothic tracery

185

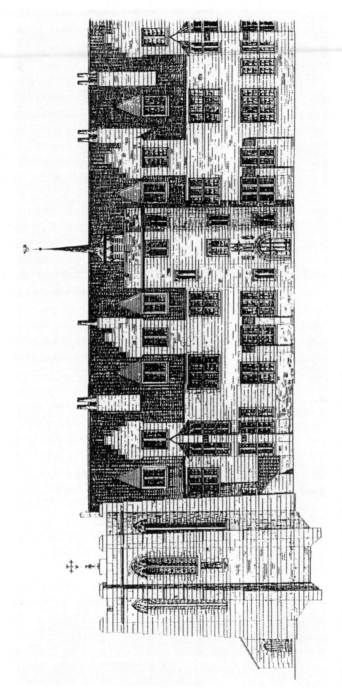

The convent that never was. Sir Ninian Comper's original design for the Convent of St Margaret's, Aberdeen. The chapel is on the left. Unless otherwise indicated, the illustrations in this chapter appear by courtesy of the Mother Superior and the Convent of St Margaret's.

set forward at the south-east end. A splendid turret sits in the re-entrant angle, its conical hat reminiscent of the Round Tower at King's College. Two entrances were planned for the south gable. For guests an imposing Gothic archway lead to an open porch and four panelled door. To its right a cross in pink granite bore the legend 'the Lord will provide'. The girls' entrance was nearer the rear of the building where stone steps gave access to Froghall Road, a stone's throw from the Jute Works.

The census returns of 1891 reveal that the Comper household consisted of the Reverend and Mrs Comper, three daughters, one of whom, Sister Mary Ellen was a sister of St Margaret's, and three servants. Their architect son, Ninian, was absent. He had set up his own practice in London and in the years to come Sir Ninian Comper would acknowledged as the most renowned church architect of the age.

As it happened, the twenty-seven year old Comper was just beginning work on a commission closer to home, next door in fact, a chapel for the sisters in the gap between St Margaret's Brae and the Bay View cottages. These in turn would be replaced by living quarters in the same idiom as the chapel when the latter was finished. A drawing owned by St Margaret's Convent opposite, possibly the only one in existence, shows how the scheme would have looked when completed. The buttressed and battlemented apse or east-facing end of the chapel, left, resembles a small castle high above the Spital road. Comper used the Church of the Holy Rood in Stirling as his model. Adjoining the chapel is the proposed convent, an ornate neo-Jacobean range, inspired perhaps by the rather simpler Jacobean mansion house at Drum Castle where young Ninian spent school holidays with the Irvines of Drum who were family friends.

The chapel was ready for consecration by 1892. It was Ninian Comper's first completed work and the cost was £3000. Its interior with its high barrel-vaulted ceiling, is a gem, a place of beauty and of peace. Designed specifically for a convent, without the need to accommodate large numbers of lay worshippers, the nave at the west end is small, with a gallery above. It is the larger choir, the ceremonial area, whose high-backed stalls of oak, presented as a thanksgiving at the end of the Second World War, that is mostly in use these days. Within the apse is the chancel, paved in green Scandinavian marble and belying the martial appearance of its exterior. When marguerites are in bloom, great bunches of these simple white flowers, adorn the chancel in honour of Saint Margaret. On the north wall is a magnificent sacrament house or aumbry where the holy vessels were kept. Several fine sacrament houses survive in the pre-Reformation chapels of the North East, but Comper's design is a modern interpretation of the

The chapel and the section of the convent that were completed according to Comper's plans. (Frank Donnelly).

mediaeval style. Above it is a lofty spire of filigree work high up in whose centre niche is a stone statue of St Margaret of Scotland. The sisters once ran a mission connected with Holy Trinity Church, Stirling, and the statue was gifted by the congregation in commemoration of their work. Opposite the sacrament-house are the *sedilia* or seats reserved for the celebrants which are little more comfortable than the usual wooden ones.

The high altar is in the centre of the chancel, encompassed by three lancet windows, each with two 'lights' divided by a mullion. From the outside these windows look like elongated archers' slits, in keeping with the fortress theme, but from inside they glow with translucent colours, especially a jewel-like red. Ninian Comper was a master of stained glass work. St Margaret of Scotland, St Columba and St Andrew are depicted, with several other of the Apostles, as well as scenes from the Annunciation. The window to the left as one faces east includes a scene with St John the Evangelist standing and Father Comper kneeling. Fine stained glass work also enriches others parts of the interior. High in the south wall is a window is dedicated to the memory of Mother Annis Mary, Mother Superior from 1878 until 1919, while in the back chapel a another depicting St John the Baptist and St Sebastian, commemorates the baptism of Ninian Comper's son, Sebastian. In the sacristy, a stained glass window, brilliant in green and white, marks the centenary, in 1964, of the original founding of the convent

Right: The choir and chancel of the chapel. Below left, the Neale Window and right, Father Comper kneeling in prayer.

In memory of John Mason Neale, Priest 1818-1866, Founder of S¹ Margaret's Community

in Ferguson Court. It features a pensive John Mason Neale, first patron of the Aberdeen convent, The window was designed by Sebastian Comper and bears the motif of the white strawberry. The handsome wrought iron gate at the west end of the chapel is a more recent addition, dating from the 1980s. A former St Martha's girl, a postal van driver, was killed in a crash. The gate was erected in her memory by the postmen of Aberdeen.

No sooner was the chapel complete than the building of the south end of the new convent was underway. However only one bay, the section linking chapel and cottages was completed when work was halted, as was Comper's ambitious extension to St Margaret's-in-the-Gallowgate. His father had established another mission, this time to minister to the poor of the harbour area, and it may be that funds were now more urgently needed for the new St Clement's mission. The neo-Jacobean convent was never finished and Captain Henderson's sturdy cottages, converted to form a single, comfortable, unostentatious dwelling, permanently house the Convent of St Margaret's. Given the level of maintenance required both for the chapel and the surviving bay, one detects a feeling of relief that the new convent was never completed. To this day, however, the distinctive stonework and red pantiles of Sir Ninian Comper's work at the two St

The original Bay View cottages still form the living quarters of the convent.
(Frank Donnelly).

Margaret's, in the Gallowgate and in the Spital, each complement the other and remain a delight.

The census returns of 1891 provide an interesting glimpse of life at Bay View - the original name of the cottages remained in use for many years. Mother Annis Mary, Mother Superior for some forty years is shown as head. With her were three embroideresses, one visiting embroideress, two teachers, two organists, one embroiderer, one nurse, one housekeeper, one visiting plain sewer, three visiting sisters of sick and poor, one boarder teacher, one outdoor servant, a cook, one inmate nurse, and three kitchen maids. There was probably no subtle difference between 'embroideress' and 'embroiderer', while 'visiting' would not indicate a guest, but a visitor to the community outside. By this time the distinctive grey habits of the sisters were both familiar and welcome in the east end of Aberdeen. Work in slum areas was hazardous and one sister fell to her death down rickety stairs after visiting a poor family. Their sheer dedication and hard work did not go unnoticed. Gammie wrote in 1909:

> Sister Katherine Mary and her devoted band are unwearied in visiting and ministering to the poor. Their helpful presence has brightened many a dark and squalid home; while the lapsed have been reclaimed and the fallen won back by their gentle and sympathetic dealing.

In addition to their duties in the Gallowgate, the sisters worked in the harbour area with Father Comper's St Clement's Mission and went wherever they were needed. They founded a school and chapelry in Cove in 1867, and later when the seasonal herring fishery began, they tended the fisher girls who followed the fleet, binding their fingers against the brine. This explains the pattern of mission houses which were established. In 1892 a house opened in Kirkwall and another in Lerwick in 1904 which continued until 1918. The mission in Stirling, already noted, ran from 1881 until 1919 and the sisters also worked in Fraserburgh, Stornoway, and Oban between 1904 and 1930. Rather more unusual was the 'seconding' of Sister Margaret Anne from the Spital to Tanganyika in 1910 to help with the establishment of a new community there at the request of the right Reverend Frank Weston, Bishop of Zanzibar.

But sadly, one of the earliest 'travelling' sisters, Sister Martha, sent from East Grinstead at Father Comper's request to nurse those suffering from typhus in Peterhead died from the fever herself. This happened in 1879, and she, alone of the sisters is buried in St Machar's Kirkyard. Near the ornate tomb of the artist James Giles, a cross in pink granite simply engraved 'Jesu

Mercy' marks her last resting place. The convent has had its burying ground in St Peter's Cemetery for many years now, and Father Comper's own grave, anonymous, but marked by a recumbent tombstone bearing the insignia of St Margaret, and a slender obelisk of the crucifixion, designed by his son, is nearby. He died suddenly in 1903, while walking in the Duthie Park. He had just bought strawberries for his wife when some Gallowgate children who were playing in the park ran over to greet them. Father Comper was in sharing out some strawberries with the children when he collapsed. All Ninian Comper's subsequent work would incorporate the motif of a red strawberry in memory of his father. His son Sebastian was to follow suit, his strawberry 'differenced' by being white.

The sisters had devoted teachers among their number. Sister Katherine Mary was headmistress of the school attached to St Margaret's-in-the-Gallowgate from 1884 until she was elected Mother Superior in 1919 on the death of Mother Annis Mary. In 1886, St Peter's Hall, No 137 Spital, was built near the junction with Sunnybank Road. Here the sisters took Sunday School classes as well as evening classes for boys. Dorothy Gerrard, born and brought up in the Spital, clearly recalls Sister Elizabeth taking Sunday School classes, a striking figure in her dark grey habit. She remembers each child being given a daffodil from the convent garden to take home to their mothers on Mothering Sunday. It was here too that nursery schooling was introduced to Aberdeen by the matron of St Martha's Home, Miss E M Kennedy and her friend Mrs Lily Falconer. As a result of their initiative the city's first nursery school was opened in St Peter's Hall by Lady Astor in 1933. The sisters were responsible for in running it until 1937 when the local authority took over responsibility for nursery schooling in Aberdeen.

Miss E M Kennedy, matron of St Martha's and a pioneer of nursery education in Aberdeen.

The Jute Works girls who originally lodged at St Martha's Home would work the early shift for 6am till 8am, return to the Home for breakfast, then work till 8 pm at night. After that they sewed. A hard life. From 1887, however, the sisters ran St Martha's as a non-denominational children's home. In the 1890s Sister Maria Teresa was sister-in-charge with an assistant matron and eight of a staff, plus twenty-one girls, either working or still at school. Local people of a later generation recall how well the sisters looked after their charges, and still remember the children's excitement when deciding what to buy with their Saturday penny. A memory of those times comes from Alex Slessor whose childhood home in Merkland Road was not far from the Convent. At the rear of the building the sisters had (and still have) a garden, where they grew flowers and vegetables, and at one time kept hens and pigs. Kitchen waste suitable for the pigs was gratefully received, and Alex Slessor can remember delivering leftovers to the rear of the convent, then going round to the front to get a sweetie.

Accommodation at St Martha's in those days consisted of refectory, sitting room, waiting room, sisters' room, kitchens, lavatories, and washhouse all on the ground floor. A large dormitory for twenty girls and the sisters' bedroom were situated on the first floor while the second floor contained a large night nursery, day nursery and three bedrooms. By 1955 a playground was opened for the girls at the rear of the building where a former allotment in Froghall Road had been concreted over.

The opening of the St Martha's playground in 1955, from Froghall Road. St Martha's is glimpsed behind the trees, top right. Courtesy, Elizabeth Weston.

The girls of St Martha's in the 1950s.

Mother Verity Margaret, Mother Superior of St Margaret's since 1965, has many memories of St Martha's particularly during the last war. These were dangerous days for the chapel was used by the Luftwaffe as a landmark. There was no official air raid shelter within the convent, so a passage-way at St Martha's which had no windows and consequently no glass to shatter, served instead. If an air raid came after midnight, the children would be allowed cocoa and a bun, but if it occurred before midnight they had to go straight back to bed. 'A stingy little raid,' said one lad disapprovingly when they had to return to bed before the witching hour. The children, en route to St Margaret's School in the Gallowgate were told that if they had reached Mounthooly when the air raid siren went off, then they should go straight on to school. If it sounded before Mounthooly, however, they were to hurry back to St Martha's. She remembers small figures loitering around Canal Street in the hope of hearing the familiar wavering wail.

Canon Kenneth Strachan, rector of St Margaret's-in-the-Gallowgate and chaplain to the convent for thirty years, was a great source of strength during the war years and after. When he died in 1994 the sisters wrote movingly of Father Strachan's wisdom and sense of humour: 'He shared all the joys and sorrows of the sisters, the children, the old people and the staff, regarding them all as his family'. He was succeeded by St Margaret's is Canon Donald Nicholson.

At the door of the convent from left, Sister Mary Joan, Sister Mary Thelca, Mother Verity Margaret and Sister Columba.

Mother Verity Margaret, born Margaret Campbell into a Church of Scotland family, learnt about the Episcopalian faith from an aunt and worked with children before joining the order as a postulant in 1939. She took her final vows in 1942. After the war, as sacristan at St Clement's-on-the-Quay, the church which grew out of Father Comper's last mission, she remembers the horror of hearing rats scuttling nearby and the difficulty in finding flowers to decorate the church for the first service held there at the end of the war. It was something of a triumph eventually to find six yellow daisies. St Clement's later relocated to Mastrick.

In common with the other sisters who presently form the community at St Margaret's, Sisters Mary Thelca, Columba and Mary Joan, she could not have entered a convent without an overwhelming sense of vocation. 'There was no doubt about what God was calling me to do.' Over a period of years the postulant becomes a novice, then a junior sister. She may leave during that period, before taking her final vows of celibacy, poverty, obedience, charity and commitment to God, if it becomes apparent that she is not cut out for the life.

Apart from the mother house at East Grinstead and St Margaret's Convent in Aberdeen there are three further autonomous houses, in London, Walsingham, and in Boston, Massachusetts as well as mission houses at Chiswick and in Sri Lanka. A photograph which has pride of place at the

Convent shows a reunion of all the sisters of the Society taken in East Grinstead in 1985. As well as their commitment to the education and welfare of the young, the Aberdeen-based sisters have given devoted service to other sections of the community. The old Comper family home, St Margaret's Brae, was left to the Convent by the Reverend John Comper's widow and from 1945, for some forty years, the sisters ran a non-denominational eventide home there, St Margaret's Hostel for elderly women. From 1959 until 1964 they worked in Dundee, and during the late 1970s, gave medical assistance at Aberdeen's model lodging house.

During the latter half of the twentieth century, standards of living have improved vastly and the work for which communities such as St Margaret's were founded has largely been taken over by the social services. A reduction in the number of postulants and novices coming forward has been inevitable, and at St Margaret's as the sisters themselves have progressed in years there has been a scaling down in the amount of work they are able to undertake. Sister Columba has been involved in chaplaincy work at Cornhill and at the City Hospital. Sister Mary Joan continues to visit the elderly and is organist at St Ninian's Episcopal Church and assistant organist at St Margaret's-in-the-Gallowgate. Members of the public continue to turn to them for help, and some of those whom they have recently befriended now assist in the convent garden.

Within the convent, the day begins with private meditation. Matins is at 7am, Terce at 9am, the Mid-day office at 12.45, Vespers at 5.30 and Compline at 8.30. Eucharist is celebrated daily In addition to attending the offices in chapel, each sister spends two hours a day in private prayer and some meals are taken in silence. One day each month the sisters go into retreat, and there is also a longer retreat for five days once a year. The community is also used by members of all denominations for private retreats.

Several of the buildings that were connected with St Margaret's for so long have other uses these days. St Martha's ceased to be a children's home in 1973 and two years later, after a reorganisation of local government, ownership was vested in the then Grampian Regional Council. In October 1985, the building was gutted by fire, though fortunately it was empty at the time. The exterior stood firm and a year later the Langstane Housing Association purchased the property and remodelled the interior into seven furnished flats to provide a halfway house to rehabilitate up to twenty-seven persons who had experienced 'an unsettled way of life', including former prisoners. A senior resident senior housing assistant collaborates with agencies such as the City Council's homeless unit in settling those between sixteen and sixty that are eligible for replacement, and guidance is given on payment of bills and rent, budgeting, shopping, cooking, job applications and domestic and social skills. Thus St Martha's, or No 19 Spital as it is now known, continues to give succour and shelter to those who need it, just as it has always done.

St Margaret's Brae became the headquarters of the Diocese of Aberdeen and Orkney in 1991 after its closure as an eventide home. At No 39, it is the

The shared entrance. To the right work is underway on the Welfare houses.

last building in King's Crescent, and shares an entrance with St Margaret's, which at No 17, is the first building on the west side of the Spital. Neither the sisters nor anyone else knows where Nos 1 - 15 have gone.

The chapel continues to command the Spital, though there was much concern during the 1980s when damp and dry rot necessitated a lengthy restoration. During this period the sisters used the refectory as a chapel, and ate in the kitchen. By the end of 1990, after five years' refurbishment, the chapel was pronounced ready again for worship. By 1995 there had, unfortunately, been further outbreaks of dampness, followed by more remedial work. The hope is that it has at last been eradicated.

Mother Verity has written:-

However widespread our activities in the peak years, the worship of God and the intense life of the chapel has always been the first call on our energy and devotion...The chapel is the power-house through which we get our strength. Prayer, for strengthening the spirit, and for intercession on behalf of others, remains the most important part of the sisters' day.

Chapter 14

North Spital
Rose Villa to Spital Walk

A spokesman for the city architect's department confirmed that great care had been taken to blend the redevelopment with the established character of the area in choice of materials and style, which have made the houses in the first phase unique.

Evening Express, 8 July, 1968

We now cross back to the east side of the Spital and begin the descent to Old Aberdeen. On the other side of Merkland Road from Glamis Cottage there once stood Rose Cottage, a late eighteenth century dwelling tucked in the north corner of a substantial feu, approached from the Spital by a wooded driveway. A long walled garden, three times the length of that of Glamis Cottage, ran down to the East Back Road, as Merkland Place used to be. A long time Spital dweller, Thomas Yeats the flesher lived here with his family and mother-in-law (he had married the boss's daughter) for over twenty years from the mid 1850s. His slaughter shop would have been down in the Back Road.

At a rather later date, Alex Slessor remembers a small-holding and ponies in the long 'back rig'. In the inter-war years, the house was owned by Henry Brown sheriff's officer and a well known figure in the area. Around 1926 he reconstructed the house, creating a smart, modern, south-facing dwelling. Rose Cottage having turned its side on the Spital, became No 38 Merkland Road and was promoted by Mr Brown to Rose Villa. Mr Dick Christie, who had a workmen's cafe on Regent Quay, then went into road haulage, succeeded Henry Brown, and during his time there, the Town Council took over much of the long garden. These days Dick Christie's son

Rose Villa, 38 Merkland Road replaces an older house, Rose Cottage built on the same site.

and daughter-in-law live opposite. Rose Villa later became, as it remains, the home of another well known local family, the Leiths. Mrs Chrissie Leith, who knows more about the area than most, also ran the little store on the other side of the Spital for a number of years along with her sister-in-law, Miss Ivy Leith. Chrissie Leith's older sister was one of the last pupils at Primrose School, a real link with the past.

By the 1960s plans were afoot to replace the old houses on the east side of the Spital, right down to the Red Lion. Rose Villa was originally included in this scheme but the Leiths fought a successful battle to save it from demolition. It was still a relatively new house and common

Mrs Chrissie Leith at 38 Merkland Road in the early 1960s. Courtesy Ronald Leith.

The council-built houses of the early 1970s. Despite appearing as two-storey houses from the Spital, full use has been made of the sloping ground to the rear where they are four-storeys deep. The exteriors are in granite and harl.

sense prevailed. Rose Villa, neat and gleaming, survives. Next to it there stretches a long terrace of dwellings, and below them, further groupings of flats, taking advantage of the gentle slope to Merkland Place. This three acre scheme, unique in Aberdeen, was designed by the city architect's department and erected during 1970-71. Its sixty-odd houses, some gable-end to the street, some with stair towers, is nevertheless not a quaint olde-worlde pastiche, rather an understated mediaeval *mélange* presented in a modern idiom.

Mark you, the old row of cottages and tenements that stood here for so long were uncopyable. Many dated from the eighteenth century, direct successors of those in Parson Gordon's Plan, and were built in a do-as-you-please mixter-maxter of Seaton brick, random rubble, undressed granite, dressed granite and wet harl, with canted dormers, half-dropped dormers, lofty tympana, slated roofs and red pantiles and the whole crowned with an amazing assortment of lums and chimney stacks. The terrace was girded with iron railings to prevent the unwary from tumbling into the sunks, some of which were used as coal cellars, though many were occupied.

The first section of these houses, No 46-94 in modern numbering, ran as far as St Peter's Cemetery, and for a short time in the 1860s was known as Spital Terrace. As indicated in Chapter Nine there was a robust mix of residents here, fleshers, farmers and gardeners, milliners and dressmakers,

*Built in a do-as-you-please
mixture-maxter of Seaton brick,
random rubble, undressed granite
and wet harl, these houses had an
Alice in Wonderland quality.
Courtesy John Souter.*

shoemakers and booksellers - located here as well as at Glamis Cottage to catch the passing College trade. Some of the houses had an Alice in Wonderland quality; urban dwellings from the front, country cottages at the rear with long rigs of ground sloping, like their neighbour, Rose Villa, down to Merkland Place. Many were laid out with gardens, and seats, some had woodlands; a few had sheds indicating agricultural pursuits.

Many houses had a tale to tell. We can start at the beginning with No 46 - 50 the Spital, (Nos 33-34 old style), next door to Rose Villa. It is on the right of the photograph above, the low house with a street sign, 'Auckland Place', at the side endowing it with an unlikely whiff of the Antipodes; included in this group are the next two dwellings with canted dormers. The feu charter dates from 1758, granted by George Moir of Scotstown and Spital in favour of James Michie, a Spital gunsmith. By the mid-nineteenth century James Booth, a Spital farmer and his wife Elizabeth were the liferenters and the property was held in fee by William, George and John Booth. In 1866 John, a shipmaster living in the Green, had come into possession. Presuming his brothers William and George to be dead, he sold the two houses and their yards to Edward Mackay, licensed grocer, who lived across at No 26 Spital (the present No 39, the house with the ironwork on the front cover) for £40.

Twenty years later a long lost heir was found. John Booth, son of the deceased James, the farmer and John, the shipmaster's heir-at-law, had gone off to seek his fortune, and was traced to Auckland, New Zealand, where, nostalgically, he had christened his home Bon Accord Cottage. Thither the Spital's own solicitor, Williamson Booth, dispatched his apprentice to redd things up. Whether the young man travelled by steamer or one of the last of the clippers is unknown but it must have been an invigorating break from routine. It seems that John Booth had no wish to return to Aberdeen and take up his inheritance. In 1888, from his home in Auckland, he granted his relative, Mrs Jane Sharp, née Booth, wife of the Spital tailor, his right in the two houses and yards 'for love, favour and affection', that is he gifted them to her.

In 1892 Mrs Sharp cleared the decks paying £30 in settlement of claims by the representatives of the late Edward Mackay. Again, the deed was drawn up by the solicitor, Williamson Booth, surely another member of the clan. He pops up frequently in Spital transactions, a cross between a wadsetter and a building society, frequently lending money against the security of property. The Sharps thought much of Williamson. The census returns of 1891 show that the household consisted of William Sharp, tailor, his wife Jane, his daughter, also Jane, an envelope maker, two sons who were tailors and a third son, a message boy, and a further three daughters and three sons, all scholars. The two youngest sons were called Williamson and Booth. Alex Slessor's father had his suits made by Mr Sharp - 'one every five years.' Another link with the past.

In 1892 the laird of the Spital, H W Knight Erskine, George Moir's great-great-grandson, granted a charter of *novodamus*, ('we grant anew') to Mrs Sharp, altering terms of the original few charter by allowing further development. Provision was made for the building of a back house to the value of at least £300, to be approved by the laird's architect who was none other than the distinguished Dr William Kelly. A plan, signed by Kelly, is extant, though perhaps a trifle too plain to be considered one of his master works .

A sizeable building, in sneck-coursed rubble and named Auckland House in token of John Booth's generosity duly appeared in the long back garden. It was tenanted by three families and the upper house was entered by forestairs. Meanwhile the houses on the Spital were undergoing expansion. Two dwellings were added to the rear of No 46. These became Nos 1-2 Auckland Place, No 1 being sunks. The dwelling built behind Nos 48-50 became No 3 Auckland Place, and Auckland House itself Nos 4-5 Auckland Place. This name was introduced in December 1894, at the time when the Town Council had proposed 'that the names Mounthooly, King's Crescent, Spital and College Bounds, should be abolished, and the whole line of street between Causewayend and the Old Aberdeen Town-house named High

202

Left, No 2 Auckland Place, built at the rear of No 46 the Spital. Below, No 3 Auckland Place, at the rear of No 48-50. To the right are the twin gables of the 'farmhouse' No 52-54, while beyond is the Big House. Courtesy, the Leith family.

Street'. A high-powered deputation of Aulton divines and academics saw to it that such heresy on the part of the city fathers was quickly abandoned. But Auckland Place was a perfectly acceptable name for the backlands of Nos 46-50 the Spital, while the East Back Road became Merkland Place and nearer Old Aberdeen, Churchyard Wynd, became St Peter's Gate. Indeed, all the Old Aberdeen wynds were officially named at this time.

In the wartime, an air raid shelter went up in the gap between Auckland House and Nos 1-3 Auckland Place. No 5 was the home of Ronald Leith's grandfather and Ronald recalls 'a warren of interesting houses, some with ornate doors and windows.' Mrs Yule, an elderly lady with a walking stick lived at No 1, Miss McDonald at No 3, and the McLennan family at No 4 Auckland Place. In spite of the additions, there still remained a sizeable garden to Merkland Place, with trees, flowers and a sundial. There were ruinous buildings nearby, and much of the Merkland Place area at that time was covered in rough grass. Ronald and his friends could run up Merkland Place, barking to annoy Willie Weir's Airedales at the far end, then make a quick dash for safety. 'It was a great place to play.'

The scene as Auckland House, Nos 4-5 Auckland Place, centre, is taken down. Top left is Rose Villa. The length of the garden, sloping down towards Merkland Place made it, 'a great place to play'. Courtesy, the Leith family.

Mr Sharp's tailor shop which fronted the Spital later became, William Troup's cycle and radio shop. 'There was always a queue of kids waiting to hire cycles,' recalls Iris Donald who has lived in the neighbourhood all

The terrace of old Spital houses demolished by the early 1970s. The slates visible at the rear right belong to No 2 Auckland Place. Courtesy, Aberdeen Journals.

her life. Elizabeth Weston whose family lived in Froghall Road remembers the heavy accumulator cells for the old wirelesses being taken there to be recharged. This complex of buildings remained in Sharp hands until the Council acquired them in 1967.

The next house Nos 52-54, (Nos 37-40 old style) to the right of the hoarding, its dormers in dressed granite, looks like an old farmhouse. Here, from the late 1860s onwards, we find the Duncan family of fleshers noted in Chapter Eleven, probably the next generation of the family that had lived at Glamis Cottage. Resident here was William Duncan, flesher, Alex Duncan cattle dealer and William's son, John Duncan, cattle salesman, whose office was at the King Street cattle market. Yes, this was our renowned auctioneer who would later build a fine home, Zetland House, nearby on King Street. (Merkland Road makes a good attempt at encompassing the globe, what with Auckland near its west end and Zetland at the east). To the rear of the Duncan dwelling was a conglomeration of sheds fronting onto Merkland Place where William Duncan did his slaughtering, and Alexander Wilson's nauseous horns were piled. Wilson's pigsty was another feature of the landscape but fortunately a belt of woodland in the long back garden shielded the Spital house from any unpleasantness. Later

Nos 11-15 Merkland Place
with its country-style porch
Courtesy, the Leith family.

Nos 11-15 Merkland Place was built near here, a tenement with a country-style porch.

Back up in the Spital, beyond the hoarding was Nos 68-70, the Big House, a tenement, built around 1900. Its tympanum, carrying the chimney stack, rose high above the others. Sasine of this land had been granted as early as 1725 to 'John Taylor shoemaker and his spouse'. Nearly thirty years later Taylor sold 'that piece of land lying in the Spithill with the houses built or to be built' to a wright, William Duncan and two masons, clearly a team of builders. In 1755 the team was ready to sell 'the land and houses' to John Strachan, a journeyman smith and his wife. Then a hiccup occurred. James Aberdour, a brasier or brassworker had taken up residence in one of the houses. He was in unlawful possession, but the description of his household suggests that he was more than just an opportunist squatter. By 1756 he was undertaking 'to flitt, red (vacate) and remove myself, wife, bairns and family servands and goods from Whitsunday next so that John Strachan, his Tennents and others in his name may then peaceably enter'. Whether Aberdour had to pay damages for illegal possession (violent profits) is uncertain.

By 1900 John Booth Sharp, engineer, and his brothers, William Sharp, tailor, and James Sharp, joiner both residing at Auckland House, had acquired the property and Williamson Booth was waiting in the wings as ever, ready to give financial assistance. It seems that at this time they replaced the old dwellings with the Big House, which remained in the hands of John B Sharp's heirs until sold to the Town in 1966 for demolition.

Beyond was another of the older houses, No 74, the entrance forming a bridge over the sunks below. Here one of the Spital's wee shops was located. In the 1880s, as No 46, old style, it had been Miss Henderson's dressmaking establishment, but by the early years of the century she was running a drapery there. Some forty years later the business was taken over by Philips the draper and the Slessors can remember this haberdashery being run by two sisters, always clad in black.

The next house Nos 80-82 was one of the later tenements, owned in the 1920s and 1930s by another Booth, Andrew, sub-postmaster in Old Aberdeen. The feu charter was originally granted by George Moir of Scotstown in 1786 to William Milne of Horse Crook, Udny. In 1828 the original buildings were owned by a flesher, Peter Davidson who also had his yard there. Later, a builder's yard operated in the 'lang rig' at the back.

The group of houses Nos 84-94, was the last of those whose long gardens ran down to Merkland Place, (after that the graveyard intervened). The title deeds here could be traced back to 1779 when Andrew Craig, tailor in Spital, sold part of this property to Andrew Creighton, candlemaker in Aberdeen. Two years later the adjoining properties were also disponed by David Ferrier to Creighton who had overreached himself and went bust. A later owner was Alexander Collie, threaddlapper, and during his time there is mention of neighbouring ruinous house, and subsequent rebuilding.

The properties were later split among various owners, but by 1829 had come together again in the ownership of the Weaver Incorporation of Old

Merkland Place today. The site of Willie Weir's farm was at the far end.

*The group of the Spital houses
which were bought by Willie Weir.
Courtesy, John Souter.*

Aberdeen, who owned the houses right down to St Peter's Gate.

Nos 84-94 used to be numbered Nos 54-60, old style. No 60, the most northerly of the group had long been a farmer's dwelling and behind it, a range of byres and biggings ran down by the side of the cemetery wall to Merkland Place. In 1898, the tenant of No 54, a dairyman, William Weir, son of a farmer, John Weir, successfully offered the Weaver Incorporation £815 to buy all the houses. He had raised £215 himself and granted bonds of £600 over the property. Thus Willie Weir one of the great characters of the Spital became a landlord.

He is remembered as a big man, well made, while his wife was petite. They had a family of four daughters and three sons. 'You couldn't see much of the farm from the Spital, but if you walked along Merkland Place you came upon it - there was a slight rise in the ground,' recalls Gordon Cardno. Alex Slessor, remembers as a boy taking Willie Weir's cows to graze where Linksfield Academy was later built. He herded them via King Street and Pittodrie Street and took them back at night. As a milk boy he went out with the yoke round the neck and the cans attached. Jimmy Yule ran with milk twice a day, for folk had no means of keeping it cool . He remembers being afraid of the dark in College Bounds which was pitch black. Willie had a primitive refriferator at the farm, a concrete shed at the end of Merkland Place, where he sat the milk bottles on stone shelving which ran all the way round the shed. Jimmy has a traumatic memory of a fire when he had to

208

run to West North Street fo fetch Napier, the knacker to put the beasts out of their misery. A happier memory was of stealing the occasional locust bean on which the cows were fed - they were fine to eat. The pay for a milk boy was not great, but the additional reward of a quart of milk to take home every day, made up for it. Dorothy Gerrard recalls the cows coming from Sunnyside to Froghall Terrace. They would walk up Froghall Terrace to Merkland Road, then along Merkland Place to get to their byres.

Willie Weir had fields where the University Refectories now are. Local legend has it that one evening in the Red Lion he was heard to declare that the beast was not yet born that could get the better of him. Whether or not he had the Horseman's Word is unclear. The next day he was ploughing a field for neeps when something snagged on the plough and the two horses bolted, alarmed, it is thought by hooting from the railyards at Kittybrewster. He was dragged along for some distance, his leg badly cut by the 'sock' of the plough. Gangrene developed and he died in hospital a few weeks later, in April 1924.

Willie Weir Jnr was a big man like his father, with a shock of black, that later became a shock of white hair, and a moustache. Alex Slessor's first memory of Willie Weir Jnr, was during the First World War. He had come home on leave very late one night and had slept in the loft above the byre so as not to disturb the household. Here Alex met him in the morning, still in his army uniform. After his father's death, Willie Weir Jnr developed a market gardening side to the business, across at Sunnyside Farm. His round with the vegetable cart, pulled by Sandy the horse and accompanied by the handsome Airedales which he bred and which snapped at Sandy's hooves, is recalled by older Spital residents. He supplied neeps, carrots, potatoes, Brussels sprouts, and eggs as well, for ducks and hens were kept at the Merkland Place farmyard. Gordon Cardno remembers what was for him an unhappy event when his grandmother decided to give up the few hens that she kept out in the back at Hillhead Terrace. Willie Weir took them away, grabbing them unceremoniously by the legs, crossing the Spital with two handfuls of squawking bundles of feathers.

Mr Cardno also remember the day a wheel buckled during Willie's vegetable round. Instead of returning to base and thus disappointing customers, Willie - and Sandy - carried on resolutely in the lop-sided cart. Sandy would be taken round to a field in Sunnybank for rest and relaxation once a year, and on one memorable occasion, seems not to have been impressed with the holiday arrangements. The gate to the field was left open so the horse decided to return home himself, trotting along Sunnybank Road, past the Red Lion (a shock for tipplers), down the Spital, down Merkland Road and along Merkland Place and so into his own stable.

Tales of Willie Weir abound. He was not dress conscious ('he'd aye on the same claethes') and invariably donned a curious antique garb for funerals, stiff collar and tails, following the cortège on his bicycle. Iris Donald remembers that this outfit so irritated his family that it was one day surreptitiously cast into the flames of the washhouse boiler. Great was Willie's wrath when the next funeral came around and the mourning apparel was nowhere to be found.

Harry, Willie's brother, had the milk cart. Gordon Cardno can remember when it was a two-wheeled contraption with a bar across two chains, the cans attached and milk controlled by a tap. Bessie, one of the sisters, 'a bonny lass' dressed for work in green wellies and overalls, ran the dairy side of the business. 'Once a week my sister or I visited the farm to pay our weekly milk bill,' Dorothy Gerrard remembers. 'Bessie always gave us a penny back to spend on sweets or whatever'. She married Harry Anderson the hairdresser whose business was across at No 121.

Such then were the cottages and tenements which backed down to Merkland Place. The next group of houses, still part of the row, sat in front of the St Peter's graveyard, though their back gardens were still of reasonable length. Nos 100 -104 traced its history back to a feu charter of 1777 by George Moir in favour of 'Robert Ogg, indweller in Spittal', noting the house and yard of David Ferrier on the south, George Barron on the north and the Spital Churchyard on the east. Harold Bishop recalls that his mother Jean Smith Bishop was born at No 104 in 1879, 'a little woman, well kent and respected', a member of St Machar's Cathedral who worked for Aberdeen University Press and later emigrated to Canada where she married a farmer. She subsequently returned to the Spital with her three young sons and cleaned for Professor Harrower in College Bounds. Mrs Bishop died in 1949.

Mrs Jean Smith Bishop, born at 104 the Spital. This photograph dates from around 1900. Courtesy, Harold S Bishop.

210

No 106 also traces its origins back to 1777. James Kerr, a writer (lawyer) owned the property from 1856 until 1872, by which time he was working in Glasgow. In that later year he sold No 106, which sat back from the road, to George Troup an iron-moulder, a native of Rhynie, 'now residing at Santo Amaro, Bahia, South America' for £115. Troup, when he came into possession of No 106 must have looked across the road and noticed a nice empty space waiting to be filled. It was there that he built Boa Vista Place, to which we will return. A later owner was a policeman, John Pirie who bought No 106 for £200 in 1897, lived there for many years, and on his retirement from the force became a house agent. By 1936, the owner, an engineer, Alexander Macintosh, was having problems. The graveyard wall to the rear of the house was bulging and unsafe. There are tales of the contents of crypts becoming exposed, and of prolonged disputes with the proprietors of St Peter's Cemetery.

Also opposite Boa Vista place was 'Jobbie' Nicol's radio and cycle shop at No 108 Spital. Iris Donald remembers soldiers quartered in Sunnybank School during the war queuing to get their accumulators charged here.

Mrs Iris Donald lives in one of the modern Spital houses with a view across to the former Primrose School.

We now move on to the houses that once stood on either side of St Peter's Gate, the old Churchyard Wynd. At one time, according to the title deeds, those on the south side included a 'close, yard, and two forehouses high and laigh towards the King's common highway...' No 122 Spital, the ground floor house nearest St Peter's Gate, was entered from the Spital while the flat above, No 2 St Peter's Gate, was entered from round the back. The 1868 ordnance survey shows 'PH' here, the site, by that time, of the old Red Lion tavern.

By the 1920s No 122 was purveying eats rather than drinks. Dorothy Gerrard remembers: 'There was a cooked meat shop at the corner of St Peter's Gate. They sold lovely pies, potted meat and tripe. It was owned by Mr Alexander Donald and he made lovely ice cream as well.' Mervyn Donald recalls his grandfather Alexander Stewart Donald, founder of what was for many years Aberdeen's most famous ice-cream firm: 'He was an orphan who came in to town from the Alford-Marnoch area. He married an Aberdeen girl, and they decided to set up a cooked meat shop in the Spital. When the trade was thin in the summer, he turned to making ice-cream. It proved so popular that he later moved to bigger premises at 18 Whitehouse Street.' And he recalls one of his grandfather's favourite stories. While waiting at the North of Scotland Bank near the present Marks and Spencer, hoping the manager would allow him an overdraft to help start up, he got chatting with another young man, Gammack Clark, in the same circumstances, but whose project required a larger overdraft than Alexander Donald's. Both men got their overdrafts and did well, and Gammack Clark, became Alec Donald's first customer. Everyday a half gallon of ice cream would be sent from the Spital to Clark's successful project - the Douglas Hotel.

The Donald family lived literally over shop at No 2 St Peter's Gate. Gordon Cardno across in Hillhead Terrace was a pal of A S Donald's son, and there was nothing he liked better than to be invited by young Alec to test new flavours for the firm in the work shop at the back, giving them his considered opinion. When A S Donald died suddenly of a heart attack, it was Alec who had to step in and run the business. This property, along with Nos 118-120 Spital, which had long been ruinous, was acquired by the Council in 1969.

On the other side of St Peter's Gate was another group of houses, laid out along similar lines. No 124 Spital was on the corner with Nos 1-3 St Peter's Gate above, while No 128 Spital was next door with Nos 5-7 above. Was this, I wonder, the site of James Sheriffs' lunatic asylum? It certainly for a time was earmarked as the site for St Margaret's Convent, the property being disponed to Father Comper by Ann Presslie - for a time the Red Lion's landlord - in 1871. Five years later the property was back in Mrs Presslie's hands, and the sisters more suitably accommodated at Bay View. It was in one of these houses that a chimney sweep who played the bass fiddle lived, right up until the time of demolition. Shades of Johns Ross the blind fiddler.

All these houses were purchased by Aberdeen Corporation between

1962 and 1971. Willie Weir held out to the last. He did well, receiving nearly £2050. By the time that his property was compulsorily purchased, most of the old houses had not only been demolished but fifty-six of the new houses were complete. Six more houses were added where his property had been. Apart from the main Spital terrace, Merkland Place had an attractive scattering of new homes for the elderly, and the old name, Auckland Place was retained. The St Peter's Gate area had its own little development and

Mr Neave contemplates his garden at Merkland Place. Brought up in Gerrard Street, he used to play in the Spital as a child.

the arched stone gateway of St Peter's cemetery, with the coat of arms of the Moirs, a poignant reminder of the past, was retained

Perhaps the old houses were too far gone to be worthy of preservation, though the example of the University's painstaking restorations of the most unlikely property in Old Aberdeen is always held up to Doubting Thomases. These Spital houses of the 1970s have comfortable interiors and charming flowers beds at their doors, but one reservation remains. When the terrace was newly built, its exteriors were

Gateway, St Peter's Cemetery.

pristine to the extent that they dazzled passers-by. Alas, modern buildings do not always wear well; if this exercise in quasi-mediaeval modernism is to retain its impact, regular external maintenance is a *sine qua non.*

In the 1880s the Red Lion had flitted from its site at St Peter's Gate, just three houses down the north Spital slope to premises that would have dated from the late eighteenth or early nineteenth century. It was now numbered No 90 (having had several other numbers) and became No 130 at the great renumbering of 1903. Like holy places, built and rebuilt on the same sacred soil, inns hover near the place where they were originally located for restorative purposes; in this case, to refresh the weary traveller halfway between Aberdeen and Old Aberdeen.

Immediately beside it was the narrow gap of St Peter's Place. 'The lane ran down the side of the Red Lion, and came out in Orchard Street,' Mrs Gerrard recalls. 'Quite a few people lived in the little houses there, and at the foot there was a small saw mill run by Mr James Geddes. During the General Strike of 1926, we used to buy wood for our fires as no coal was being delivered.' On the other side of the St Peter's Place gap houses similar to the early tenements of College Bounds would have carried on down to the Old Aberdeen boundary at Orchard House, No 2 College Bounds. There was no break, apart from the narrow Susie's Close which stood almost opposite Firhill Place and whose condition had distressed the *Aberdeen Journal* reporter in the course of his 1878 safari.

Major changes came about in 1890 when H W Knight Erskine decided to lay out a new road on part of his Spital Lands which the Town Council agreed should be called Orchard Street. It would run between King Street and Orchard Place, where it came to an unsatisfactory termination. Access to the Spital was barred by the 'long rigs' of the Spital houses, now free of the constraints imposed the St Peter's graveyard whose northern boundary wall we have just passed. Many of these 'rigs' were built over with back houses and assorted rickles and backed against Orchard Place. For a time a row of newly built houses at Nos 47-63 Orchard Street was caught in a triple pincer movement between the little houses in St Peter's Place to the south, the back rigs of the Spital to the north and the terraced dwellings of the Spital itself on the western front. In 1899 the Town Council decided that the sensible thing was to extend Orchard Street to join the Spital, thus linking it directly with King Street. It was also decreed that Susie's Close a few yards to the north, running between the Spital and Orchard Place, be closed.

The Council now entered into an agreement with a local carpenter, James Green, who removed a house and back biggings, possibly a little dairy, on the line of the proposed extension. The Council meanwhile set about acquiring and taking down a neighbouring property, No 100 Spital (old numbering). A fair gap was created by these demolitions, allowing

The early twentieth century development at the Orchard Street corner. Wilburn was on the corner and the Sunnybank Dairy was the second shop beyond. A playhouse stood here in the eighteenth cenury.

room not only for the planned Orchard Street exit, but for putting up new buildings immediately south, up the hill. Here, in 1901, after several hitches, James Green was given permission to build three tenements with shops on the ground floors, the present Nos 138-140, Nos 142-146 and No 148 on the Orchard Street corner which was the first to appear. This development has all the hallmarks of an Northern Co-operative initiative - many such are still identifiable throughout Aberdeen. By 1903, a grocery branch of the Co-op was open for business at No 148, followed in 1908 by a Co-opie butcher at No 146. No 142 was occupied by Charles Bain, dairyman, who also had the neighbouring premises, at No 140 next to the Red Lion. For years these two shops ran as dairy and fruiterer.

Having noted these changes, Robert Forrest, landlord of the Red Lion carried out additions to his building in 1904. Even so, he must have felt that the old inn was still not in keeping with the smart new shops and tenement houses next door. In 1906 the entire building was reconstructed to blend in with its neighbours. The plaque on the wall commemorates this rebuilding. Though there was a similar, smaller development across on the Spital-Sunnybank corner, this new block, breaking into the east side of the Spital, where many of the dwellings still dated from George Moir's day, must have stuck out like the proverbial sore thumb. But it would have been well

215

received. No thought of 'sensitive' redevelopments that harmonised with the area then. At the turn of the twentieth century it would not have occurred to the developers to do other than to build in the style of the time.

The Co-opie subsequently flitted round the corner to Orchard Street and other shops took its place. No 148, the corner shop, became for many years a branch of Wilburn, one of at least fifteen retail outlets owned by the wholesale supplier William Watt Hepburn (hence Wil-Burn). Hepburn died in 1953 but tales of his extraordinarily sharp business flair, his famous waistcoat grown green with age, his habit of walking on to the next tram stop to save a penny, are still recalled by older Aberdonians. Wilburn shops al-

The plaque on the wall, centre, indicates the 1906 rebuilding of the Red lion.

ways had a distinctive smell and a flavour of the hard-up. Iris Donald recalls the barrels of syrup and the brown bags at No 148, the wooden floors being swept and damped down with water to keep the dust at bay.

The St Machar's branch of Aberdeen Savings Bank made its debut at No 146,(the former Co-opie butcher), from the early 1920s and the Sunnybank Dairy was at No 142. George Gordon recalls that it was occupied from about 1934 by Mr W B Paterson and his wife who had previously spent some time in Canada. They lived across the way in an interesting cottage on the north side of Sunnybank Road. In more recent years there have been a number of changes. Wilburn has been a radio and television engineer and now offers contract furnishings. The Savings Bank moved across the Orchard Street divide in the late 1950s and the former branch is now a hairdresser's. The Sunnybank Dairy is long gone: the Gehlan Newsagent and General Store is here now, as well as Bismillah who specialise in Indian, African and Aribian comestibles, while No 140, the former fruiterer, was for a time a music centre.

Gulzar Gehlan and his son Bilal in the well-stocked Spital shop. This was once the Sunnybank Dairy.

The Red Lion has not changed its spots. It remains a traditional pub frequented by both locals and students, its upstairs lounge renowned as the 'Beastie'. It has changed its landlords down the years, though. John Deans Snr and his son of the same name are the best remembered of recent times while Sandy Pirie became landlord in the late 1980s. As Aberdeen's

Sandy Pirie, mine host at the Red Lion.

international golfer, he had a fabulous career, winning his first junior tournament as a fourteen-year-old in 1955. He was a scratch player at eighteen, and in the 1960s and 1970 and won every trophy in the North East. He represented both Scotland and Britain on numerous occasions, with great distinction - not to mention his club, Hazlehead, where he was an outstanding greenkeeper. Back down to earth at the Red Lion, Sandy has restored the bar in traditional style, and at time of writing has plans for upgrading the frontage.

Across the Orchard Street divide, two older houses have been modernised, and next door to them we find the former Susie's Close in person. The closure order of 1899 was not implemented, indeed, the reverse. In December 1902, the Council decreed that Susie's Close, which had slipped through the net in the naming of wynds of 1894, 'be renamed Orchard Lane'. This sounded much more posh, but went ahead only because sections of the original ancient, winding Orchard Lane had been renamed. We know them as Orchard Walk and Orchard Place - the north and east sides of the old east Spital rectangle.

Next door to Susie's Close the St Machar's Branch of Aberdeen Savings Bank had settled down for a time in a plain custom-built building, No 164 Spital. By 1976 the Bank was on the move again, to another custom-built branch on the School Road-King Street corner, one that retained the ASB's low key but distinctive style of architecture. In November 1978, the Spital bank building re-opened as a mosque, to serve Aberdeen's Mos-

Susie's Close, now Orchard Lane looking towards Orchard Place.

lem community, many of whom live in the area, though some twenty years on the building still looks more like a redundant bank than a mosque. The Spital throngs when the mosque skails, and it is understandable that the community would prefer to invest in a new place of worship, built specifically to cope with their increasing numbers.

At No 182 was James Gordon's store. 'A little shop with groceries, paraffin and coal at the back. Mr and Mrs Gordon were real old characters.'

recalls Harold Bishop. 'Close by, where the Spital and College Bounds meet was Jim McOndich's coal and firewood store. We got pocket money for bunching sticks. Mr McOndich smoked about a hundred Woodbines a day. A fag was always hanging from his mouth.' Tommy Donaldson remembers the kindling machine that 'bundled' the kindling which was then wrapped round with soft wire.

These shops, and a handful of neighbouring buildings that had become derelict, were demolished and replaced in 1968 by the Spital Walk scheme, which runs from the mosque to College Bounds, and from east to west, between Orchard Walk and 'the King's Highway'. It was the first phase of a redevelopment of the east side of the Spital (the bold essay in quasi-mediaeval modernism up the road was the second). Built by Aberdeen Town Council at what now seems the remarkably economical cost of £90,000, twenty-five two, three and four apartment homes are grouped round traffic-free courts. This attractive scheme which takes us to the threshold of Old Aberdeen has rightly won high praise.

Journey's end, Spital Walk. Orchard Cottage is to the left.

Chapter 15

North Spital

The Last Lap

Proposals for this area should aim at preventing further erosion of its character
and encourage its upgrading.

Old Aberdeen Conservation Area Report, 1993

Back now on the west side of the Spital we start down towards Old
Aberdeen on the last and possibly the most interesting lap. The photograph
opposite, taken in 1978, reveals the dilapidations of the post-war era. The
three blocks of tenements on the extreme left follow on from St Martha's at
No 19. It is good to report that, like much else in the area they have since
been attractively refurbished. In the photo, the junction with Froghall
Terrace is hidden by a van but on the corner, at No 29, Elizabeth Weston
recalls a shop 'which sold ice-cream that my mother wasn't very happy
about'. It was also, she says, a lending library at one time.

Nos 35-37 (No 25 old style) across the Froghall Terrace divide is shown
boarded-up. The Victorian author, George Macdonald digged here in his
student days. His dashing tartan and velvet jackets would have been kept
in the press in the attic of No 37, the most northerly of the two houses. The
ground floor was a grocer's, John Johnston in Macdonald's time and for
many years after. The fascia is still visible in the old photograph opposite.
Our contemporary shot shows how the Spital frontage has been altered.
The entrance is now from Froghall Terrace and more space has been created
in the attic storey. The finish is in granite chip dry dash, quite common in
the Spital nowadays though not traditional.

Next door is Nos 39-41 (old style No 26) the distinctive house with the
veranda that everyone notices. Mr John Argo and his wife Moyra have lived

The Spital in 1978. Extreme left, the row of tenements beyond St Martha's. The van hides the junction with Froghall Terrace. Centre, George Macdonald's digs at No 37, boarded up, and right, No 39-41 when still a bakery. Courtesy, John Souter.

Contemporary shot of the same area in 1996.

here since 1966 and their title deeds show the feu charter to have been granted in 1746 by George Moir in favour of Alexander Smith, square wright, or cabinetmaker as we would now say. This is one of the oldest extant houses in the Spital and John Argo is convinced that it was originally a one storey but and ben. A brick upper storey, now covered with rendering, has been added. At the time of George Macdonald in the 1840s a bootmaker, Stephen Airth, lived and worked here, followed by a number of grocers of whom Edward Mackay was the longest *in situ*. It was he who once bought the houses across the road, only to be foiled by John Booth, the man in Auckland.

John Argo, born in New Pitsligo and a baker to trade, estimates that baking must have been done on these premises for a hundred years. In the days when John Wiseman had the shop, folk queued for rolls at two for three farthings. John Argo himself was baker here for ten years and is the last of the line. The bakehouse at the back has now been taken down and a patio is being built over the site. But behind it, backing onto the access lane from Froghall, the shed once used to store bakery supplies, and later by the famous boxers of Froghall as a gym, still stands, bordered in autumn by Mr Argo's colourful display of chrysanthemums, dahlias, gladioli and sweet peas.

This is one of the Spital's secret gardens. But it is the iron work on the veranda that everyone notices, a simplified Vitruvian 'running dog' design as a border with anthemion scroll

Mr John Argo indicates where bricks take over from the stonework.

work forming the main body. When viewed from the street, the 'running dogs' are running in the opposite direction from usual, indicating that the owner, looking out towards the street, enjoys the correct view. It was probably added when the house was heightened.

The Argos have one of the Spital's haunted houses and they have a few tales to tell. One night, not long after moving in, they heard loud footsteps on the stairs which stopped outside the living room. Thinking their young

222

No 39-41 c.1965, while still a bakery and right, the old No 43 whose demolition caused much activity in the spiritual world. No 45 is behind. The iron work on the veranda is a Vitruvian 'running dog' design with anthemion scroll work forming the main design. The correct view is from the inside looking out.
Courtesy, Alexander Reith.

family was romping about, John opened the door, ready to give them a ticking off. The passage was deserted and the children, three sons and a daughter, were all sound asleep upstairs. In the weeks that followed, noises and thumps continued. The assistant baker refused to work in the bakehouse alone at night. One evening three loud knocks were heard at the front door. No one was there and no one could have hidden or got away in the few seconds it took John to answer the door.

Finally the ghosts appeared in person, materialising from a wall cupboard in the ground floor bedroom one night. A short, fat man wearing a gabardine coat tied with a bit of twine round the waist accompanied by a black and white dog on a string lead began to cross the room, vanishing about halfway across. John described the ghosts to an old neighbour who immediately recognised them as Mr Alexander and his dog who used to live next door. They appear to have been disturbed by the demolition both of the bakehouse and of No 43 next door. A new house was built on the site of No 43 and when complete, all the ghosts - there is another one - settled down again.

Next door, the old No 43 (No 27 old style) used to be a shop and house, gable-end to the street as shown on the photograph on page 223. Maggie Sermon, Mrs Connor, was the shopkeeper. 'She sold everything including lucky tatties,' Muriel Slessor remembers. 'Sometimes if you bought a penny one you found a halfpenny inside. You could also buy bits of candy and cinnamon which she made herself.' Maggie sold potted heid and vegetables as well, and bairns going to school bought their pieces there. She lived over the shop with her husband Jake who was confined to a wheelchair. Local folk remember him playing the bagpipes and shouting - 'Maggie - shop,' to let her know that a customer had come in. Dorothy Gerrard, born in Boa Vista Place in 1918 recalls that Jake and Maggie lost their only son in the First World War. They bought a coach on retiring form the shop and Mrs Gerrard remembers seeing Jake being lifted into it at the start of an outing.

To the north of No 43, and set back from the road was No 45, (No 28 old style) dating from around 1745. The claim that this was once a leper hospital may be taken with a pinch of salt since leprosy had died out a century and a half before this house was built. This was a building of dignity and elegance, the back and front roofs piended to form a mirror image, and altogether superior in quality to its neighbours. It probably began life as a merchant's house. Between 1842-59 it housed the Female Penitentiary, as we know, and one wonders if George Macdonald 'just about the handsomest man in the university' *en route* to his nearby digs was ever propositioned by those young women.

After the penitentiary closed it became an ordinary dwelling again, the Greig family taking up residence in 1860. It was home to a grocer for a time and in 1934 it had three tenants, Alex Marr, tailor, Andrew Hall, boxmaker and John Wood, labourer, and their families, some of whom are still in the area. One lady recalls as a child throwing disciple spoons down the famous trapdoor on the ground floor where the secret tunnel allegedly starts. Around 1900 the two top floors had been occupied by the McRobb family and after Sandy Reith announced plans for its conversion in 1971, he had a letter from a Mrs Houston of Ontario, whose father had once apparently received a letter addressed to Mr J McRobb, Old Penitentiary, Spital. The old name must have lingered on for half a century at least.

Sandy Reith, who was later responsible for the conversion of the 'Welfare Houses', bought No 45 in 1971 for £350. At that time he was an assistant architect in Aberdeen City Architect's department. The house had lain derelict for twenty years, and it took an architect's eye to see that it had possibilities. He did much of the restoration work himself and he and his family lived there from 1972 until 1980. He received an Aberdeen Civic Society Award in 1978 and his conversion alerted others to the potential of the Spital. His work on No 45 is a revelation. When I called on Muriel McCulloch who has lived there with husband Simon and family for twelve years, it was to experience something of a culture shock. Having just researched the history of the penitentiary I was not prepared for the Scandinavian sense of space and light now created within. A tiled hall (with that trapdoor on the floor hermetically sealed) gives access to a granny flat into which the family has now spread. The open plan sitting-room, dining area and kitchen is at first floor level and one looks out at another of the Spital's secret gardens . On the third floor are master bedroom, bathroom and study. Access to this point is by an open wooden spiral staircase, but the bedrooms and playroom of the fourth floor are gained by a small attic stair. Like all houses on this side of the Spital, the views are panoramic; the great sweep of the city from the west windows, the Links and sea from the east.

Mr Reith also designed a new house on the site of Maggie Sermon's old shop at No 43. At that time it appeared to be past saving, though he says nowadays, given modern techniques, he would attempt to restore it. It was while the old No 43 was being demolished that Mr Argo's ghosts appeared, while at No 45 Mrs Reith also had a visitation, a lady in grey who seemed perfectly benign in spite of her bunch of keys. In Chapter Ten it was suggested that, 'perhaps Mrs Anderson (the matron of the penitentiary) did come back for a time...' She vanishes from records in 1858 the year before the penitentiary closed and may have died there. Like the shades of Mr

Alexander and his dog, that of Mrs Anderson (if indeed it was she) must have been temporarily disturbed by the works going on around them.

The modern No 43 is now the home of the Spital's most distinguished resident, Dr Leslie Macfarlane, mediaeval scholar and author of the celebrated biography on Bishop William Elphinstone.

Next door to No 45 though set even further back, towards the Lands of Froghall is No 49, (old style No 31) another of the Spital's handsome houses, and like No 43, a listed building. It too has an interesting past. On 5 June 1798, the *Aberdeen Journal* carried the following advertisement:

To let that house and garden called Rosemount lying on the west side of the High Road leading from New to Old Aberdeen Four rooms, three closets, a kitchen, cellars and a garret. One of the rooms is 14 feet by 16 feet and all are nearly finished. Commanding a complete prospect of the whole bay and harbour of Aberdeen with an uninterrupted view of the adjacent country, and as it is only about five minutes' walk from the Gallowgatehead, may be said to be in town and country. A more wholesome and pleasant situation in not to be met with in the vicinity of Aberdeen. Apply to the proprietor, John Sutherland, merchant, Schoolhill. Mr Sutherland still continues to deal in groceries, spirits, porters and good linen and yarn.

The advertisement creates the impression that the house was new. In fact there were two owners before Sutherland, Robert Paterson, blacksmith, then William Symmers, and it dates from around 1750. This John Sutherland, a Schoolhill wine merchant, and not to be confused with the later John Sutherland of Viewton Place, had just finished upgrading his house adding a new frontage. The symmetrical gable-end, built of Loanhead granite faces out to the street. Its well-proportioned fenestration, balanced curving skewputts, the whole surmounted by a chimney-head finial combine to convey a keen sense of proportion.

At this time two little mirror-image shops were erected on the line of the pavement, flanking the entrance to the house, rather like lodges. As a merchant, Sutherland doubtless thought in terms of shops and trade, and the whole complex is a parody in miniature of the great house with its entrance lodges.

Three years later John Sutherland's house and one of the little shops in front, were both tenanted, but he was anxious to sell. On 8 July, 1801, the *Journal* ran another advertisement:

For sale house and garden in the Spital possessed by Major Corbet, with the shop or sale shop in front, possessed by Thomas Clark... Apply to the proprietor,

The former 'Rosemount' No 49 in 1978, with its shop-lodges. No 45 'The Old Penitentiary' is to the left. Courtesy John Souter.

John Sutherland, merchant Aberdeen or John Watson, Advocate, Aberdeen.

Rosemount subsequently served as lodgings and as the home of a solicitor, and much later like No 45 underwent a long period of neglect. In 1976 it was bought by George Massie, principal planning officer with Aberdeen District Council. He found raging dry and wet rot and the original rafters had almost been completely eaten away by woodworm. Over the next two years, he gutted most of the interior and rebuilt a large part of the exterior, restoring it as far as possible to its original condition. He received the award of Aberdeen Civic Society Award in 1979.

The little lodge-like shops, Nos 47 and No 51, old style No 30 and No 32 may well be the oldest in Aberdeen. No 47 was a shoemaker's for a time but is best remembered as a newsagent's and general store. In the 1930s Miss Weir, no relation to Willie, was shopkeeper there. Elizabeth Weston recalls: 'this was where I first used to telephone, one of the old candlestick variety.' In 1955 Mr Henry Leith bought the shop which was run by his wife Chrissie and her sister-in-law Ivy. By a coincidence, the previous owner had also been Henry Leith, a sea-faring man who vowed he would never return to sea which was exactly what he did. The Leith ladies were very popular and thoroughly enjoyed their time behind the couner.

They were succeeded by Mr Jimmy Smith who worked extremely hard

No 45 left, with No 49 visible right. The shop at No 47 just prior to closure with the troublesome tree towering above it.

to make a go of the shop. Sandy Reith pictures him still coming along the Spital, briefcase in hand. 'He worked there from 5.30 am till 8 pm come hell or high water.' He would take an hour or two off in the afternoon, relieved by his sister. He stayed open at Christmas and New Year, and the Argos would send him along a helping of their own festive fare. Since his day, the shop has had a number of tenants, none of whom were to stay very long. The opening of Safeway in West North Street and the 'link' road between King's Crescent and King Street has had an adverse effect on trade. In spite of the hard work of the last tenant, the shop closed in September 1996, the situation compounded by the self-seeded tree to the rear which has caused structural damage to the roof.

The other little shop, No 51, has had an even more chequered career. Towards the end of the nineteenth century, we find bootmakers there, one of whom, Mr Daniel was a member of a long-established Spital family. By the early twentieth century the souters had been replaced by butchers and sometimes No 51 was used as a store by the shopkeeper resident in its twin. It was a chipper in the 1930s. 'Matt Ferguson had the fish and chip shop,' recalls Dorothy Gerrard. 'It was very good.' He lived at No 49, the old Rosemount. Having a little shop at pavement level and a prestigious house back from the road was a west Spital trend. Latterly, the use of No 51 as a shop or even a store became sporadic and in 1985 planning permission was

228

applied for change of use to a domestic garage to serve No 49. This was refused by Aberdeen City District Council but granted two years later by the Scottish Office. The Reporter had sympathised with objections, agreeing that:

the pair of small symmetrical buildings in front of the Georgian house at No 49 the Spital enhances the setting of the listed building and adds interest to the conservation area because of the unusual layout and distinctive appearance

But given the neglect the building had suffered the Reporter felt that the garage proposal 'represents the most tangible, and probably the only way to secure the future of this unusual building.' Who knows, one day its opposite number might became a garage as well.

No 53 Spital (No 35 old style) adjoins the shop that became a garage, and though derelict in our picture, it was clearly a house of some dignity

Left, No 53 prior to demolition. Courtesy, John Souter and below Nos 53 and 55-57 in 1996.

and character. The charter was granted by Alexander Moir in favour of Robert Ferguson wright in Aberdeen on 18 July, 1792. 'All and whole that piece of ground or yard on the west side of the Spital with the house built thereon as presently possessed by Andrew Reid'. On the west a dyke divided it from the Lands of Froghall. Between 1841 and 1851 it was owned by Alexander Stronach, Advocate in Aberdeen (of Stronach and Grainger, not Stronach and Sons). To the rear he would have enjoyed the view to Sunnybank House which he subsequently rented then bought. In 1976 the house was acquired and restored by Susan and Roger McGowan, who also created a ground floor flat with a three bed-roomed house next door at No 55-57. The McGowans were among the first to appreciate the potential of the Spital.

On now to the former Primrose School. No 65, the ground floor flat is the home of Mr and Mrs G. McKenzie. He is a local man, she is from Colombia; both have a keen interest in the history of the area and are delighted that Miss Primrose's great gift to the Spital has not been forgotten. The house has survived its days as a school surprisingly well. Consuela's kitchen was once one of the entrances though whether the boys or the girls is unclear. The McKenzies would dearly love to see the building becoming an entire house again, and hopefully one day this will come about.

Beyond Primrose House, we climb the heights to visit Hillhead Terrace and Boa Vista Place on the high ground of the west Spital. On 19 November 1834, the *Aberdeen Journal* announced:

That small park called the Hillhead of Spital at present occupied by Alex Robertson will be sold by public bargain. This piece of ground commands one of the finest views about Aberdeen. Building stances will be fenced off at a moderate rate in the meantime.

Not a great deal appears to have happened over the next few years. The ordnance surveys of the later 1860s show that there was still a gap between Primrose School at No 67 and No 113 the Spital. But by the 1870s, Hillhead Terrace and its companion, Boa Vista Place had made their appearance, plain and severe tenements with a certain dignity, not unlike the old buildings of Stevenson Street in Gilcomston, though today the ill-assorted windows of this terrace are frowned on in a conservation area. Some of the buildings have great toothed-ends, waiting to bond with houses that never appeared while Nos 11-12a is a modern 'rebuild' which probably explains why all the windows match, if not the stones. The 1891 census returns show

The 'rebuild', Nos 11,12, 12a Hillhead Terrace.

large families in Hillhead Terrace. No 7, for example, part of the middle block had three tenants: Catherine Webster, a former nurse with five children all at school, John Murray a railway wagon examiner with his wife and seven children and Alex Rae, with his wife and nine children.

Gordon Cardno is Hillhead's, if not the Spital's, oldest inhabitant. He was born in 1915 in Elmbank Avenue, but after his father was killed in 1917 during fighting at Mons in the First World War, he moved with his mother to Hillhead Terrace to live with his grandparents the Williamsons. His grandfather tended St Peter's Cemetery, cutting grass for each individual lair and being paid by the individual owner. His mother took a part time job in the Old Aberdeen Library acting as relief for the librarian, Mrs

Mr Gordon Cardno, Hillhead's oldest resident.

231

McPherson. He remembers her looking out for him at the library window as he came home from school at dinner time and would give her a wave as he passed.

He had originally attended Sunnybank Public School, but when it became an Intermediate in 1924 for twelve to fourteen year olds, he had to finish his primary education at Old Aberdeen. His class marched in a crocodile down College Bounds on the way to their new primary. It was a poor area in those days, he says. The only traffic was milk carts, though he remembers the coal carter, Bubbly Harry, from King's Crescent whose nose was always running. He has seen numerous families moving in and moving out and remembers one of the Hillhead families who shared a tenement. 'The old people, the Kirktons were upstairs with the Beverleys, a daughter's family in the middle. They were succeeded by the Ritchies, another of the daughters, while Tam Reid and his family were on the ground floor.'

These days, the flats of Hillhead and those of its neighbour, Boa Vista Place are popular with students. The name Boa Vista (Portuguese: beautiful view) endows these plain buildings and their brick outhouses with an aura of the exotic. This 'Place' was built by George Troup in the 1870s. He had made his money as an iron-moulder in Bahia, (Salvador), Brazil. No 1 Boa Vista is probably contemporary with Hillhead, but Nos 2-3, not such a tall building as most of its neighbours, was erected for Troup by Daniel Macandrew in 1884. Troup lived at Boa Vista himself for a time but in the 1890s retired to Netherfield, Inverurie.

Nos 69-75 the Spital, (Nos 45-51 old style) sit at the foothills of Hillhead Terrace, at pavement level. Neatly finished in granite, and today the premises of Windmill Printing, this little building is still well-remembered from the days when it was a row of shops, grocer, shoemaker and chemist. George Keith, who owned quite a bit of Spital property, had a licensed grocer's at No 1 Hillhead Terrace, but moved down to become the first occupant at No 69-71 in 1885 when these shops were new. In Spital tradition, he also went to live a little further along at the secluded Prospect Cottage.

By the 1930s he had been succeeded by Henry G Morice, though the shop was still called Keith's. Muriel Slessor has a vivid memory of the aftermath of the great air raid of April, 1943. St Peter's Cemetery and Merkland Place had been among the targets and goods on display outside the grocer's were strewn all over the pavement. No one would have dreamt of looting them. At No 73, next to Keith's was the shoemaker's, where for much of the first half of the twentieth century, George Milne was the souter and Harold Bishop's brother, Bill, now over eighty, served his time here.

Hillhead Terrace with Nos 69-75 at pavement level. The two blocks of Boa Vista Place are at the far end.

Last in this little row, No 75, was the chemist's. Before the First World War William MacPherson was in charge, assisted by his daughter. 'When he retired,' recalls Dorothy Gerrard, it was taken on by Mr J Guthrie Aitken.' In turn he was succeeded by Mr William Ewen whose sister, Nan was a Sunday School teacher at St Mary's, Old Aberdeen.

Continuing our stroll past former Spital shops, No 101 a little shop for some years occupied by John Clark fishmonger, sits at the foot of No 1 Boa Vista Place. It is now an office. A few yards further along was a licensed grocer's, another of the Spital's early shops, built sometime before 1840. Early in its life it was No 57 Spital, owned by William Keith, grocer, tea and spirit dealer and probably a forebear of George's. By 1859, Keith still at No 59 is describing himself as 'farmer', a retirement job perhaps! while at the same address is his successor, John Farquharson, tea and spirit dealer. Three generations of Farquharsons John, Alex and John would now carry on the business. The shop became No 113 after the renumbering of 1903, while No 111 was the back house, with access by steps at the side. Again following the west Spital fashion, John acquired No 109, Westview, the most southerly of a handful of 'secret' Spital houses which occupy the high ground between Boa Vista Place and St Peter's Nursery School. He was still living there in retirement at the time of the Second World War while

Boa Vista Place. No 1 is behind the small office, while Nos 2-3, was a later addition.

Nos 2-3 Boa Vista (Portuguese: beautiful view) Place.

William R Beaton, who himself became long-established grocer had taken over at No 113. No 109 in more recent times has been the home of Aberdeen's leading lady of the theatre, Annie Inglis, and subsequently of the late Gordon Mackay, one of the city's most respected journalists. His family still live there.

Now we head on to an attractive old house gable-end to road. Its distinctive shape is described in the feu charter of 1790, the east and west sides only twenty -five and thirty-one feet respectively, its north and south sides one hundred and nineteen and one hundred and eighteen feet, and bounded on the west by 'a dyke dividing the same from the Lands of Sunnyside'. This is No 117, once the home of 'Puddin' Allan whose pudding factory in Canal Road was noted in *Round About Mounthooly*. Roddy Allan, son of the family was, with Alec Donald, one of Gordon Cardno's schoolboy chums.

Next door were two little semi-detached shops, John Adam, butcher at No 119, and, in the 1920s and 1930s, Harry Anderson the barber (and bookie's runner), husband of Bessie Weir at No 121. Mr George Keith, brought up in College Bounds writes:

As a boy of twelve I got a job as a 'soaper' with Harry Anderson. The wages, 4/6 for a part time week, was a princely sum when one considers that I was to get

No 117, gable-end to the road, with No 119, right.

From left, Boa Vista Place, No 111, No 117 gable-end to the road, and Nos 119-121.

8/- a week when I served my time. A soaper would lather up the face to soften the beard which Mr Anderson then came round and shaved, I repeated the process on the second chair. In those days men got shaved two or three times a week at 3d. On as Saturday I can assure you that the fingers on my right hand were lily white and fair sookit.

Nos 119-121 is now Dr A M Barrett-Ayres' surgery. No 123, the back house, was a separate dwelling behind Nos 119 and 121, consisting of ground floor and upper storey and was entered from the rear by a staircase. Susan and Roger McGowan have done a fair deal of restoration work with this particular grouping. A sunroom has been added to No 117 which is their own house. At No 123 they created a three-bedroomed house, though this has now been incorporated into the surgery.

No 123 before conversion. It sits behind Nos 119-121 and is now incorporated with them. Courtesy, Susan McGowan.

Mrs Alison Whimster at the doorway of No 125, Prospect Cottage.

Beyond, and far above the Barrett-Ayres surgery is Prospect Cottage, No 125, the most secret of all the Spital's secret cottages, and the highest. For fourteen years now it has been the home of Peter and Alison Whimster, their two sons and daughter. The cottage, dating from the 1850s, sits at the end of a long garden, a riot of Russian Vine in the autumn with hollyhocks, creepers, a cobbled path and Brodie a delightful Scotty that keeps up the Spital's terrier tradition. The Whimsters have made the best imaginable use of space. Downstairs two rooms have been knocked into one to provide a long lounge with windows at either end. A dining kitchen and a small bedroom complete the ground floor; books are ranged round the staircase; upstairs, two bedrooms and a bathroom have been enhanced by the addition of new dormers on the west side, creating an even more spectacular prospect. Looking across the Spital Lands one can envisage the great nurseries, Sunnypark, where Alec Cocker started out in business stretching to the north west, and its more southerly neighbour, Froghall Nursery. One of the joys of writing about the west side of the Spital has been to observe the great panorama of the city, gradually changing as one edges northwards.

Another interesting group with shop below, houses above were to be found next door to Prospect Cottage, No 129, No 135 and No 131 Spital. The past tense has been used because the shop, No 131 is no longer with us. The high wall to the centre of our photograph below, marks the spot. The land in question was feued by George Moir of Scotstown to Charles Gordon, messenger in Aberdeen in 1778 and other owners included James Chalmers, Farmer in Spital in 1788, John Collie, Surgeon in Aberdeen in 1815 and John Yarrol or Yarroll carrying on business as John Yarrol de Neville, Ostrich Feather Manufacturer in Aberdeen in 1867. I had always understood that ostriches had the monopoly of manufacturing ostrich feathers, so this is surely one of Aberdeen's least known nineteenth century industries. By this time a house, Amelia Cottage, No 67, had been built on the land 'with fixed presses and garret beds' appearing in solitary splendour on the 1868 ordnance survey. By 1872 John Yarrol had sold on to John Lendrum, wincey manufacturer. The next owner, in 1876 was Thomas L Shaw, house proprietor in Aberdeen who was about to go bankrupt.

John Fowler, shipmaster in Aberdeen bought the house from Shaw's creditors in 1877 and two years later acquired ground immediately to the north where a second house No 69 was built. They subsequently became No 129 and No 135. Fowler's daughter sold on to Aitken Malcolm, iron-moulder in 1882, and by the following year, H W Knight Erskine had disponed further ground at pavement level to Malcolm. Thus was that little enclave formed.

Malcolm's family continued to live at No 135 for many years. No 131 was a butcher's shop but by the 1930s was occupied by Troup, recalled as

Nos 129, left and No 135 form a small terrace. The block of masonry below indicates the site of No 131.

238

a first class shoemaker. Jimmy Yule remembers his father, a fellow souter, swapping many a yarn with Mr Troup, when as union representative he would come to collect the empolyees' dues. (Mr Yule was paid £2.50 a year to collect these). The road bulged where the shop was located and in 1973 the Council acquired No 131 from John S Troup, retired shoemaker, for £1300 which sounds like a good deal, and shop and bulge were removed. The two houses above are still with us and form a secluded terrace, quite striking when viewed from St Peter's Gate.

Now we move on to St Peter's Nursery. The first part of the story, when the nursery was under the auspices of St Margaret's Convent is told in Chapter Thirteen. Aberdeen Town Council took over the running in 1937, the Grampian Region as the incoming education authority in 1974, and Aberdeen City again in 1996. (One could argue that the Convent is due for the next shot). There has been much upgrading of the building since its days as St Peter's Hall. It is a friendly, welcoming place, set in a leafy garden,

St Peter's nursery, set in a leafy garden.

much of it planted out and nurtured by the staff. To the rear is yet another of the Spital's secret gardens. Mrs Catherine Cameron who previously taught the nursery class at Kaimhill and infants at Willowpark has been head at St Peter's since 1984. She and Mrs Linda Dillon each take a class of twenty children, the former in the hall, the latter in the annexe and all forty children gather for lunch which is set out on small tables on the stage of the Hall. There are also three nursery nurses on the staff, a secretary and a

Some older snaps from the St Peter's archive.
Above left: Jimmy Sim, Charlie, Roy and Bertie with cartie, before the grounds were landscaped. Behind, left, the Red Lion and No 128 the Spital prior to demolition. Above right: A tea party in the front garden. Across the Spital is the Aberdeen Savings Bank at No 146.

Above: Playing in the front garden. In the background are, left the Sunnybank Dairy, and A Mitchell. Left: St Peter's childern at party time in 1948. Miss Forsyth, one of the early head teachers, is pictured centre. All photographs, courtesy, St Peter's Nursery.

St Peter's Nursery, class of 1996, with the new St Peter's sweatshirts much in evidence. Head teacher, Mrs Catherine Cameron, is in the back row, extreme right, with other members of staff. Courtesy, St Peter's Nursery.

janitor, Norman Collie, Councillor Alex Collie's son. School hours are between 8.45am and 2.45.pm

The children have a carefully structured day, playing in a stimulating environment, learning social skills, adapting to their companions. When I visited the nursery soon after the beginning of term, one or two souls still looked a little timid and were getting the extra attention on which the nursery prides itself, but most were enjoying themselves hugely, those in the hall 'baking' with plasticine and bathing dolls with lots of noise and splashing, while those in the annexe were listening to a story. Birthdays are always celebrated and for festive occasions a special children's disco has been provided by Charlie Flett of Creative Sound and Lighting formerly of No 140 the Spital.

One anomaly, inherited from the region is that as far as entrance is concerned, the oldest children living in the St Machar Academy catchment area (Powis of yore) have priority so that a four-year-old from Bridge of Don will receive priority over a three-year-old in the Spital, a policy that local parents find impossible to understand. Having said that, there a number of local children on the register, and the situation is being reassessed by the new authority. A number of children with non-English speaking back-grounds are on the roll, and receive special encouragement to integrate. The nursery has visited the mosque across the road, and been made most welcome.

The Sunnybank corner.

Unlike the east side, the west side of the Spital did not form an unbroken terrace for beyond St Peter's was a gravel pit. Nevertheless at the time the Sunnybank estate was being laid out in the later nineteenth century, a small group of buildings was erected, somewhat daringly there, at the junction with the Spital, balancing the Orchard corner development opposite. For a time, before Sunnybank Road materialised in its present situation, this group of buildings sat in splendid isolation. They consisted of two small shops, Nos 143 and 145, and as a corner showpiece, a fine tenement, No 147-149, complete with tympana, string courses and half-dropped dormers, one of which wears a stylish conical cap.

Of the two smaller shops, No 143 (old style No 74) was in earlier days, another of the Spital's numerous shoemakers. James Thomson was the souter there from around 1900 for the best part of half a century. Then in the early days of weight-lifting the shop became the Health and Strength Club. Next door at No 145, the other single storey shop had been McDonald the baker and William Sharp, fishmonger, but is best remembered as Dod Shepherd's fish and chip shop 'We gathered there at night.' recalls Harold Bishop. Fish suppers were twopence.' Folk used to come up from Froghall as well. Though No 145 closed after a fire, Spital folk and Froghallers did not go hungry. Coletta's had to relinquish their West North Street fish and chip shop during the Gallowgate demolitions so moved to No 143 the Spital. After Mr Coletta's retirement, there came a string of owners and tenants. The shop is now an Indian takeaway, advertised as the geographically

242

breathtaking 'Khyber Pass, 143 Spital behind King Street'.

The shop on the ground floor at No 149, the lofty tenement, was for many years a chemist's. By 1908 George Glennie was in command and remained so until about 1938. 'Glennie was an amiable little man,' says George Gordon, 'who had a curious habit of sniffing - he seemed to sniff the air when speaking.' Iris Donald remembers: 'Mr Glennie had staring eyes.' Harold Biship recollects: 'We called Glennie the chemist, "Blinkie". He was always blinking'. In spite of sniffing, staring and blinking, Mr Glennie appears to have been a popular and competent chemist. He was succeeded by George L Dickie. The shop itself was a big one for the Spital. 'You went through to the back where there was a large counter approached by steps which ran the length of the frontage.' says Iris Donald. By the 1950s, however, the pharmacy tradition had ended. The shop became the Modern Method Dry Cleaners, and later, and for many years now, the intriguing Spital Gems, which also sells second hand clothes.

Across the Sunnybank Road divide we come on the houses of Firhill Place, set at right angles to the Spital. The Firhill itself, removed long ago for its sand, was within the Lands of Sunnyside some distance from the Spital. From it there sprang the healing waters of the Firwell, better known as the Gibberie Wallie whose story belongs to *The Spital Lands*. Firhill Place got its name because it marked the start of the road to the Firhill from the Spital and the buildings we see today were developed in the 1880s from older dwellings by the omnipresent Daniel Macandrew. His trustees owned the property well into the twentieth century. The group originally consisted of five dwellings and a grocer's shop, No 159, the gable-end that fronts on to the Spital.

'Firhill Place was our playground,' Harold Bishop recalls, looking back to the 1920s. 'The Bowers family were at No 1. Mr Bowers was a stone polisher. Then there was the Wright family. - Alec Wright was a champion Links golfer - and the Breslins who reared Scotties.' The gable-end building, though now a house, continued its career as a shop well into the twentieth century. In 1934 it was Annie Phillips grocer's shop, but by the 1950s James Coutts, the baker was there. Iris Donald recalls sisters there making their own baps and softies through in the back before bringing them through to the front shop for sale.

By the postwar era these houses had become derelict, ripe for demolition. Instead, a programme of restoration fortunately was adopted and this unique group is now attractively harled, with handsome windows, astonishing skewputs and neat canted dormers and chimney pots. They could well be a row of country cottages for there are trees on either side, grassy banks, and bright gardens that come right up to the windows.

Nos 1 and 2 Firhill. The gable-end with the arched windows, No 159 was once a shop.

Beyond No 159 lay derelict ground which was acquired and land-scaped by the Council in 1978. Lying between Firhill Place and Primrosehill, this was the site of a now forgotten enclave which included the original Red Lion Inn and Hall. No 177, ('The Doll's House'), flattened these days, alone survives, on high ground above the Spital. The homes of Dr Iain Davidson, its title deeds cast light on this interesting area which will be discussed more fully in *The Spital Lands.*

A requiem is perhaps fitting for the little row of houses and shops that once stood below it, numbering No 179 to No 193. George Gordon recalls a shop dealing in second-hand furniture 'and probably much else' which was run by Danny Morgan, and his sister Bella, and which later became ruinous. Next door at No 193 was the barber's shop of Danny McCann. George Gordon recalls him as:

> a tall, well-built, heavily-moustached man of about fifty-five. He came to work dressed in a heavy overcoat, hat, umbrella a pair of highly polished leather leggings and carrying a voluminous Gladstone bag. He never varied, summer and winter. He was as a nice friendly man, very keen in politics and so was I though I was only fifteen or sixteen at the time. As he busied himself with my hair he would discuss the politics of the day. It was the time of the National Government and Ramsay Macdonald, and just down the road (at Powis House) J G Burnett had been elected MP for Aberdeen North. McCann went away well before the War and the shop was closed.

'Ghostly reminders of the past are still visible in the surviving stonework.' No 177 is perched to the left.

This area has been turned into a miniature park though vestiges of doors and windows, ghostly reminders of the past, are still visible in the surviving stonework. These were the last of the Spital's amazing number of shops. Those of College Bounds then took over.

The City of Aberdeen's *Old Aberdeen Conservation Area Report* of 1993 gave the Spital a 'could do better':

there have been many insensitive alterations to buildings; inappropriate window replacements are particularly in evidence. There is, however, plenty of townscape interest and the potential for making more of it. Added interest is given to the area by the topography which allows views over the City (and) out to sea and by the dramatic scale of trees in King's Crescent.

And the note on the Spital concluded: 'Proposals for this area should aim at preventing further erosion of its character and encourage its upgrading'.

So be it. The Spital has survived a long period of decline. It has taken a new generation of enterprising young people to make us aware that this is an area with great character and an identity of its own.

Postscript

More About Mounthooly

'Fit wye are ye nae up in Aiberdeen makin pies?
London security guard to Garth Jessamine

Since the publication of *Round About Mounthooly* more information about the area has come to light, a few loose ends have been tied up and readers have made contact with a wealth of memories.

On the purely historic side, interesting facts about Mounthooly itself have emerged. A smallpox hospital was in existence there between 1872 and 1875, working on an 'as needed' basis. The medical attendant received a fee of £1.11s 6d per case, although when the number of patients exceeded nineteen, this was reduced to one guinea. In January 1875, for example, the hospital re-opened after a period of closure to cope with a fresh outbreak; by June it had closed again after discharging the last patient of the current epidemic. During this period seventy-six patients had been admitted of whom sixty-four had recovered and twelve had died.

By June 1877 'the Epidemic Hospital at Cunnigarhill' (the City Hospital) was almost complete and a new use for the former Mounthooly Hospital was considered by the Town Council as stabling for their carting and cleansing departments - and was rejected. Instead, on 19 August, 1878, the *Aberdeen Journal* announced:

the southmost portion of the Mounthooly Hospital is now being adapted for a Reception House, containing six rooms with kitchen, dining-hall (etc). Edward Brown, late seaman RN has been appointed keeper at 12/- per week with food when the house is in occupation and 2/6 with no rations when not in use.

The Reception House did not prove popular and in 1882, ground at Mounthooly, including the former smallpox hospital was auctioned for £605 to Mr James Fraser, washing powder manufacturer, who was already tenanting part of the building. Thus the Mounthooly Smallpox Hospital became Fraser's Balmoral Soap Powder Works and the Aberdeen Margarine Factory, whose existence, if not its earlier pedigree was noted in *Round About Mounthooly;* an interesting new use for an old building. The Soap

Works appears in the 1901 ordnance survey, located in the cul-de-sac which is now Canal Place. At a later date, Mr Green's well known stables, which a number of readers visited as children, were also based in this area.

The Mounthooly Riot of August 1874 also deserves documentation. Two unfortunate policemen, attempting to arrest a man for a breach of a bye-law, were surrounded by a crowd of several hundreds who knocked them down, kicked, punched and beat them with sticks. Reinforcements arrived and four persons from Canal Road were arrested. A woman in the crowd was heard to exclaim: 'Dod, can we nae hae a riot as weel as at Fraserburgh?' The Canal Road Four were later convicted and fined sums ranging from 7/6 to 15/-.

Moving round to Hutcheon Street, a little more has been gleaned about John Stewart and Joseph Rowell, founders of the mighty Aberdeen Comb Works. They were brothers-in-law, and Rowell was a native of Yorkshire rather than Devon. He resigned from the firm around 1848 with a substantial fortune, though he continued to run an ironmonger's business from the Upperkirkgate. The ambitious Stewart became heavily involved in the Aberdeen-London steamship wars, which he eventually won, though not before committing himself to an outlay of over £46,000 for the purchase of three vessels. Worse still, he had invested much of his fortune in Great North of Scotland Railway shares, and when a panic set in and share prices fell, Stewart lost everything including his fine estate of Craigiebuckler. Well, not quite everything, for the Comb Works weathered the storm, enjoyed some years of good trading and by 1872 Stewart was able to afford the estate of Banchory (Devenick) which had come on the market at £76,000.

Now for some personal memories, and firstly, the Gallowgate area.

John Gray of California has written of his widowed grandmother, the remarkable Annie Bain who brought up a son and three daughters in the Gallowgate and Spring Garden areas. The girls at one time attended the Socialist Sunday School at the Porthill and later became active in the Independent Labour Party (ILP) and the peace movement. They continued the fight for social justice throughout their lives. Annie with her son John set up a second-hand furniture business in Spring Garden and later opened a second shop in the Gallowgate while developing a trade with the Orkneys. They would wheel the furniture, sewn into sacking for protection, down to the harbour on a handbarrow to be loaded on to the Orkney boat.

Chrissie Leith remembers childhood days in Seamount Place, a world of its own, perched high on the east side of the Gallowgate, where the folk were all friendly, ready to help each other. One of her earliest memories was of the coastal blackout during the First World War which applied, not to the city as a whole, but to areas such as Seamount Place whose twinkling lights were visible to those at sea. She remembers how alarmed her mother was when two policemen called to say that she was infringing the blackout. By the following night they came back to report that no chinks of light were visible. It was in those days that she once heard the cry, 'Zeppelin overhead!' going up.

She perfected her Highland dancing steps in Causewayend, courtesy of Bendelow's famous bakery. A mirror in the shop window, primarily intended for display purposes, also afforded passers-by an opportunity to observe their feet and ankles. She practised her steps on the pavement outside the shop, watching her feet in the mirror.

Garth Jessamine recalls that Bendelow's - the name may be of Polish origin - was founded by his grandmother, Jane Bendelow, daughter of John Bendelow, hotel waiter; or, perhaps by John himself, given that one of the many poems inspired by the firm's products has the refrain: 'Jist ane o' John Bendelow's Pies'.

'The business,' says Garth, 'was carried on first by my grandfather, R S Jessamine, then by his oldest son, my uncle, R B Jessamine.' His

Bendelow's, No 42 Causewayend dressed overall for the Coronation in 1953. R B Jessamine, left is in shirt sleeves and baker's apron. Courtesy, Gordon Jessamine.

A formal portrait of the Jessamine family, with R S Jessamine in the centre of the front row with his wife Jane, nee Bendelow on his right. The photographer painted in an additional six inches of her skirt which R S deemed had shown an indiscreet amount of ankle. Their sons and daughters are as follows: Back, from left, Edith, R B Jessamine, Hilda, Austin and Alice. Seated, left, Edmund, and on the right, Elizabeth and JEB. Courtesy, Garth Jessamine.

grandparents had lived at No 64 Powis Place, but by the 1930s they had moved to No 48 Elmbank Terrace.

'Saturday lunch for the girls working at 'The Shop' in Causewayend was prepared at No 48 and I, as a spindly youngster had the weekly chore of transporting it on my bicycle down Canal Road, with the heavy containers dangling from my handlebars. On only one occasion did I come to grief but did not have the courage to advise the waiting staff that some of their potatoes had to be retrieved from the traffic on the wooden bridge at the top.'

Garth Jessamine recalls family and friends gathering of a Sunday at No 48, a fine house with a large garden. After the evening meal there was hymn singing. 'In a corner of the dining-room stood a pedal organ to the accompaniment of which a repast befitting the table of a successful baker would be digested to the lusty rendering of hymns. I can still recall my surprise at the number of people who would gather outside in the street to listen to the choral renditions from within. '

Of his uncles, Dr Austin Jessamine had a particularly fine baritone voice. Another uncle, Edmund, was the Belmont Road dentist, while, a third, J E B Jessamine was appointed Military Governor of the Cocos-Keeling Islands in 1943. He had previously been attached to Lord Mountbatten's staff in Colombo after escaping Malaya in the face of the Japanese invasion. Garth's own brother, Dr Gordon 'Curly' Jessamine was awarded a Canadian Centennial Medal in 1965 for services to medicine and other members of the family have enjoyed equally fulfilling careers.

On a lighter note, Garth's father and a friend had the distinction of getting themselves locked in the cellar of the Red Lion Bar in the Spital one night. 'Absolutely no one heard their cries of despair to be released.' Garth himself, on giving his name to a new security guard in the west end of London was asked: 'Fit wye are ye nae up in Aiberdeen makin pies?'

Moving along from Causewayend to Powis Place, Dr May G Williamson writes: My interest was particularly in Powis Place, where my mother's old family home, No 11 was a plain-fronted house of two storeys and attics set back from the street by a patch of drying-green, with a large garden behind. The attics, apparently intended for letting, were reached by an outside stair at the rear. In those attics Harry Gordon was born, (not at No 7 as is usually stated). Nos 7 and 9 made up a solid granite tenement from the rents of which No 11 was no doubt maintained. The builder of all three houses was my mother's grandfather, Robert Robertson, a quite exceptional character for the time in which he lived. He was a Chartist and one of the founders of the Unitarian Church in Aberdeen.'

Dr Williamson continues: 'You write of the hawthorn hedges in which the children once played. I can just remember my mother pointing out a rather dilapidated hawthorn hedge behind a low dyke where she played with her sisters, climbing into the gnarled branches which formed 'chairs' and 'thrones'. That must have been about 1923 or perhaps a little later'.

Finally to the kirk and the thorny problem of the union of congregations. After *Round About Mounthooly* went to press, proposals to unite John Knox, Mounthooly and St Stephen's, Causewayend, foundered. The announcement that John Knox would be the chosen place of worship would not be countenanced by the Cassie-enders and when the decision was reversed, the Knoxites would have no truck with St Stephen's. Now the latter kirk gings its ain gate while John Knox is to unite with its mother kirk of Greyfriars, Broad Street, which will be the chosen place of worship. A new fate awaits Mounthooly's most famous building.

Select Bibliography

Books consulted

Anon, *Freedom Land Marches*, nd
Burnett, John George (ed), *Powis Papers, 1507-1894*, Third Spalding, 1951
Carnie William, *Reporting Reminiscences*, Aberdeen 1902
Douglas, Francis, *A General Description of the East Coast of Scotland*, Paisley, 1782
Fraser, G M, *Historical Aberdeen*, The Bon-Accord Press 1905
Gammie, Alexander, *The Churches of Aberdeen*, Aberdeen Daily Journal, 1909
Gill A J M, *Families of Moir and Byres*, D Wylie, Aberdeen, 1885
Gordon James, *Aberdoniae Utriusque Descriptio*, Spalding, 1842
Innes, C (ed), *Fasti Aberdonensis*, Spalding, 1841
Innes C, (ed), *Registrum Episcopatus Aberdonensis*, Edinburgh 1845
James, I E, *The Goldsmiths of Aberdeen 1450-1850*, Bieldside Books, 1981
Kennedy William, *The Annals of Aberdeen*, London 1818
Littlejohn, David, *Records of the Sheriff Court of Aberdeen*, New Spalding, 1906
Macfarlane, Leslie J, *William Elphinstone and the Kingdom of Scotland 1431-1514*, AUP, 1985
McLaren, John, *Sixty Years in a Granite Yard*, Aberdeen University Centre for Scottish Studies, 1982
Meldrum, Edward, *Aberdeen of Old*, 1986
Maclean, Neil, *Life at a Northern University*, The Rosemount Press, 1917
Milne, John, *Aberdeen, Topographical, Antiquarian and Historical* Aberdeen Journal, 1911.
Munro A M M (ed), *Records of Old Aberdeen* , New Spalding, 1899
Rait, R S , *The Universities of Aberdeen*, Aberdeen 1895
Smith, John (ed), *Old Aberdeen: Bishops, Burghers and Buildings*, AUP 1991
Spalding, John, *Memorialls of the Trubles in Scotland and in England*, Spalding, 1850
Stuart, John (ed). *Extracts from the Council Register of the Burgh of Aberdeen 1643-1747*, Edinburgh, 1872
Tayler, A & H, *Jacobites of Aberdeenshire and Banffshire in the Rising of 1715*, Oliver & Boyd, 1934
Taylor Louise B, *Aberdeen Council Letters 1552-1681*, v, vi, (Oxford, 1942-61),

Reports, Prospectuses
Old Aberdeen Conservation Area Report: City of Aberdeen Planning Division 1993
St Peter's Nursery School: Prospectus, 1996-97.

Works of Reference
Aberdeen Post Office Directories
In Memoriam, Wm Kay & Sons, Aberdeen, 1892, 1899, 1904, 1912
Scotland of Today Part II, Historical Publishing Coy, 1889

Monographs

Gordon, George, 'A Short History of King's Crescent', Aberdeen, 1985

Wyness, Fenton, "The Story of an Aberdeen Property, 37 Belmont Street', 1973

Aberdeen City Archives: Aberdeen Extension and Improvement Act, 1883; Accounts: Guild Brethren's Hospital, Vols I & II; Box No 16, miscellaneous items; Commutation Books, 1811-1812, 1824-25, 1839-1840; Contract of Marches, 1759; Council Registers, LXI-LXIV; Letters received, Vol XIII; Log Book, Primrose School; Minutes, Old Aberdeen Police Commissioners, from 1860; Old Aberdeen Police Assessment Rolls; Miscellaneous deeds relating to Spital; Miscellaneous Valuation Rolls from 1855.

Aberdeen City Libraries: Aberdeen Council Minutes from 1893; Census Returns, 1851, 1871, 1881, 1891; G M Fraser - Notebooks; Cuttings on the Spital.

Aberdeen University Special Collections: Aberdeen Female Penitentiary: Minute of the Seventh Annual Meeting of Subscribers, Aberdeen 1846.

Records of the Society of Advocates in Aberdeen: Writs relating to the Lands of Gallowhill and Mardyke.

Newspapers: Items relating to the Spital from the *Aberdeen Journal,* by courtesy of George Gordon. Items relating to the Spital's council-built housing and the King's Crescent Fire Station from the *Press and Journal* and *Evening Express.*

Index

What the Press said about 'Footdee'

Footdee book tops sales list.
Aberdeen Press and Journal

A model of what a local history should be.
Scottish Book Collector

She writes with warmth and affection.
Bob Smith: Leopard Magazine

ISBN 1 898645 01 9

What they said about 'Mounthooly'

200 pages of tightly written fact and
anecdote, leavened with archive photographs and documentation...a book that
does Aberdeen a great service.
Aberdeen Press and Journal

ISBN 1 898645 02 7

There is a strain of warmth and humour running
through the book that I found particularly attractive.
Aberdeen University Review

The second in a ground-breaking series...Diane Morgan
has rescued from impending oblivion, the story of
Mounthooly and its people.
Scottish Local History

The second volume in the 'Villages' series uses original
sources, maps and interviews to provide a detailed
account of this community since earliest times.
Scots Magazine

...A companion volume, *The Spital Lands* is in preparation, covering
Sunnyside, Froghall and Sunnybank, to the west of the Spital, King
Street, Pittodrie and the Links to the east.